Miller's Children

*The publisher and the University of California Press
Foundation gratefully acknowledge the generous support
of the Anne G. Lipow Endowment Fund
in Social Justice and Human Rights.*

Miller's Children

WHY GIVING TEENAGE KILLERS
A SECOND CHANCE
MATTERS FOR ALL OF US

James Garbarino

UNIVERSITY OF CALIFORNIA PRESS

University of California Press, one of the most distinguished university presses in the United States, enriches lives around the world by advancing scholarship in the humanities, social sciences, and natural sciences. Its activities are supported by the UC Press Foundation and by philanthropic contributions from individuals and institutions. For more information, visit www.ucpress.edu.

University of California Press
Oakland, California

Library of Congress Cataloging-in-Publication Data

Names: Garbarino, James, author.
Title: Miller's children : why giving teenage killers a second chance matters for all of us / James Garbarino.
Description: Oakland, California : University of California Press, [2018] | Includes bibliographical references and index.
Identifiers: LCCN 2017030347 (print) | LCCN 2017036539 (ebook) | ISBN 9780520968363 (epub) | ISBN 9780520295674 (cloth : alk. paper) | ISBN 9780520295681 (pbk. : alk. paper)
Subjects: LCSH: Juvenile delinquents—United States. | Juvenile homicide—United States—Psychological aspects. | Correctional psychology. | Criminals—Rehabilitation. | Juvenile corrections.
Classification: LCC HV9104 (ebook) | LCC HV9104 .G35 2018 (print) | DDC 365/.6019—dc23
LC record available at https://lccn.loc.gov/2017030347

Manufactured in the United States of America

26 25 24 23 22 21 20 19 18
10 9 8 7 6 5 4 3 2 1

*To the men and women who have made the journey
of rehabilitation and transformation*

CONTENTS

ACKNOWLEDGMENTS

My thanks go out to all the men (and a few women) who shared their stories of rehabilitation, transformation, and redemption in prisons around the country, most especially the men whose words are included in this book. Together, they have taught me more about the path from troubled teenage killer to wise and compassionate man than I could have learned otherwise. They have walked this path, and they have been generous and gracious in sharing with me how they did it and what they learned along the way.

I also must express my gratitude to my colleague Kathleen Heide. Her research and insight have informed and improved my own. Her support and encouragement in the writing of this book have sustained me and improved the end result (as it did before in writing my 2015 book *Listening to Killers*). Kathleen was joined in reviewing the first draft of the manuscript by Barry Krisberg and Christopher Slobogin, and I thank all three of them for the helpful suggestions they made, suggestions that I have incorporated into the final version of this book.

Many thanks to "my" editor at the University of California Press, Maura Roessner, whose belief in the project and astute comments and suggestions have supported me from start to finish. And my thanks to Richard Earles for his excellent copyediting that improved the book's clarity and focus.

And I thank all my teachers—at East Rockaway High School, where my intellectual life began; at St. Lawrence University, where it really took hold; and at Cornell University, where my professional education began. Thanks also to the academic institutions that have been my professional homes for more than forty years as a professor—Empire State College; the Boys Town Center for the Study of Youth Development; Penn State; the Erikson

Institute for Advanced Study in Child Development; Cornell University; and, since 2005, Loyola University Chicago, where I have found a home for the spirit as well as the mind.

Finally, thank you, Claire, for your insights and spiritual perspective. They led me to this work in the first place.

PREFACE

In 2012, the U.S. Supreme Court handed down a decision in the case of *Miller v. Alabama.* Fourteen-year-old Evan Miller had been subject to an automatic sentence of life without the possibility of parole for a murder he committed in 2003. His sentence was appealed on the grounds that it constituted cruel and unusual punishment, thus violating his Eighth Amendment rights. The ruling came because the court accepted the proposition that he was "less guilty by reason of adolescence" (as the research from developmental psychology that was brought before the court indicated). After considering this evidence, the court ruled, in a 5–4 decision, that mandatory sentences of life without the possibility of parole for murderers under the age of eighteen are unconstitutional.

This decision led to efforts around the country to get the courts to apply the substance of the *Miller v. Alabama* decision retroactively to the some 2,500 cases in which defendants under the age of eighteen had received such sentences. These efforts, which have included both litigation to force resentencing hearings and legislation to require them as a matter of social policy, have found success—for example, in Illinois (legislation) and Florida (litigation).

Given the political intransigence of many state legislatures and the general climate of "getting tough on crime," it was not clear that the *Miller* decision *would* be applied retroactively on any widespread basis. Then, in 2016, the Supreme Court ruled, in the case of *Montgomery v. Louisiana,* that the *Miller* decision was to be applied retroactively throughout the country—and this opened a floodgate of hope for men (and a few women) who had been convicted of murders as teenagers and had been incarcerated with the expectation that they would never leave prison except in a coffin.

The *Miller v. Alabama* and *Montgomery v. Louisiana* decisions set in motion an important "social experiment." Teenagers who had entered prison with no prospect for release ten, twenty, thirty, or more years before were now adults who might become eligible for parole if they were given a resentencing hearing. Imagine what this meant for them! A door that had been locked shut might open up.

In 2015, I published a book titled *Listening to Killers: Lessons Learned from My 20 Years as a Psychological Expert Witness in Murder Cases.* I was finishing that book just as the social experiment ordered by the Supreme Court was getting under way. What is more, I began to be asked to serve as an expert witness in some of these cases—especially in Illinois and Florida.

In *Listening to Killers* (and in my 1999 book *Lost Boys*), I had dealt with teenage murderers, but mostly in their initial trials, before they had begun their life sentences. I had been involved in a few cases in which men were applying for parole who had committed murder when they were teenagers (and in some cases young adults—nineteen to twenty-one years of age), and I included these cases in my 2015 book as part of a chapter titled "Tales of Rehabilitation, Transformation, and Redemption."

In the years after *Listening to Killers* was published, I came to focus on the resentencing of men under the *Miller v. Alabama* decision. At the time they committed murder as kids, it was difficult to see the developmental path these killers might take as they came of age in prison. In some cases, clinicians who evaluated them as part of their original trials and sentencing hearings said as much. But now it is not necessary to speculate and predict, because the intervening years have answered the questions that could not be answered ten, twenty, thirty, or more years earlier. These teenagers had become adults. I have come to know some of them, and in many cases it has been an honor and a privilege to do so. This book is about what I learned from them, and what their experience can teach us about the human capacity for change through rehabilitation, transformation, and redemption.

I must note at the outset that I cannot, with any certainty, say anything definitive about how statistically representative these cases are. I do know that in some states there is a "triage" process for deciding which cases to bring forward first. In Michigan, for example, I was told that the cases going first are "felony murder" cases—that is, cases in which the teenager was involved in a felony during which someone was killed but the teenager did not pull the trigger. These appear to be the easiest cases to resolve, because the inmate involved was not actually a killer, despite his legal status.

Also, I can't say for sure that the invitations I receive to participate in such cases are not selectively offered (e.g., asking me to work only on "the best cases" among the legally eligible inmates, those who have demonstrated the best records in terms of rehabilitation). But I can say that in presenting the cases in this book, I have tried hard to represent what I have seen and heard and learned. I have not "cherry picked" only the best cases. My principal goal throughout the book is to demonstrate what is possible for teenage killers serving life sentences, without going so far as to offer conclusive data on exactly how statistically common these stories of rehabilitation and transformation are. That will take years of further study.

ONE

Adolescence Squared

WHY ARE KIDS WHO KILL DIFFERENT?

This chapter outlines how the Supreme Court ruling in *Miller v. Alabama* in 2012 (and the follow-up decisions that made this ruling universally retroactive) changed the lives of juvenile murderers originally sentenced to life without the possibility of parole. I also look at how it changed my own life.

COOK COUNTY COURT, CHICAGO, ILLINOIS: Two decades ago, seventeen-year-old Javell Ivory, fifteen-year-old Darnell Foxx, and two other members of a gang called the Mafia Insane Vice Lords stole a van to transport them on a mission of retaliation. Days earlier, a member of their gang had been shot by their archenemies—the Gangster Disciples—who controlled the adjacent territory. Now it was time to restore the balance of power, avenge their loss, and uphold their honor. The four "soldiers" carried three weapons among them on their mission—two pistols and a semiautomatic rifle. Crossing Cicero Avenue on Chicago's South Side, they entered into "enemy territory" and zeroed in on a gas station, where they identified someone they *thought* was an appropriate target: twenty-one-year-old Joshua Thomas (who, it was later reported, was not a member of the rival gang). While Javell (who was carrying a .22 caliber pistol) sat in the van, both Darnell and one of the other "soldiers" opened fire in classic drive-by-shooting style. Joshua Thomas was killed in a hail of bullets, but he was not the only victim. Standing next to him was twenty-four-year-old Salada Smith, six months pregnant with her second child. She, too, was killed in the fusillade. Two other innocent bystanders, both male, were also hit but survived. Thus, as is sometimes the case in such attacks, the "collateral damage" exceeded the "intended damage." Within days, Javell and his three companions were identified and arrested. They soon confessed. Javell was tried for murder, despite the fact that he did not fire a shot in the fatal attack, under the legal principle of "felony murder" (which considers everyone involved in a felony in which homicide occurs accountable for the crime and guilty of murder, regardless of whether they wielded the weapon). Under the law in effect at the time, although they were juveniles, Javell and Darnell received mandatory sentences of life without the possibility of parole. Now, two decades later, both of them sat in a courtroom in the Cook County Courthouse for a resentencing hearing. They hoped for a decision that would open the prison door for eventual release if presiding judge James Obbish imposed a limited number of years, rather than the existing sentence that would have them dying in prison.

I have served as a psychological expert witness in murder cases since 1994, focusing on issues of child and adolescent development (as chronicled in my 1999 book *Lost Boys* and my 2015 book *Listening to Killers*). As a result, I was asked to serve as a psychological expert witness for Javell Ivory. In court on May 24, 2016, my testimony focused on the immature brains and behavior of juveniles, the power of peer influence on teenagers, the destructive impact of growing up in a socially toxic family and community environment, *and* the reality of rehabilitation and transformation that exist in the minds and hearts of adolescent killers despite the severity of the crimes they commit. I prepared a twenty-four-page, single-spaced report, in which I laid out a developmental analysis of the life that brought Javell to that terrible day in 1997. This analysis included his experience with childhood trauma in an urban "war zone," the effects of that experience on his judgment and feelings (what I called the "war zone mentality"), and the larger picture of abuse, neglect, social deprivation, drug abuse, and crime that shaped his life. I also laid out the evidence that he had become rehabilitated and transformed during his twenty years in prison. I summarized my conclusions in this way:

> All of these factors must be understood in the context of him being a seventeen-year-old adolescent from a traumatic and unsupportive social environment when he committed the crime for which he is being sentenced, and thus plagued by the kind of developmental immaturity characteristic of teenagers in general, and most especially of teenagers with traumatic histories. . . . What is more, he exemplifies the principle that because of the "malleability" of even adult brains, there are possibilities for rehabilitation inherent in juveniles, even juveniles with traumatic life experiences and who grew up in social environments loaded with trauma and antisocial influences.

It worked. Here's how the *Chicago Tribune* reported on the resentencing decision handed down by Judge Obbish, which replaced life without parole with eventual release dates:

Obbish said he weighed several factors before returning the new sentences, including the men's impoverished upbringing and early initiation into street gangs. The judge also said he took into consideration what Foxx and Ivory have accomplished during their incarcerations. Both men earned high school equivalency diplomas and completed a program that seeks to teach young offenders to appreciate the consequences of their actions. Obbish also cited a growing body of scientific evidence suggesting that teenage brains aren't fully developed and therefore lack the impulse control and the understanding of consequences that come with maturation . . . . "I think by and large both of these men have displayed serious potential for rehabilitation," Obbish said Monday.

But why were Javell Ivory and Darnell Foxx in court for a resentencing hearing in the first place? After all, they had been sentenced to life without the possibility of parole. They weren't seeking clemency or a pardon. They were in court that day for resentencing because of the U.S. Supreme Court's 2012 *Miller v. Alabama* decision, in which the justices ruled 5–4 that mandatory sentences of life without the possibility of parole for juveniles who commit murder are unconstitutional. This was one of a series of rulings by the court that recognized juveniles as a class of defendants who merit special attention in the criminal justice system. These cases are outlined in box 1.

The *Miller v. Alabama* decision set in motion the process that brought me to the courtroom to testify on behalf of Javell, and it stimulated the writing of this book. As psychologist-lawyers Tom Grisso and Antoinette Kavanaugh wrote in 2016, in their excellent review of the legal and psychological issues arising in and from the *Miller v. Alabama* decision and its follow-up legal and policy development:

> Developmental science now faces a new challenge. Its research served well to provide normative information with which the U.S. Supreme Court distinguished adolescence as an immature class. Now we must consider what role developmental science can play when applied, case by case, to describe legally relevant developmental characteristics of young people as evidence for individual mitigation in *Miller* sentencing and resentencing cases.

This book arose from my work to do that case-by-case application of developmental science, which includes forty such individual cases at the time of this writing.

A year before I testified on behalf of Javell Ivory, the first resentencing hearing of this kind was held in Illinois, and the judge in that case, Angela Petrone, reimposed the sentence of life without the possibility of parole

**BOX 1. RECENT U.S. SUPREME COURT DECISIONS
ON SENTENCING OF JUVENILES**

Roper v. Simmons (2005). Ruled that capital punishment for crimes committed by juveniles is unconstitutional.

Graham v. Florida (2010). Ruled that juvenile offenders cannot be sentenced to life without the possibility of parole for non-homicide offenses.

Miller v. Alabama (2012). Ruled that mandatory sentences of life without the possibility of parole are unconstitutional for crimes committed by juveniles.

Montgomery v. Louisiana (2016). Ruled that the ban on mandatory life-without-parole sentences for crimes committed by juveniles was to be retroactively applied to the cases of all juveniles sentenced to mandatory life-without-parole sentences.

Tatum v. Arizona (2016). Reaffirmed that life-without-parole sentences for juveniles are to be imposed only for the "rarest of juvenile offenders, those whose crimes reflect permanent incorrigibility."

upon Adolfo Davis, who, at age fourteen, was involved in a gang-related double murder. I didn't participate in that case. As for Darnell Foxx, although I wasn't a witness for him, since his and Javell's cases were heard by the same judge simultaneously, it seems likely that whatever influence I had on him in considering Javell's fate probably spilled over to his sentencing of Darnell.

After the judge delivered his verdict, I received this email from David Owens, the lead attorney working on Javell's behalf:

> Today Judge Obbish issued his decision. . . . He ultimately sentenced Javell to 30 years for the 2 murders and 12 for each aggravated battery, which were required to be consecutive, giving him a total sentence of 54 years. That's at 50–50 time, so it's a total sentence of 27 years and he's served 19 already. It's probably best to describe this as bittersweet. One thing is clear: the Judge was deeply influenced by, and took to account, your testimony. He pointed to it repeatedly during his decision. It was crucial to this result.

I quote this message not to draw attention to myself, but to highlight the point that when the "adolescent development" case is made, it is possible for judges to hear it and incorporate it into their thinking as they make these weighty decisions (which, as we will see, has even led to some of these juvenile offenders walking out of prison soon after their resentencing hearings with "time served"). That, in turn, leads to a more complete report of the Supreme Court's thinking in the decision that put David Owens, Javell Ivory, and me in Judge Obbish's court and opened the door for thousands of others. It created a new legal category that I call "Miller's Children."

MILLER v. ALABAMA

The Supreme Court decision in the case of *Miller v. Alabama* specifically dealt with the case of Evan Miller, a fourteen-year-old boy who had been subject to an Alabama law that provided for an automatic sentence of life without the possibility of parole for a murder he committed in 2003. Along with a friend, Miller beat up his neighbor and set fire to his trailer after an evening of drinking and drug use. The neighbor died. Miller was originally charged as a juvenile, but his case was removed to adult court, where he was charged with murder in the course of arson, while his friend pled guilty to a lesser crime.

Although it is the *Miller* case that has given the name to the decision banning mandatory life-without-parole sentences for juvenile killers, there were actually two cases considered by the court in reaching its landmark decision. The other (*Jackson v. Hobbs*) came out of Arkansas, where fourteen-year-old Kuntrell Jackson accompanied two other boys (one of whom was his cousin) to a video store to commit a robbery. On the way to the store, he learned that one of the boys was carrying a shotgun. Jackson stayed outside the store for most of the robbery, but after he entered, one of his co-conspirators shot and killed the store clerk. Arkansas charged Jackson as an adult with capital felony murder, as Illinois had done with Javell Ivory. The jury convicted Jackson of both murder and aggravated robbery, and this resulted in a statutorily mandated sentence of life in prison without the possibility of parole.

In *Miller v. Alabama,* the jury likewise found the defendant guilty, and the trial court likewise imposed statutorily mandated life without parole. The sentence was affirmed by the Alabama Court of Criminal Appeals. This decision was itself appealed and eventually reached the U.S. Supreme Court. The court's 5–4 majority opinion struck down the Alabama law, reasoning thus:

> Two strands of precedent reflecting the concern with proportionate punishment come together here. The first has adopted categorical bans on sentencing practices based on mismatches between the culpability of a class of offenders and the severity of a penalty. See, *e.g., Kennedy* v. *Louisiana,* 554 U.S. 407. Several cases in this group have specially focused on juvenile offenders, because of their lesser culpability. Thus, *Roper* v. *Simmons* held that the Eighth Amendment bars capital punishment for children, and *Graham* v. *Florida,* 560 U.S. ___, concluded that the Amendment prohibits a sentence of life without parole for juveniles convicted of a non-homicide offense. *Graham* further likened life without parole of juveniles to the death penalty, thereby evoking a second line of cases. In those decisions, this Court has required sentencing authorities to consider the characteristics of a defendant and the details of his offense before sentencing him to death. See, *e.g., Woodson* v. *North Carolina,* 428 U.S. 280 (plurality opinion). Here, the confluence of these two lines of precedent leads to the conclusion that mandatory life without parole for juveniles violates the Eighth Amendment.

In addition to the legal arguments presented, the justices cited the scientific evidence presented to the court in *Miller v. Alabama* and in earlier, related decisions (such as *Roper v. Simmons* in 2005, which outlawed capital punishment for juveniles). This included an amicus brief by the American Psychological Association. It's important to note that the court ruled that *mandatory (but not discretionary)* sentences of life without the possibility of parole for murderers under the age of eighteen are unconstitutional. This is the loophole that permitted the Chicago judge in the Adolfo Davis hearing to simply "resentence" him to the sentence of life without parole that he started out with. As we will see, however, that too may be coming to an end.

In its 2016 ruling in the case of *Tatum v. Arizona,* the majority summarily reversed the convictions of five juveniles who had been sentenced to life without parole, writing: "On the record before us, none of the sentencing judges addressed the question *Miller* and *Montgomery* [*v. Louisiana*] require a sentencer to ask: whether the petitioner was among the very 'rarest of juvenile offenders, those whose crimes reflect permanent incorrigibility.'" In an opinion written by Sotomayor, the majority instructed:

It is clear after *Montgomery* that the Eighth Amendment requires more than mere consideration of a juvenile offender's age before the imposition of a sentence of life without parole. It requires that a sentencer decide whether the juvenile offender before it is a child "whose crimes reflect transient immaturity" or is one of "those rare children whose crimes reflect irreparable corruption" for whom a life without parole sentence may be appropriate. . . . There is thus a very meaningful task for the lower courts to carry out on remand.

Alito and Thomas dissented, but their dissent appears to make it clear that the court has now extended the principles articulated in both *Miller v. Alabama* and *Graham v. Florida* to *all* life-without-parole sentences for juveniles, not just such sentences when they are mandatory rather than discretionary. Alito wrote:

In any event, the Arizona decisions at issue are fully consistent with *Miller's* central holding, namely, that mandatory life without parole for juvenile offenders is unconstitutional. . . . A sentence of life without parole was imposed in each of these cases, not because Arizona law dictated such a sentence, but because a court, after taking the defendant's youth into account, found that life without parole was appropriate in light of the nature of the offense and the offender.

Alito goes on to say:

It is true that the *Miller* Court also opined that "life without parole is excessive for all but 'the rare juvenile offender whose crime reflects irreparable corruption,'" . . . but the record in the cases at issue provides ample support for the conclusion that these "children" fall into that category.

Then, of course, he highlights what he sees as the most egregious facts of each crime. By granting that even Alito thought that this was the issue (i.e., the nature of each individual juvenile's case), it appears that the court has made clear now that the sentencing court is required to make the "irreparable corruption" finding before imposing life without parole for any juvenile offender. This rule still leaves open the possibility of life-without-parole sentences for juveniles (which, I believe, is a wrong yet to be righted), but it effectively nullifies the mandatory/discretionary distinction. That's progress, even though it does leave the loophole that permits discretionary sentences of life without parole for juveniles.

From my perspective, the loophole that allows teenage killers to receive *discretionary* sentences of life without the possibility of parole is why I hope the court will take the next steps in the process of the United States joining the rest of the "civilized" world in exempting *all* juveniles from life sentences without the possibility of parole. Amnesty International put it this way: "The United States is believed to stand alone in sentencing children to life without parole. Although several countries technically permit the practice, Amnesty International knows of no cases outside the United States where such a sentence has been imposed in recent years" (www.amnestyusa .org/).

The Eighth Amendment precludes punishments that are "cruel and unusual." Acknowledging that the court has not yet gone far enough to bring us forward to where the rest of the world is, why did the court (five of the nine justices, anyway) find automatic life-without-parole sentences for juveniles cruel and unusual? Because juvenile killers are "less guilty by reason of adolescence" and are more capable of rehabilitation as their brains and personalities mature. That was 2012.

Then, four years later, in 2016, the Supreme Court ruled in the case of *Montgomery v. Louisiana* that the *Miller* decision was to be applied retroactively throughout the country. This made it applicable to about 2,500 men, according to data collected by The Sentencing Project—a national advocacy group dealing with criminal justice issues (www.sentencingproject.org). This decision opened the floodgates for these men to seek resentencing hearings in the thirty-one states that have had mandatory life-without-parole sentences for juvenile murderers on the books, although it still did nothing whatsoever directly for the 7,500 inmates who are serving *discretionary* life sentences for murders they committed (or were involved in) as juveniles. That was a matter for another day in court. In my view, also in need of a Supreme Court ruling are what might be called "Methuselah" sentences (so called after the Biblical figure who reportedly lived to be 969 years of age). These are sentences so long that they exceed the expectable life span of any human being—as in the case of Paul T., who at the age of fifteen received a sentence of 120 years before he would be eligible for parole. Having noted them here briefly, I will return to these issues in chapter 6, where I consider how to translate this hope into law and practice.

One important consequence of the *Miller v. Alabama* decision (and the follow-up cases) was to send a message of hope to men who previously had no earthly basis for hope. My colleague Kathleen Heide wrote movingly about this in a letter to me in 2017, which I will quote here because her observations are crucial:

> One of the problems with giving juveniles life without parole is that it may take away hope, which can be a significant motivator for change. Many juvenile homicide offenders (JHOs) have had a multitude of adverse events, which affects their ability to mature to the level of their counterparts who have grown up in healthy families and good neighborhoods and who have been blessed with positive role models and excellent opportunities. These JHOs may feel intense anger and despair when sentenced to life without parole, thinking that it is just one more "unfair break" in their lives. From my experience, sometimes this anger continues and escalates in prison. These youths feel "what is the point" of bettering themselves when they are denied access to many prison programs and will never get out of prison. So instead of examining themselves and moving forward, these individuals act out, that is, they rebel against the correctional authorities, for years. For some, it is one of the very few choices that they see themselves as having. Many of their transgressions are minor. For example, they may refuse to make their bed, sit on their bunks during count, etc.

Miller v. Alabama brought these individuals hope that someday they might be released. For some, their thinking, decision making, and behavior changed when the possibility of having a chance to start over suddenly appeared on the horizon. Individuals in their thirties who had defied rules since being incarcerated as teens started to reevaluate their behavior. For them, the decision to grow came late, but it eventually arrived.

I recall a conversation I recently had with the parole commissioner of a northeastern state. He was relating how dramatic the change was in the behavior of juveniles sentenced to life without parole when the *Miller* decision came down. He stated that prior to the court's decision, these kids were unruly and acted out, making supervision in the prisons very difficult. After *Miller,* their behavior radically improved. I am reminded of the words of Nobel Prize winner Archbishop Desmond Tutu: "Hope is being able to see that there is light despite all of the darkness." Amen to that.

But this hope is not the whole story. Before going any further, I should say two things. First, waiting until after a teenager commits a murder is hardly good social policy, no matter how humane the sentencing guidelines are. Preventing the murders in the first place is the first priority. There is some good news on this front to be found in the empirical work of Chicago psychologist Robert Zagar. Zagar developed an extremely effective approach to identifying youths at high risk for committing murder—correctly identifying more than 90 percent of the youths who eventually did commit murder and correctly ruling out more than 90 percent who did not (in contrast to the success rates of other measures, which rarely achieve 70 percent accuracy).

Based on Zagar's identification of such high-risk youths, the City of Chicago spent $50 million to support a preventive program that screened twenty thousand youths and identified nearly five thousand of them as being "at high risk." The intervention involved three components: anger management, mentoring, and job opportunities. In the wake of participating in the program, the murder rate was reduced by 47 percent among the high-risk group (from what it was predicted to have been)—saving 193 lives and $1.4 billion. Javell Ivory and many other kids like him might well have profited from participating in such a program. Unfortunately, he did not have such an experience *before* he was incarcerated. Nonetheless, the prevention message is clear. What is more, as we will see at a later point, these findings offer some guidance in understanding what kind of programming focus can help Miller's Children after they are incarcerated, namely the important role played by mentoring, anger management programs, and occupational opportunities in prison.

The second point I want to make here concerns the implications of the *Miller* decision for sentencing juvenile killers in general (assuming it leads eventually to a prohibition of *discretionary* life-without-parole sentencing). A number of important questions arise. What *is* the developmentally appropriate length of the sentence for a juvenile killer? Should there be minimums as well as maximums? Must it all be done on a case-by-case basis? What is the prognosis for teenage killers when they are released—is recidivism likely? Could Zagar's approach to screening play a role in sentencing decisions? How soon should eligibility for parole kick in? What are the appropriate grounds for granting parole? Again, can Zagar's approach provide a scientific foundation for making these decisions? I will address these questions at various points throughout this book, and return to them systematically in the concluding chapter. But this entire discussion hinges on the recognition that teenagers are not yet adults, and teenagers who grow up with high levels of adversity tend to be *less* rather than *more* mature than their fortunate peers.

TEENAGERS ARE DIFFERENT, AND TRAUMATIZED TEENAGERS ARE MORE DIFFERENT

Put most simply, the *Miller v. Alabama* ruling (like the *Graham* and *Roper* decisions before it) requires the courts to consider the fact that a teenage killer is not just any defendant, not just any violent criminal. The teenage killer is in court because of an insidious interaction of his (or her) adolescence and background. For a start, teenage killers are not playing with a full deck when it comes to making good decisions and managing emotions because of their immature brains. But many of them are also playing with a *stacked* deck because of the developmental consequences of adverse life circumstances.

Both their immaturity and their social histories impair their capability to make good, prosocial decisions and manage their emotions effectively. This is why so many of Miller's Children represent a kind of "adolescence squared." The psychologically traumatic and socially toxic nature of their families and communities exacerbates the immaturity of thought and feelings intrinsic to adolescence, not just additively $(4 + 4 = 8)$ but exponentially $(4 \times 4 = 16)$. Research on the developmental impact of "childhood adversity" makes this clear.

The CDC—the federal government's Centers for Disease Control and Prevention—has endorsed an approach to risk accumulation that focuses on the impact of ten "adverse childhood experiences" (ACEs). These risk factors are assessed through a series of ten questions, including inquiries about childhood experience of physical, sexual, and psychological maltreatment, poverty, domestic violence, household substance abuse, parental separation or divorce, depression or suicide in a family member, and incarceration of a family member. While not encompassing all possible negative influences on development (for example, the impact of racism and educational impairment), these ten factors have proved to be powerful in accounting for differences in negative outcomes extending into adulthood.

Among these are a constellation of problems involving precisely the issues of "executive function" and "affective regulation" with which teenagers struggle by virtue of having their behavior shaped by adolescent brains, namely violent behavior directed at self or others, substance abuse, and depression. ACE scores account for 65 percent of the variation in suicide attempts, 40 percent of the variation in violence toward others, 55 percent of the variation in substance abuse, 45 percent of the variation in depression, and are associated with poor health outcomes generally. When you consider that exposure to secondhand smoke accounts for only about 15 percent of the variation in lung cancer rates, these are very impressive numbers.

For purposes of understanding the lives of the "general population," it may be sufficient to report measures of health and well-being in which the lives of adults who had a score of zero (some 35 percent of the general population), one (26 percent), two (16 percent), or three (10 percent) ACEs are compared with those with four or more (13 percent). But to appreciate the developmental damage experienced by many killers, it is necessary to understand the impact of extraordinarily high scores that are rare in the general population but relatively common in this group—38 percent having more than five of these risk factors (vs. 10 percent in the general population) according to a 2014 study conducted by Michael Baglivio and colleagues.

Prosecutors sometimes try to dismiss the importance of childhood adversity by saying, "Lots of kids have tough childhoods and *they* didn't kill anyone." Data on the ACE scores of teenage killers can provide a powerful rejoinder. Of the approximately 27 million kids ages twelve to seventeen in the United States, only about 270,000 (1 percent) have ACE scores of seven or more (and 27,000 have scores of eight, nine, or ten—about 0.01 percent). Of course, only a small minority of youths with high ACE scores commit murders—about seven hundred in total per year (about three in one hundred—3 percent—of the kids experiencing the greatest adversity in the form of eight, nine, or ten ACEs). Among all 27 million kids ages twelve to seventeen, the homicide rate is more like three in a million (0.0003 percent), *making the murder rate for kids in the highest category of ACE scores one hundred times higher.* Most kids who grow up with high levels of adversity do not become killers, and some juvenile killers do not have high ACE scores. But elevated adversity scores are as common among killers as they are rare in the general adolescent population.

What differentiates those with high levels of adversity who kill from those with high ACE scores who do not? It is only when we can see the complete picture of a juvenile's pre-murder life that the specific path he took becomes clear as an interaction of adversity, temperament, social environment outside the family, substance abuse, and idiosyncratic circumstances that led to the moment when a gun, a knife, a club, or a fist made that juvenile into a juvenile killer. Exploring these complex interactions was my principal focus in *Listening to Killers*. I cover some of that same ground here as a basis for understanding how these factors affect the process of rehabilitation and transformation in the lives of Miller's Children after they arrive at the point where they become killers. Psychology is about the accumulation of probabilities. The more you know about negative and positive factors, the closer you get from an "it depends" to a "yes or no" answer about who becomes a juvenile killer.

One way to provide an empirical context for this discussion is to note the results of a study conducted by Patrick Tolan and colleagues in Chicago. This study revealed that among abused children living in the most violent and impoverished neighborhoods who were exposed to racism, *100 percent exhibited significant psychiatric and/or academic problems between the ages of thirteen and fifteen.* No one was spared. Most kids experiencing a lot of childhood adversity may not kill, but certainly they all do suffer—even the "good" ones who demonstrate miraculous resilience in the face of extreme adversity.

The good news is that most kids overcome the damage eventually, and few take the path that leads to murder. But we must all be humble about the connection between childhood adversity and a troubled adolescence—whether it takes the form of violent behavior or not. I have heard more than one man who grew up with abuse and adversity on the mean streets of Chicago and avoided going to prison admit, when hearing the stories of Miller's Children, that "there but for the grace of God go I." Only the ignorant and the self-deceptive are smugly judgmental about this connection.

Moreover, the same trauma and social toxicity that exacerbate the risk posed by high levels of adversity (as measured by ACE scores) also mean that the *consequences* of adolescent immaturity and waywardness are more serious. It's one thing to have typical teenage problems with executive function and affective regulation when you are being raised by competent and loving parents, have a low ACE score, and are living in a safe, high-resource, middle-class community where second chances abound if you make a mistake. It's quite another to have these same adolescent issues when you are being raised by parents who themselves have compromised functioning due to substance abuse, mental health problems, and poverty and you live in a gang-dominated urban war zone where guns are common and second chances rare.

Think of this: if a boy has developed a chronic pattern of aggression, bad behavior, acting out, and violating the rights of others by age ten he can be diagnosed officially as a case of "conduct disorder." I must note at this point that although these are the criteria for diagnosing so-called conduct disorder, I resist using the term. Why? Because it is a mere name for an observation (of a chronic pattern of aggression, bad behavior, acting out, and violating the rights of others). As we will see in more detail later, it doesn't really explain anything. It is true, however, that this *childhood pattern* is often the gateway to seriously violent delinquency (leading to that outcome in some 30 percent of cases on average).

Does displaying conduct disorder at age ten strongly predict violent juvenile delinquency at age seventeen? According to research conducted by criminologists Rolf Loeber and David Farrington, the answer is that "it depends." If a ten-year-old displaying a pattern of aggression, bad behavior, acting out, and violating the rights of others lives in a "bad" neighborhood, he is *four times* more likely to end up as a seriously violent juvenile offender than if he lived in a "good" neighborhood (60 percent vs. 15 percent). Most teenage killers do not come from "good" neighborhoods.

This kind of finding makes sense from the perspective of "human ecology." As elaborated by my mentor Urie Bronfenbrenner, an ecological perspective on human development focuses on the critical importance of context—social, cultural, historical, biological, and psychological. One way to capture this idea is to point out that when the question is "Does X cause Y?" the best scientific answer is usually "It depends."

We must remember this when we look at the developmental impact of *temperament,* the package of attributes that a child arrives in the world with: "impulsive vs. reflective," "reactive vs. easily soothed," "stress allergic vs. stress resistant." Do these genetically originating predispositions affect development? The answer, of course, is "It depends." One important illustrative example of this latter temperamental issue is to be found in the operation of the *MAOA* gene.

About 30 percent of males (vs. 9 percent of females) have a form of the *MAOA* gene that reduces the levels of an important neurotransmitter (monoamine oxidase A), and this impairs their ability to deal effectively and prosocially with stressful situations (like living in an abusive family or being bullied at school). Thus, according to research conducted by Avshalom Caspi, Terrie Moffit, and their colleagues, 85 percent of males who have this genetic vulnerability *and* who live in abusive families (an environment of chronic and severe stress) end up engaging in a chronic pattern of aggression, bad behavior, acting out, and violating the rights of others by the time they are ten years old. That is to say, they exhibit conduct disorder.

It is worth noting here that recent research by R. James Blair, Ellen Leibenluft, and Daniel Pine demonstrates that a majority of children who develop conduct disorder are characterized as "anxious and reactive" to stress rather than "callous." Even in the case of those who are "callous," the origins are usually in a reaction to abuse and trauma, rather than some inherent emotional insensitivity.

On the other hand, relatively few males who grow up in well-functioning, non-abusive families end up exhibiting problems with severely violent behavior, *whether they have the MAOA vulnerability or not.* In good family circumstances, within a supportive environment, their genetic vulnerability is "neutralized" by a positive environment and effective child rearing. Neuroscientist James Fallon provided an illuminating demonstration of this in his 2014 book *The Psychopath Inside.* Fallon addresses the question of why, although he was born with the vulnerable *MAOA* gene, he nonetheless escaped a childhood and adolescence of conduct disorder and became a prosocial adult. It took him ten years to complete his analysis, and this is his conclusion: he grew up with very positive and effective parenting, in a community with very positive and effective community institutions and schools. As a result, he was tamed, whereas other boys who enter the world with the risky "warrior" version of the *MAOA* gene are faced with abuse, neglect, and community violence. That describes a lot of Miller's Children, of course.

DEVELOPMENTAL ASSETS

On the positive side, the Search Institute's research on "40 Developmental Assets" provides a compelling picture of the role that positive influences and attributes have in prosocial development in general, and in violent and aggressive behavior in particular. The 40 Developmental Assets include positive elements within the family (e.g., "family provides high level of love and support"), the school (e.g., "school provides clear boundaries"), the community (e.g., "at least three people who are not your parents take an interest in you"), mainstream cultural activities (e.g., "three hours a week of music, art or theater lessons"), and positive belief systems (e.g., "my life has a purpose").

Only 6 percent of youths with thirty-one to forty of these assets are involved in antisocial aggression, as opposed to 61 percent among youths with zero to ten of these assets. The same pattern emerges with respect to some of the factors that either contribute to aggression or prevent it. Thus, as the number of assets goes down, substance abuse increases; and as the number of assets goes up, delay of gratification and being successful in school also increase. The average number of assets reported by American youths is seventeen. As we will see, most teenage killers report fewer.

THE MALLEABILITY OF ADOLESCENT BRAINS WORKS IN BOTH DIRECTIONS

In an important way, the same factors that make juveniles likely to "choose" to kill also point toward considering the possibilities for rehabilitative intervention that are particularly promising in the case of young defendants. Not being fully formed, adolescents are highly malleable. This includes their brains, which don't really mature until their mid-twenties for the most part, as outlined by psychologist Laurence Steinberg in his 2015 book *Age of Opportunity: Lessons from the New Science of Adolescence.* In general, adolescent brains are more malleable than those of adults, although even the brains of adults are responsive to changes in environment, as amply demonstrated by Norman Doidge in his 2007 book *The Brain That Changes Itself.*

Being especially susceptible to peer influence is usually thought to reduce prosocial behavior and increase antisocial behavior, but that can change when kids are put in alternative environments and given positive direction. By the same token, to the best of my knowledge, there is no evidence that the severity of an adolescent killer's actions in committing a murder predicts less capacity for eventual rehabilitation. This means that in statistical terms, there is no evidence (of which I am aware) that the severity of a teenager's lethal behavior is strongly and negatively correlated with the possibility of socially significant improvement in thinking, feeling, and behaving in prosocial ways to the point where he will be "safe" for release into the community.

For example, although the magnitude of the crimes they have committed is enormous, "school shooters" may in fact be quite amenable to rehabilitation, because their violent outburst is generally not rooted in a long history of criminal behavior and violence. Rather, it is generally linked to an unfortunate intersection of crises in adolescence, crises that could have been resolved—and, in many cases, would have been resolved—had they not taken the dramatic action that led to multiple deaths and injuries. This seems clear to me in the analysis presented by Katherine Newman and colleagues in

Newman's book *Rampage: The Social Roots of School Shootings*. They identify five necessary conditions for a school shooting to occur:

- shooter's perception of himself as extremely marginal in the social worlds that matter to him
- shooters must suffer from psychological problems that magnify the impact of marginality
- cultural scripts—prescriptions for behavior—must be available to lead the way toward an armed attack
- a failure of surveillance systems that are intended to identify troubled teens before their problems become extreme
- gun availability

Setting aside the issue of prevention, each of these factors represents a "cause" that could be addressed and neutralized after the crime has been committed, and thus lead to the rehabilitation of a school shooter despite the magnitude of his crime. (It's almost always a male who does the shooting, so male pronouns are correct 99 percent of the time.)

How could this be done? Through changed circumstances, such that the teenage shooter no longer feels so socially marginal. Maturation will accomplish some of this as he gains perspective on just how little high school really matters in the big picture of life. Efforts to help the shooter find a positive place in life will help too—even in prison, where he can become involved in educational and service activities. Psychological intervention and treatment can deal with the psychological problems that Newman and colleagues note are a direct contributor in the first place. Education and "consciousness-raising" efforts can reduce the allure and perceived validity of the cultural scripts that "rationalize" the murderous behavior of the school shooter. Administrative procedures that provide better accounting for the social and mental health status of the shooter in adulthood—including an assessment using Robert Zagar's algorithm—can help. Limiting access to guns can play a role. High-quality probationary services when he is released can offer the surveillance needed to make sure the community is safe.

My point is that while the school shooter's crime is severe and morally enormous, the task of rehabilitating him is manageable in most cases. I have met some of these school shooters in the course of my work, and they verify my hypothesis on this score. My larger point is that the horror of violent crimes committed by school shooters does not mean they are impossible to rehabilitate; they can be made "safe." The overt correlation between the severity of a teenager's crime and his prospects for rehabilitation is weak, where it exists at all.

THE SCIENTIFIC FOUNDATION OF
MILLER V. ALABAMA

In its sixty-two-page ruling in *Miller v. Alabama,* the Supreme Court did more than make legal and moral arguments. It laid out five scientific grounds for rejecting mandatory life without parole for juveniles, grounds that have become the focal point in the resentencing and parole hearings that have been ordered as a result. These five grounds are related to decision making, dependency, the context of the offense, legal competency, and rehabilitation potential:

- Immaturity, impetuosity, less capacity to consider future consequences, and related characteristics that impair juveniles' ability to make decisions
- A family and home environment from which a child cannot extricate himself or herself
- The circumstances of the offense, including the role the youth played and the influence of peer pressure
- Impaired legal competency that puts juveniles at a disadvantage in dealing with police or participating in legal proceedings
- The youth's potential for rehabilitation

Considering each of these five grounds in turn—decision making, dependency, context of the offense, competency, and potential for rehabilitation—I will illustrate them with examples from actual *Miller* cases.*

Decision Making

Thompson State Prison, Pittsburgh, Pennsylvania: As a fifteen-year-old, Martell A. joined a group of older boys on their way to rob the home of

---

* Names and identifying information have been altered for purposes of confidentiality here, as they have been throughout the book—with a few exceptions, such as the Javell Ivory case with which I began this chapter (in which my role was a matter of public record in the mass media).

sixty-seven-year-old Ronald Paul, a retired social worker. While two of the older boys had a long history of drug abuse, violence, and antisocial behavior, Martell did not. When the crime was discovered on April 17, 1997, even the police were struck by the "mystery" of why a teenager like Martell, without a history of prior violence, would come to be involved in the brutal murder of a man who was a stranger to him. I was trying to unravel that mystery myself as I sat with him nine years later.

What I discovered was a case study in what the Supreme Court called the "immaturity, impulsiveness, and less capacity to consider future consequences and related characteristics that impair juveniles' ability to make decisions." Martell has lived his whole life in the shadow of the fact that his mother died in his presence when he was four years old. This was compounded by the fact that he has lived his life without any knowledge of his father, except that he was murdered. In figuring him out, we must add to that the fact that Martell was moved around from relative to relative after his mother died, and some of this moving around felt like rejection to him. In any case, the instability of care meant that by the time he reached adolescence, Martell says he "never had a best friend" and "felt lonely a lot" and "wanted to be accepted by my peers." Thus, he was socially estranged and craved peer acceptance. He was outwardly placid but nonetheless volatile and carrying a load of rage. When asked of his childhood, "Did you often feel that no one in your family loved you or thought you were important or special or your family didn't look out for each other, feel close to each other, or support each other?" Martell said "yes" and was moved to tears.

When it is touched directly even now (as it was in my interview with him), Martell's residual sadness is hard to bear. Looking back, he admits that sometimes "I didn't want to live anymore" and that he had thoughts of suicide. When asked about his role in the fatal assault, Martell admitted that he hit Mr. Paul with a baseball bat "fifteen times." Such a prolonged assault requires substantial emotional energy to sustain it. Where did that come from in Martell's case? After all, Ronald Paul was a stranger, a nonaggressive old man. When asked what he did when he hit Paul, Martell said, "I was shouting." When asked how he felt when he hit him, he said, "I was full of anger." That's about all he had to say in the way of explanation. Even nine years after the crime, he demonstrated an infantile interpretation of himself and his life, driven by his extreme emotional neediness.

Martell was fifteen at the time of the incident for which he was sentenced, and twenty-four when I met him in 2015. Like many adolescents, under the stress of the situation created by his older co-conspirators, he engaged in criminal behavior that was both impulsive and stupid. Listening to him closely reveals a wellspring of sadness—even despair—about the lack of intimate connection in his life, and correspondingly (and ironically) his intense yearning for connection—friendship and care. I think Martell's rage came out of his chronic suffering from feelings of abandonment, rejection, and shame. His conduct is very much the behavior of an untreated traumatized child inhabiting and controlling the body of a teenager.

The rage directed at Ronald Paul was infantile. It was a kind of lethal temper tantrum, provoked in part by the emotional neediness that led him to follow his older friends into Paul's house in the first place to participate in the robbery. The group's twenty-year-old leader and instigator thought that Paul had a substantial amount of cash hidden in the house. Martell's behavior in the fatal attack was classically immature, impulsive, and undertaken without an appreciation of future consequences. It was thus classically adolescent.

Problems with "emotional regulation" are observed frequently among children who have had disrupted childhood relationships as Martell did. Of course, he had an especially heavy load of powerful emotions to regulate, and it should come as no surprise that he evidenced many problems with emotional regulation—for example, anger and depression. In this, he is typical of adolescents who have had to cope with unprocessed psychological trauma and neglect in childhood. All this put too much pressure on his limited ability, as an adolescent, to think clearly about the consequences of his behavior, and thus represented problems with "executive function." This limited his ability to process information effectively, particularly in stressful situations. It also undermined his ability to form a coherent sense of himself. That he has a fractured self even now, in his mid-twenties, is evident in the contradictory nature of many of his behaviors (caring and hostile) and feelings (rage and fondness)—and testimony to the work he needs to do to become a man at peace with himself and safe to release into the community. I think all of this contributes to Martell's characteristic suspiciousness of people. As he says, "I don't trust nobody."

Children facing traumatic loss must accommodate their psychic realities so that they allow for the processing of life's atrocities (like witnessing the death of your mother when you are four years old). Lev Vygotsky's model of development provides additional dimensions to this analysis. By focusing on the intrinsically social nature of development, this approach highlights the role of adults in mediating the child's experience of trauma. The key is the concept of the "zone of proximal development," which posits that children are capable of one level of functioning on their own, but a higher level in relationships with the "teacher" (i.e., anyone who guides the child toward enhanced development by offering responses that are emotionally validating and developmentally challenging).

This provides a developmental grounding for understanding the "natural" therapeutic efforts of adults (as parents, relatives, and neighbors) and for the "programmatic" efforts of professionals (as teachers and therapists). It is why having even one parent who is psychologically available, stable, and nurturing can go a long way toward helping a child heal from even chronic trauma. Often the people available to help children and adolescents by serving as a source of support and care for them are unable to do the job that needs to be done. This happens for a variety of reasons, most notably because their own issues make it impossible for them to be "psychologically available." Martell A. was let down by his peers who led him astray in adolescence *and* by the adult world that should have helped him cope with his tragic and excruciating childhood losses.

Dependency

Lima State Prison, Cleveland, Ohio: Ronald B. experienced father absence growing up. The identity of his biological father was unknown to him, and this mystery plagued him. He says, "I've always had questions, but my mom kept me in the dark." His mother, Luanda, exposed him to her multiple partners (who did not operate as father surrogates), and he lived in chronic poverty that translated into sporadic neglect of his basic needs for food and shelter. More importantly, Ronald experienced traumatic family disruption and rejection when he was fifteen years old. He was "expelled" from his mother's household when he intervened in a violent conflict between his mother and her then partner, Tyrone. As Ronald put it, "She chose him over me," and he was sent to live with his older sister, Judy—whom Ronald describes as a "second mother." His junior year in high school went well, and he held a part-time job. However, because of a change in her family situation, Ronald's sister told him he had to leave her household when he was a senior in high school, a rejection made all the more powerful because Ronald was strongly attached to his nephew. He says of this time, "I was hurting. I had become so attached to my little nephew." When he tried to return to his mother's home, he found conditions difficult to live with (she was still with

Tyrone), and he soon left again, becoming essentially homeless until he was arrested for his part in a robbery gone bad. It is worth noting that Ronald had accumulated enough credits to graduate from high school, even though his arrest precluded his attendance for the latter part of his senior year.

Ronald's precipitous descent into criminal violence is a testament to the power of family rejection (the lifelong abandonment by his biological father, the adolescent rebuff by his biological mother, and the ejection by his sister). The neglect at home was related to the structural factors that defined his family's existence as well as his mother's erratic behavior with respect to money and residence. Ronald reports that "we moved around a lot, got evicted, and all that, and sometimes didn't have food in the house." As a result, school was an oasis of stability and care for Ronald all through childhood and into adolescence. He says, "I'd be taken care of there." However, in a period of months he went from being vice-president of his sophomore class in high school and a columnist for his high school newspaper to being charged with murder and sentenced to life without the possibility of parole.

In a very important sense, child development is about building brains that are effective in guiding prosocial behavior, moral development, intellectual competence, emotional regulation, and a sense of meaningfulness and positive identity—in short, becoming fully human. Thus, child development is, first and foremost, brain development. Modern neuroscience is demonstrating that the initial neurological status of the newborn infant provides the raw material, but that the quality of the physical and social environment of the infant plays a crucial role in building that raw material into an ever more sophisticated brain, and thus an ever more advanced human being.

All the elements of the social environment influence this process of development through childhood into adolescence—family, neighborhood, school, community, and the larger society. An "ecological" perspective on the "family and home environment" is essential in understanding how and why some infants become prosocial, smart, ethical, and emotionally effective teenagers, and why others develop the kinds of intellectual and emotional limitations and chronic patterns of antisocial behavior and mental health problems that dramatically increase their risk of becoming teenage killers.

In the first year of life, perhaps the most important of the core challenges for children is to develop secure and positive attachment relationships (initially with immediate family members but increasingly with other human beings). Accomplishing this task creates a model for future relationships. Developing negative, ambivalent, or insecure attachment relationships puts the child at risk for later social and emotional problems. Failure to develop any attachment relationships at all can prove developmentally catastrophic, putting the individual at heightened risk for many mental health and social problems, and for becoming a teenage killer.

Parental "psychological availability" and acceptance are crucial to child development. Children cannot develop on their own. They need social support; neglect stifles child development in all domains. They need and thus crave acceptance; it is an essential psychological nutrient. Researcher Ronald Rohner and colleagues call parental rejection a "psychological malignancy" and report that it accounts for about 25 percent of negative developmental outcomes.

Chronic trauma in early childhood (fear, violent assault, witnessing domestic violence, torture, etc.) can lead to pervasive psychological problems—because the child's brain is "incubated in terror," as one leading researcher, Bruce Perry, puts it—and to an adolescence plagued by problems with emotional regulation and executive function. Teenage killers did not choose to be born into families that are abusive and neglectful or to live in "socially toxic" neighborhoods and communities from which "the child cannot extricate himself or herself" (to quote the Supreme Court's language on this matter).

Chronic trauma tends to lead to the overdevelopment of the more primitive parts of the brain (e.g., amygdala) that process emotions (particularly anger and fear), to the detriment of the more sophisticated parts of the brain (e.g., cortex) that are involved in reasoning. This negative effect is most clear when chronic trauma is experienced in early childhood, but given the malleability of the brain even in adulthood, adolescents who experience chronic trauma can also be affected.

The Supreme Court's majority was moved by this kind of evidence in *Miller v. Alabama,* describing Evan Miller this way:

> No one can doubt that he and Smith committed a vicious murder. But they did it when high on drugs and alcohol consumed with the adult victim. And if ever a pathological background might have contributed to a 14-year-old's commission of a crime, it is here. Miller's stepfather physically abused him; his alcoholic and drug-addicted mother neglected him; he had been in and out of foster care as a result; and he had tried to kill himself four times, the first when he should have been in kindergarten.

When I went into court to testify in the resentencing hearing for Ronald, I could only hope his judge would show the same insightful compassion that five of the nine Supreme Court judges did in that landmark case.

Context of the Offense

Raulston State Prison, Philadelphia, Pennsylvania: On July 2, 1999, Alonzo W. drove to the corner of Downy Lane and Sixth Street, with his ten-year-old son, James, in the car. It was well known in the neighborhood that Alonzo was a drug dealer who moved a considerable volume of drugs, wore expensive jewelry, and typically carried a large amount of cash at all times. As he stopped to chat with a former girlfriend who was standing at the corner, three teenagers approached the car and attempted to rob him. One of them pulled James out of the car and entered it on the passenger side. Another went to the driver's side and attempted to take Alonzo's necklace. Alonzo resisted, drew a gun, and both teens started shooting during the struggle. The third teen was standing by as a lookout. Alonzo was killed by a bullet to his head.

One of the shooters was seventeen-year-old Joshua B., who was indicted for first-degree murder; he was subsequently convicted and sentenced automatically to life in prison without the possibility of parole. All three teens say that they never thought that the robbery would be anything other than "easy money." The crime itself appears to be a case study in how adolescents engage in impulsive and stupid behavior—particularly when in a group. Joshua was part of a group of kids, one of whom suggested they commit a robbery. They had a couple of guns available to them. They were high from smoking weed. They had a simple plan—"point the gun at the guy and tell him to give up his money"—and did not anticipate that the victim might refuse to comply with their demand and draw his own weapon in response. Joshua "panicked" and, in the presence of his peers, stupidly shot their victim because "I didn't know what else to do." Now, seventeen years later, Joshua says of his adolescent crime,

> I didn't have the courage to say "no." I just wanted to be accepted. I did it to please somebody else. Loyalty is love. I realized as I got older that you expect to get it from your parents, but when you don't get it you want it from someone. I realize now that there is a different way of thinking and living.

Adolescents are particularly prone to the effects of their peers, whose mere presence can degrade the quality of adolescent decision making. For example, a study conducted by Laurence Steinberg found that when teenagers are placed in a driving simulator by themselves, they can make good decisions (in this case responding to a yellow light by stopping and thus being rewarded for not continuing through the light when it turns red). However, simply the presence of two teenage friends leads to the irresponsible behavior of running the red light, thereby forgoing the prizes due them for "responsible behavior" that they were able to claim when peers were not present.

But it goes beyond the *physical* presence of peers. Sociologist Erving Goffman developed the concept of "imaginary audience" to refer to the fact that many people believe the world around them is so focused on what they are wearing, saying, and doing that their behavior is based on unrealistic anticipation of how that imaginary audience will respond to them. Adolescents are particularly prone to this effect, as is clear in the accounts of many teenage killers, including Joshua. His behavior in the murder appears to have been linked to the kind of impulsive and stupid behavior often demonstrated by adolescents in general when in crisis, particularly in the presence of peers—that is, with an audience.

Competency

Barrington State Prison, St. Louis, Missouri: Thomas M. was sixteen in 1995 when he was brought in for questioning by police in connection with a gang-related shooting, for which he was eventually convicted and sentenced to life without parole. They questioned him for six hours. They slapped him and threatened him with the death penalty. They lied about the crime (which they are legally permitted to do during an interrogation). They told him that if he cooperated he could go home with his mother, who had been waiting outside the interview room for the last hour of the interrogation. After all of this, Thomas confessed to pulling the trigger on the gun found at the scene, despite the fact that he hadn't done it and knew who really had. Years later, he says of that time:

> I was scared that they would hit me some more. I heard stories about what the police would do to you if you didn't tell them what they wanted to hear. They lied to me and told me I could go home if I just signed a statement. And I knew if I didn't take the rap the guy who really did it would come after my family.

Almost everyone would have a hard time responding well in such a situation, but most teenage killers are not just "anyone." Again, although they may look grown-up and talk tough, guys like Thomas are best understood as untreated traumatized children inhabiting teenage bodies. As such, they are impaired in their ability to represent their interests effectively in the criminal justice system unless they are treated with compassion.

One of the ways in which juveniles are at a disadvantage in dealing with police or participating in legal proceedings is that they are prone to provide incriminating information without regard to their long-term interests. This includes false confessions. FalseConfessions.org is a public advocacy organization committed to raising awareness of the incidence of false confessions in criminal prosecutions leading to wrongful convictions. Their analysis of the data concludes that false confessions are particularly likely to occur in homicide cases and particularly likely to involve young men. The rise of DNA evidence analysis has brought this to light: more than two-thirds of the DNA-cleared homicide cases documented by Northwestern University's Innocence Project involved false confessions that led to wrongful conviction.

Why do people make the "choice" to confess to serious crimes (like murder) that they did not commit? While some do it on the basis of a demented desire for attention or in a state of delusion in which they really believe they are guilty, for the most part they make this choice because of the pressure and manipulation generated by police interrogation techniques, to which adolescents are particularly vulnerable. As Douglas Starr found when he looked into this matter, common interrogation techniques inadvertently convince investigating detectives that the interviewee is guilty and lead to escalating pressure to confess. After hours of interrogation, afraid and confused detainees often confess out of desperation and exhaustion, usually with the "guidance" of police and the promise of being released.

All of these issues are particularly problematic for adolescents (and especially so for African American kids, because research by Jennifer Eberhardt and Phillip Atiba Goff reveals that police officers tend to misperceive them as being four years older than they really are). The general tendency of teenagers to see the short-term benefits of acting while ignoring the long-term negative consequences of their actions plays into the hands of some actors in the criminal justice system. This includes police who are inclined to manipulate juveniles by making promises that offer relief from interrogation in the short run ("Just tell us what happened and you can go home") but result in disastrous consequences in the long run ("You confessed to the crime, now you have to do the time").

Potential for Rehabilitation

Cook County Court, Chicago, Illinois: There are two Eric G.'s. There is the sixteen-year-old boy who, in 1990, shot and killed two gang rivals "execution style." But there is also the forty-year-old man I sat with in 2015. This Eric is mild mannered, studious, respectful, and positive in his outlook on life.

When he was thirteen, Eric's parents divorced and he lost the constant presence and monitoring of his father. He says that when his father left, it was a "fork in the road, no father there meant no monitoring." With his father gone and his mother working all the time, Eric felt emotionally bereft. "If you ain't getting love or attention at home you go to the streets," he says. In the world in which Eric grew up, it was natural for him to be drawn into the gang-dominated street life, with all the adverse consequences that come from taking that path. Eric became affiliated with the Vice Lords as a matter of "geography." Like most kids growing up in such an environment in an American city, he carried a gun consistently and served as a soldier in the Vice Lords' drug enterprises (in which violence was an important currency). Two years later, he committed the crime that resulted in an automatic sentence of life without the possibility of parole.

Not surprisingly, Eric had issues with violent behavior early in his prison "career"—during 1992–98, when he had not yet matured into adulthood and reached the golden years, from the perspective of brain maturation. But after that period, the "second" Eric began to emerge—or, perhaps more accurately, began to be constructed. According to prison records, this Eric began to have a good record and has consistently improved since then. He has had only one incident since 2004—for fighting with a "delusional" cell mate whose mental health problems precipitated a conflict. He now speaks of how he has developed a mature understanding of himself and his life as a teenager. This Eric received his GED, and he now reads for pleasure and education (which he didn't do as a teenager). This Eric has become a student of American society through his independent reading and formal classes, and this Eric has increased his understanding of self and the social dynamics of his life. With his growing insight and self-awareness, this Eric even began to have an appreciation for the level of victimization he had experienced, and how it directed him toward the murders he committed back in 1992. He reports that he eventually was able to move away and distance himself from the Vice Lords while in prison.

Thus, Eric is now a good candidate for parole, ready to leave prison and engage in a prosocial life on the outside, with the guidance and support provided by the agencies and facilities indicated in the release program that has been developed for and in consultation with him. This post-release plan can build upon Eric's maturation and adult development to be the capstone experience in his rehabilitation and transformation from the dangerous seventeen-year-old boy of 1992 to the "safe" forty-year-old man of 2015. As this latter Eric puts it, "My spiritual life helps keep my mind out of prison. Despair is the enemy here." Looking back on the adolescent Eric, the adult Eric says that he realizes now that "I didn't know my impact, my responsibility—I was being selfish."

The most highly regarded review of research on the implications of psychological development for appropriate treatment of legal culpability issues among youths is found in a report in the journal *American Psychologist* in 2003 ("Less Guilty by Reason of Adolescence" by Laurence Steinberg and Elizabeth Scott). This report documents the way adolescent brains are immature (extending into young adulthood), how the presence and influence of peers tends to short-circuit the moral thinking of youths, how the ability to assess the consequences and weigh the risks and benefits of actions is often out of balance, and how adolescents often make mistakes in interpreting the emotional messages of adults. All these factors are subject to improvement with maturation, but during the teenage years they create a serious vulnerability, one that can be exacerbated by traumatic social environments and life experiences. As I've argued above, this makes for a kind of "adolescence squared" in the lives of some kids and is the developmental key to understanding Miller's Children.

Adolescence—most particularly age fourteen—is the period in human brain development when the area of the brain involved in regulating the intensity of sensation (the nucleus accumbens) reaches its peak (declining after mid-adolescence and into adulthood). Thus, in mid-adolescence *everything*—whether it is positive or negative—feels more intense than it does before or after. Shakespeare recognized this when he wrote *Romeo and Juliet,* with Juliet being thirteen and Romeo not much older. Melodrama and pathos are not far away when adolescents confront emotionally loaded situations. And, as in the case of Romeo and Juliet, people can die as a result.

The part of the brain most involved in rational thought and reality testing—the frontal lobe—is generally immature in adolescents, and this is one reason why they are notorious for doing "dumb" things. They characteristically have difficulty appreciating the consequences of their actions, being prone to overestimate positive outcomes and underestimate negative ones. Thus, they tend to do impulsive and stupid things without an adequate appreciation for long-term and negative consequences, seeing only the immediate benefits of their action.

The cause-and-effect relationship between behavior and brain development is a two-way street; each can cause the other. The bad news is that this means there is often a downward spiral in the lives of kids who experience psychologically and socially toxic environments: their brains adapt to the negativity and become more compatible with that negativity. The good news is that this same brain malleability provides the basis for a positive upward spiral toward the light when kids are involved in prosocial behavior, educational activities that foster more mature thought, and spiritually enhancing experiences that raise consciousness. Eric G. is a poster child for precisely that potential for an upward spiral of maturity and transformation.

LISTENING TO REHABILITATED KILLERS

The goal of my book *Listening to Killers* was to understand how and why lethal violence arises in human beings in America. This book goes beyond that, seeking to understand how and why teenage killers are a special category of lethally violent people—and, more importantly, how and why they can, and in many cases do, "get better" in the years that follow their terrible crimes. This chapter's exploration of the five "Miller factors" sets the stage for a more in-depth look at the lives of Miller's Children, with a focus on where they have gone and who they have become during their time in prison. In the next chapter, we will pursue these lives in more detail, with each case chosen to represent one of the distinct pathways that kids take to leave behind the "lost boys" they were, to become the good men they are today. It may take many years—at least two decades in most cases—but it does happen. I have seen it in the records of their changed behavior—their positive, prosocial behavior within the limited confines of adult prison. I have heard it in their mature voices and their insight as they talk about who they were *then* and who they are *now*.

TWO

___

Who Are They?

This chapter introduces some of Miller's Children—some of the men, originally sentenced as juveniles to life without the possibility of parole, who came into my life when I served as an expert psychological witness in their resentencing hearings. The cases presented here cover the spectrum of successful rehabilitation and transformation stories that have come to light in the process of working on their cases, providing a "developmental analysis" of how these individuals came to kill and how they have changed for the better since then.

June 16, 2016

> Dear Dr. Garbarino:
>
> I have read your books *Lost Boys* and *Listening to Killers,* and felt I had to write to you. Reading your books I feel you know me! And, I learned that there are so many men like me. Before I thought we were like a small lost tribe, "juvenile lifers" as we are called. I felt we were alone in our hopelessness. But now I know that there are groups of us all across the country, and because of what the Supreme Court decided we can hope for the first time since we got here.

Eighteen years ago, Paul T. killed four people and wounded three others. Today, he is a sensitive and thoughtful young man, infused with insight and grateful for the person he has become. When I sat with him in 2016, he was obviously still fragile but clearly had become much more than anyone might have expected, given the magnitude and severity of his crime. And he is not alone in that.

THE LOST TRIBE OF TEENAGE KILLERS

Most people will never meet an adolescent who committed murder. After all, they are pretty rare—some forty thousand or so have been arrested for committing a murder in the United States *over the past forty years,* and mostly they have disappeared into the prison system, a kind of "lost tribe" as Paul T. puts it. This includes the many thousands of teenage killers who did not receive the *automatic* sentences of life without the possibility of parole that the Supreme Court dealt with in *Miller v. Alabama.* Their sentences were handed down at the discretion of a judge. And then there are the juveniles who received sentences so long they are tantamount to life sentences—for example, sixty or even a hundred years. In one case on which I worked, the attorneys introduced into evidence an actuarial table of life expectancies (in this case for an African American male). The table showed that the sentence of sixty-five years that had been imposed on a fifteen-year-old boy would result in an 85 percent likelihood that he would die in prison, despite the fact that his sentence was *not* a life sentence. In some states—for example, Florida—there is no legal basis for parole. The only way out of prison for Miller's Children in Florida is a resentencing decision that results in a limited term, putting an end to the existing sentence before the inmate dies or becomes a very, very old man (setting aside the extremely rare instances when sentences are commuted by executive action).

Thus, although in the case of *Graham v. Florida* the Supreme Court outlawed life-without-parole sentences for juveniles convicted of crimes other than murder, the reality is that even when juvenile killers receive sentences that permit parole, and thus will eventually get a parole-board hearing, these men (and, in some cases, women) may face impossibly long sentences before parole can even be considered. And, if there *is* a legal possibility of parole, teenage killers may not be eligible to apply for many decades after they are sentenced. What is more, some parole boards seem to be ready to stamp the request "rejected" out of hand, with little appreciation for whether or not there has been rehabilitation and transformation. I note all this here to make the point that although Miller's Children are the focus of this book, I recognize that they are not the whole story, and I will return to this topic in chapter 6.

If people have any awareness of Miller's Children at all, it will be of who and what they were as teenagers—as a result of mass media reports and portrayals *at the time of the crime or the initial trial* (or in fictionalized accounts in television programs like *Law & Order*). Rarely does anyone know much about the men they have become, many of them thoughtful, sensitive men like Paul T. who have grown into lives of service and reflection.

This chapter will introduce five good men. America is full of good men, of course. What makes *these* good men special is the remarkable story of how who they are *now* is connected to who they were *then*—or at least who they appeared to be then, years and even decades ago, when they were convicted of murder. I must point out that about 25 percent of Miller's Children were convicted of what is called "felony murder" or "accomplice liability"—as noted in chapter 1, this means they were involved in the commission of a felony (often robbery) that resulted in a death but were not the actual killer. Thus, even though they did not pull the trigger, they can be held equally culpable for a victim's death. In some cases this legal distinction is not particularly significant in psychological terms. For example, in an Indiana case a sixteen-year-old had a gun with him as a carful of gang members drove out looking for "the enemy," and could well have been a shooter had he had the chance, but he was told by the group leader to wait in the van as a lookout once they identified their target and rushed out to attack him. By contrast, in another case a fifteen-year-old simply went along for the ride with a group of his friends, not knowing that they were on a murderous mission, and was shocked into immobility when he realized what he had stumbled into. These kinds of cases are common enough, but here my focus is on cases in which the teenager's role was as an active and knowing participant in the murder.

My goal in this chapter is to provide a glimpse of five such cases, and the men these five prisoners—Robert, Muhammad, Chan, Miguel, and David—have become in the years that followed their teenage crimes. I will build upon the kind of stories I told in chapter 1, about how teenagers come to kill in the first place. Collectively, these men offer a primer on some of the important themes in the foundations of the process of rehabilitation—and some of the impediments to that process. I offer each as representative of a "type" of rehabilitated teenage killer, without presuming to say just how representative they are.

As I pointed out in chapter 1, Miller's Children often come out of childhoods marked by adversity, with 70 percent having scores of five or more ACEs (adverse childhood experiences), compared to only 7 percent of the general population. A summary analysis prepared by The Sentencing Project revealed that child abuse and neglect (and particularly psychological maltreatment) and domestic violence are a common theme (present in about 80 percent of the cases), as is being immersed in the world of drug dealing and using. A majority come from neighborhoods where they have witnessed community violence on a weekly basis. Involvement in gangs is a common issue too, as is race. And African American youths are eight times more likely to receive sentences of life without the possibility of parole.

I think there is some value in considering these five examples of rehabilitated teenage killers, to get a sense of the range of issues involved in the pathway that led them to who they are today: Rehabilitated. Transformed. Redeemed.

ROBERT

A Teen Killer Crazed by Steroids Becomes a Good Man

Burris State Prison, Houston, Texas: Robert W. is a thirty-eight-year-old man with a serious manner and a hopeful air. Sitting with Robert in 2015, I was struck by the depth of his remorse. He spoke of how he sat in detention, in the hours and days after he was arrested, and fully realized the "severity of my mistake" and its magnitude: "how I had thrown everything away—nothing but the rest of my life in prison." That is the remorse of an adolescent. But now he speaks of his remorse with the voice of a grown man. He says, "You know how many people's lives you ruined when you do something like that. It's a ripple effect. There's no taking anything back. . . . I have been locked up now four years longer than I was out there in the world! For what? It was so stupid what I did." He described to me how, over the years and through a process of education and reflection, he has gained insight into the forces that drove him to commit murder when he was a month shy of his eighteenth birthday. Then, he was a high school football player—dependent on steroids and other drugs to enhance his athletic performance—who eventually killed his dealer after coming up short on the money he needed the night before "the big game." Today, Robert says of using those drugs, "It makes you feel ten feet tall and bullet proof" and "It made me snappy, more aggressive mean. . . . It destroyed my grades, made me a negative person, a bully sometimes."

Robert is well positioned developmentally and socially to make the transition from prison to success in the outside world. He has a supportive family awaiting his release, most notably his mother, who is a fully functioning, prosocial individual and has a business waiting that will provide Robert productive employment and a financial future. Research shows that this kind of family support is a very important predictor of post-release success. He is committed to a transitional living arrangement that will provide a high level of support for sobriety, and thus he is likely to avoid the negative effects of the substance abuse that plagued his pre-incarceration adolescence (and that is often a barrier to success upon release from prison). If released, he is poised to enter the year-long transition program offered by a Christian ministry that has more than two decades of successful experience helping former inmates return to civilian life. Like a supportive family, a supportive community can make all the difference in the world for someone released from prison.

The evidence of the past twenty-one years is clear. Robert has taken advantage of whatever (limited) opportunities for self-improvement have been made available while in prison. He completed his GED. He ran a canteen on the yard. He learned computer skills and serves as a tutor for other inmates. He has worked in the dental lab and the law library. He reads. He reflects. It's worth noting here that a variety of educational programs such as these have become less common in many prisons in recent years (a point to which I will return in later chapters). When prison budgets are cut, these programs are often the first to go. What is more, in a time of resource scarcity, inmates serving life-without-parole sentences are often put at the bottom of program waiting lists—if they are even eligible to participate at all. Many of Miller's Children report to me that it was not until they became legally entitled to a resentencing hearing that they were allowed to participate in rehabilitative educational and counseling programs, because they had been considered a useless investment.

In most cases, murders committed by teenagers appear to be simply the culmination of a pattern of psychological and social trouble that begins to take root in childhood and comes to awful fruition in adolescence (and I will present such stories later in this chapter). But the "pre-murder" life of Robert W. was not like that. He came from a two-parent family, a family with adequate means. He lived in a supportive community, did not face gang recruitment pressure, and was successful at school. He was white and thus escaped the toxic influences of racism that play such a powerful role in the lives of many teenage killers.

There were "issues" in his family, to be sure. His father was somewhat authoritarian, a frustrated athlete who pressured his son to perform—even to the point of encouraging his use of performance-enhancing drugs in high school—and Robert was plagued by depression. Being a high school athlete was at the core of his identity and was his principal source of connection to his father. Robert's father was so emotionally withdrawn that the only time Robert remembers him crying, and the only time he remembers him saying "I love you," was at the sentencing hearing. The aggressiveness and intensity with which Robert played football testifies to the central role it played for him, and how his father's frustrated athletic career echoed through his life.

But, all in all, Robert was not "developmentally doomed" like so many of the teenage killers I have come to know. For example, unlike most teenage killers, who have elevated ACE scores, Robert's score is one (the single "yes" item being "Did a parent or other adult in the household often swear at you, insult you, put you down, or humiliate you? Or, act in a way that made you afraid that you might be physically hurt?"). Also on the positive side, he experienced twenty-one of the "40 Developmental Assets" growing up, compared to the national average of seventeen. This is consistent with the picture presented by Robert and others of his life. In particular, he was involved in sports and other prosocial activities and had a lot of social support and connection prior to the substance-abuse crisis that precipitated the murder. Further evidence is to be found in the outpouring of community support for him before and during his trial.

Robert's behavior in the murder appears to have been linked to the kind of impulsive and stupid behavior often demonstrated by adolescents, in general and when in crisis—in this case a drug transaction gone bad, in which both the buyer and the seller were armed adolescents. His behavior does not necessarily indicate the kind of immutable and deeply ingrained habit of violent, antisocial thinking, feeling, and behavior that is captured in the oft-cited expression of "a malignant heart" or the clinical diagnosis of "antisocial personality disorder."

Robert told me that his worst memory is of how, as a thirteen- to fifteen-year-old, he "wouldn't talk with my parents except for arguing and fighting with them"—a pattern that culminated in an incident when he made his mother cry in desperation and his father assaulted him (including hitting him on the head and choking him). This kind of insight is exactly the possibility that even very troubled adolescents carry with them, particularly when the murder they committed came out of an adolescent crisis rather than a pattern of pervasive developmental damage in childhood. Why? Because adolescents like Robert are particularly likely to "age out" of their adolescent conduct problems if given the opportunity to become more emotionally intelligent through education, reflection, and the processes of neurobiological maturation. Indeed, this is one of the foundational principles contained in the Supreme Court's decision in *Miller v. Alabama*.

Listening to the thirty-eight-year-old Robert talk about the seventeen-year-old Robert, I heard good news, because what I heard was the developmental foundation for rehabilitation that was reflected in his prison records. It made sense of the multitude of awards and certificates he received for his good behavior in prison—including his success in substance-abuse treatment programs. All told, I was very confident about the good man Robert had become when I walked into court to testify on his behalf at his resentencing hearing in 2015. The judge agreed, and his resentencing decision (forty years, of which Robert had to serve twenty) meant that Robert walked out of prison in 2016, to the waiting arms of his parents.

MUHAMMAD

A Child Abuse Victim Comes of Age and Delivers Himself into the Hands of God

Cook County Jail, Chicago, Illinois: Muhammad T. is a thirty-year-old African American man with an amazing smile, the kind that lights up a room. His smile is so engaging that when I sat down to interview him in June 2016, I had to guard against responding to him with an uncritical positive bias. Even with this cautionary mentality, I came to realize that Muhammad is more than a young man with a dazzling smile. He is a poster child for the principle of "mutability" that underlies the *Miller v. Alabama* decision. He spoke proudly of his participation in a program called "The Way to Happiness" that has improved his anger management. He spoke appreciatively of the older inmates who took him under their wing and offered guidance on how to tame himself and survive in prison—positive relationships that have served a mentoring function. And he spoke of what he got out of the job-training and employment programs in the prison. As he became better educated, and as he had time and motivation for reflection, his insight grew in parallel with his mind. Muhammad received his GED, and he now reads for pleasure and education (which he did not do as a teenager). But in Muhammad's case, there is more than these "secular" experiences. There is a spiritual path that has complemented his intellectual path. He told me this: "I have taken the initiative to change my life because when I die I am going to be judged by the Creator." His involvement in Christianity in mid-adolescence gave way to an immersion in Islam (of the Sunni variety) in late adolescence, an immersion so transformative that it led him to change his name from John to Muhammad.

How are we to understand the process by which John, the violent, gangbanging teenager, became Muhammad, the peaceful thirty-year-old? I think the experiences available to Muhammad while in prison have roughly paralleled what researchers like Patrick Tolan and Nancy Guerra have identified as the keys to reducing adolescent violence, namely "cognitive restructuring" and "behavioral rehearsal." The first refers to changed thinking about violence (and larger issues of self and society). The second is about practicing changed behavior with respect to violence and its triggers. It is when they are put together, argue Tolan and Guerra, that violence and the risk of aggression subside.

Muhammad reports two experiences that sparked his transformation. The first was participating in a Black History class. The second was his involvement in the Islamic Studies program. Both were pivotal in the process by which he increased his understanding of self and the social dynamics of his life. He reports that reading *The Autobiography of Malcolm X* was the beginning of his "true" education. That book certainly had a similar impact on me when I read it in the mid-1960s. Why? Because it offers a concrete path out of the darkness of racism and toward the light of universal human respect and affirmation.

I have often thought that being sentenced to life in prison poses a critical choice: Will I become a savage barbarian or a cloistered monk? Muhammad struggled initially with the psychology of being incarcerated—with depression, aggression, and acting out—but eventually chose the monk's path. Study and reflection have led to his transformation from a teenager addicted to the "gangsta" life to a monk committed to a life of service and prayer. He told me, "I'm not attached to the things I was attached to before. I've changed in what I value."

When Muhammad first entered prison, he was depressed and traumatized. He reports that "I cried the first three days in prison. I didn't sleep a lick. I opened myself to hopelessness." Eventually he was exposed to Islam (being presented with a copy of the Koran). "I was looking for something, and Islam gave me the guidance I needed to do more than just live my life. I had to look at my life and I became more than just a product of my environment." He says of himself, "I have had a change of heart about my life." This kind of insight is exactly the possibility that even the most very troubled adolescents carry within them, if given the opportunity to become more "emotionally intelligent" through education, reflection, and the processes of neurobiological maturation.

Muhammad uses his Islamic perspective to communicate the ethical stance he has developed as an adult. He quoted to me a Koranic verse, "To kill one human life unjustly is like to kill the whole world," and then added, "The same for saving one life." Muhammad feels remorse for the life he took when he was sixteen: "I feel very ashamed—to say the least—that I have taken someone's life so unjustly and foolishly. It was pointless and I have to live with that. No matter what good I do in the future I am tied to that—I am a 'convicted killer.'"

How does his faith manifest itself in day-to-day life in the prison? He delivers a monthly sermon to the Islamic group in the prison and is devout in his practice. Beyond his allegiance to the tenets and practices of Islam (e.g., praying five times a day), he has embraced the message of love and service he finds in the Koran. Like many of Miller's Children who have accomplished rehabilitation and transformation, Muhammad has developed a strong ethic of service to his community in the prison. He mentors younger inmates, serves as a teacher, and counsels his peers when the darkness threatens to overwhelm them.

With the benefit of a more mature, adult perspective informed by an ethical and spiritual code, he has the foundation for reflecting on his violent behavior as a sixteen-year-old. He told me, "I had to look at my life after I got arrested. All the gangsta garbage I was living created this illusion in my mind. I realize now that prison is the grave of the living." He understands now that living that way was wrong. Then he was a boy; now he is a man. Muhammad looks back on his adolescent actions with regret, and he knows that the behavior that led to the murder he committed was impulsive and stupid.

Muhammad's successful rehabilitation is all the more compelling as a developmental pathway given that his experience up to the point when he became a teenage killer was one of chronic and severe adversity. Beyond growing up with an abusive, dysfunctional mother and a father who was gone at best and abusive at his worst, Muhammad lived in an urban "war zone." In our interview, he reported that he first witnessed someone being shot when he was nine years old. I then asked him these two questions: "Out of one hundred kids growing up in your neighborhood, how many would have witnessed someone being shot by the time they were nine years old?" and "If we picked one hundred kids from around the whole country, how many would have witnessed someone being shot by the time they were nine years old?"

In response to the first question, he answered, "I would say seventy." He struggled to answer the second question, ultimately saying, "Maybe fifteen." He was stunned when I told him that only about 3 percent of American nine-year-olds have witnessed a shooting. But in his world, his view is that *15 percent* of kids across the entire country experience the trauma of witnessing a shooting—a rate more than five times the national norm. This is what it means to live in an urban war zone: chronic trauma, and all it entails for child and adolescent development.

When Muhammad responded to the ten ACE questions, his score was nine. The only adverse experience he did *not* report pertained to being physically neglected at home, despite the fact that he grew up in an environment without a sufficient amount of parental guidance or supervision, and thus really merits an ACE score of ten because the lack of supervision he experienced does qualify as neglect. Part of his rehabilitation and transformation has come from his ability and willingness to reapproach his abusive and neglectful mother with love and compassion, and to let go of the idea that the man who is his biological father will ever be more than a genetic ancestor to him.

And then there is the matter of race, as there so often is in America. African Americans constitute about 13 percent of the population but commit about 50 percent of the murders. However, it is crucial to note that the racial disparity in committing murder is only present within low-income communities; middle-class African Americans have a murder rate no higher than that of the white middle class. It is the social toxicity of racism, in partnership with deprivations of social class, that explain the link between race and murder.

Racism has long been understood as a social toxin in the lives of African American children, youths, and adults (indeed for all of us, as a kind of American "original sin"). Beyond the obvious social cancer of slavery that lasted until the mid-nineteenth century, research documents that there were more than 1,500 lynchings, mutilations, and dismemberments of African Americans in the United States (mostly in the South) in the century between the end of the Civil War and the Civil Rights Act in the mid-1960s. This pattern of terrorism affected the socio-emotional life of African Americans (including Muhammad's extended family and himself). This has led to a movement to include "race-based traumatic stress injury" and "post-traumatic slave syndrome" in the list of "official" clinical diagnoses recognized by the psychiatric and psychological professional communities. Psychologist Joy DeGruy suggests that the consequences of post-traumatic slave syndrome include "extreme feelings of suspicion and perceived negative motivations of others" and "violence against self, property, and others." This is a major factor in the violence that has infused the lives of so many African American families and communities (even being linked to the disproportionate use and justification of physical punishment of children).

There exists in the black community a strong sense of vulnerability to police intimidation and violence. For example, a recent survey conducted by Jeffrey Fagan and colleagues in New York City found that 82 percent of blacks (and 71 percent of Hispanics) believe that "the police did not treat white and black New Yorkers with equal fairness." In contrast, only 45 percent of whites agreed with this statement. These different views are based on differing experiences with police. For example, research by Andrew Gelman, Jeff Fagan, and their colleagues revealed two important points about the implementation of the city's "stop-and-frisk" law. First, among the many thousands of stops made by police (which yielded detection of serious crimes in a very, very small percentage of cases), the demography of those stopped was very heavily (and disproportionately) weighted toward targeted minorities—blacks and Hispanics. Second, there is a direct correlation between the number of times an individual is stopped and frisked and their negativity and alienation regarding the police and other institutions. The researchers in this case attribute a causal connection: the more you are stopped and frisked, the more negative your views of the police become.

Research by Jennifer Eberhardt and Phillip Atiba Goff reveals that police see black youths as older and less innocent than white youths of the same age. As noted in chapter 1, on average, police (and citizens included in the research) estimated the age of black kids as being almost five years older than it actually was. As Goff has put it, "Our research found that black boys can be seen as responsible for their actions at an age when white boys still benefit from the assumption that children are essentially innocent." All of this research on the reality and impact of racism illuminates the social context in which African American males like Muhammad grew up.

Muhammad reported that "white people never came into my neighborhood unless it was to arrest people, pick up the bloodied, or give bad news." He says of his interaction with the police, "Whenever you deal with them there was hostility." His first memory of dealing with racism in childhood was at age seven, when he was forced to fight with another seven-year-old boy, a white boy. Why? According to Muhammad, he was told to fight the other boy simply as a matter of "racial loyalty." His first memory of a positive interaction with a white adult was in middle school, when a white coach took him under his wing on the basis of his athletic talent.

I think it is telling that *The Autobiography of Malcolm X* began the process of transformation for Muhammad, because he has found precisely the transcendence that Malcolm X found on his pilgrimage to Mecca. While not turning his back or a blind eye to the reality and negative consequences of racism, Malcolm X came to an appreciation that humanity could transcend race, and this insight transformed him spiritually.

That Muhammad has emerged from the heavy weight of childhood adversity that he experienced and become the man he is today is miraculous. Perhaps no one who "evaluated" him at the time he became a teenage killer could have foreseen this miraculous path. Of course, that is one reason why the Supreme Court ruled against automatic life-without-parole sentences for juveniles: you can't know what kind of men these troubled and violent boys will become.

When I interviewed him in late March 2015, I noted that our birthdays are only three days (and forty years) apart. I was pleasantly surprised when, after the interview, I received a birthday card that quoted St. Augustine: "In as much as love grows in you, so in you beauty grows. For love is the beauty of the soul." Inside the card Muhammad wrote these words:

> I pray that this greets you in a state of peace and tranquility. Hopefully you've enjoyed your birthday and life is beautiful for you. I wish you nothing but love and peace. I would love it if you can help me in my education process and grow in all areas of my life. Life is based on one word "Loyalty." With it we can build a paradise. Without it we only live in Hell.
>
> *Always Loyal, Muhammad*

Muhammad is now writing a book to both illuminate his own experience and provide guidance to others. The manuscript is titled "The 12 Steps on How to Seek and Maintain the Knowledge of Self." Having sat with him, I think he will finish it.

CHAN

A Murderous Immigrant Becomes a Good Christian

One day in 2014, I received this letter:

> Dear Professor James,
> Greetings. I would like to take this opportunity to make your acquaintance. I've recently finished a reading of your book "Lost Boys." Your concern, compassion, tolerance and understanding for the youth is palpable throughout your material. I would like to provide briefly my story.

My family immigrated here from China in 1980, and settled in St. Louis. I was three years of age then. I can't recall any memories except for that of my life in America. America is all I know. However, I've always felt an alienation from this country and most of its inhabitants. I was raised in a community without a considerable Asian presence. I always felt somewhat of an outsider. Even more so in prison. I did have an immense degree of potential. I was on the honor roll in high school right before my arrest. I even managed a 3.8 GPA despite the advanced courses (AP and college prep) I was enrolled in. My future held so much promise. But I was susceptible to peer pressure because I desired strongly to fit in and belong to some group. Unfortunately for me and my victims, I fell into the wrong crowd. Prison was the eventual outcome.

I was barely into my 17th year of life when I was arrested for the crime of armed robbery and murder in 1994. I am approaching the 20th year of my incarceration. I was sentenced to Life. So I am among the 300 plus 'Juvenile Lifers' in my state. I was the youngest of the 4 participants in said crime. . . .

During the approximately 20 years of incarceration I have undergone a substantial transformation and evolution of mind, heart, and spirit. I am no longer the wayward and lost teenager I once was. I have regained my moral bearing and compass. I have experienced a deep and heartfelt remorse for the victims. After reading your book I felt a kinship to you. I felt I finally found an adult who understands me and cares for me even though we never met. . . . My greatest desire is for us to become close friends. I need more positive influences in my life and I would gladly welcome a mentor of your stature and understanding. I hope you accept my offer of friendship. It would make a difference in my life.

Well James, I am going to bring this to a close at this juncture. Do take very good care of yourself. May God continue to shed His Grace and many Blessings upon you and your whole family. I wish you success in all your noble endeavors.

With the utmost respect and regards,

Chan L.

Thus began a correspondence that continues to this day.

The public defender's office in the state where Chan L. is incarcerated is staggering under the weight of processing the more than three hundred *Miller* cases in the jurisdiction and, as a result, has "triaged" the cases to match the office's resources. Their first priority is the seven cases in which the teenager was sentenced under the principle of "felony murder" that I explained earlier. Chan's case is not one of those: he *was* the shooter in a gang-related conflict over drug sales.

When I visited him in June 2016, I was only his second visitor in seventeen years (the other was his younger sister, who came once from out of state). His *Miller* appeal had not yet started; he had corresponded with the attorney who would be managing his case, but they had not yet met face to face. Our time together was a mix of serious discussion about his life and his boyish enthusiasm to try the treats in the visiting room's vending machines as a change of pace from the routine of prison food. I had anticipated this, bringing twenty dollars in coins so that I could feed Chan while we talked. And feed him I did! He tried the barbeque chicken wings (twice), the lemon cookies, the cheese-flavored pretzels, the salt-and-vinegar potato chips, and several different fruit drinks and soft drinks in the three hours we spent together.

Chan is a very bright young man, as his high school grades indicate, and he has harnessed his intelligence in the service of his rehabilitation and transformation. In one of his letters, he wrote this: "In an effort to understand myself I took an interest in reading what psychology books are available at the prison library. I've just finished reading material by M. Scott Peck, Carl Rogers and Laurie Ashner." It's a good list. Peck writes critically about conventional views of masculinity, Rogers about humanistic psychology as a pathway to meaningfulness, and Ashner about how to identify and replace self-defeating personal strategies in life.

I asked Chan how he understood his adolescent violent actions now, looking back on them after twenty years. He wrote this:

> I now realize how fearful I was back then and how each event in my life influenced my source of direction in life. My resolution to procure a gun was the direct result of having been attacked by a group of rowdy, aggressive guys in the parking lot of a club. I bought a gun because it made me feel safer overall. It was something I believed I could rely on in times of danger.... But as I look back on myself, I now realize how scared I was in general. How I felt life was so uncertain and that harm and danger could surface in an instant. How I didn't trust in people to aid me or support me. That I felt like I was on my own. Not only was I physically small but I felt small, and weak. And how desperate I was to be accepted and to that degree compromised my character and principles for acceptance. How immature and narrow-minded I was. How even my noble principles I lived by were misdirected for the wrong purpose, i.e. loyalty to the wrong people. Jim, as I answered this question it provided me insight into who I was back then. I didn't even realize some of these truths until just now. It was a revelatory experience. From even a better understanding of myself I am grateful. I can exert even more control and awareness over my behavior than I already have.

Like many of Miller's Children, Chan has taken almost every course to which he has had access. For example, he has received training as a mediator (as he told me, "the same training SWAT negotiators receive") and has taken courses in "Ethics and Critical Thinking" (offered by a local college), "House of Healing" (offered by a local church), and "40 Days of Prayer" (offered by church volunteers). This last program is related to the fact that Chan has pursued a spiritual path as a devout Christian. In 2015, he was selected to enroll in a four-year seminary course—the "Urban Ministry Institute"—and more recently started a two-year "Spiritual Practicum." He wrote to me about his joy in this: "So eventually I'll be both a certified preacher and a Spiritual Director. How ironic is that for a prisoner!!!??? It makes me smile. God truly works in mysterious ways."

From our conversation that day in the prison visiting room, I learned that Chan had faced many challenges as a child. After coming to the United States from China, his father had slipped into schizophrenia and disappeared from the family. I learned that Chan witnessed his father beating his mother. I learned that his mother and sister moved across the country after he was arrested, and that he has never seen or heard from his mother again. I learned that his early years in prison were full of conflict (he stabbed a bigger, older inmate who was bullying him), anger (he got written up for mouthing off to guards), and depression (he had thoughts of suicide). When I asked Chan to fill out the ACE questionnaire, his score was five—physical abuse, psychological maltreatment, divorced parents, witnessing domestic abuse, and having a family member who was mentally ill. His score puts him in the most challenged 10 percent of American kids.

However, as with many of Miller's Children, things took a turn for the positive as Chan moved beyond his mid-twenties. In the photos he sent me after he completed the "preacher" course, he is beaming. In the photo we took on the day of my visit, he is smiling with pleasure. In the Christmas card he sent me, he wrote,

> I wish you and your whole family a joyous and memorable Christmas. May God bless you and hold you in his protecting grace for all the love and good works you have shown in his Name.
>
> Love,
>
> *Chan*

All I can say is "Amen."

Over the years of our correspondence, I have slipped into a "surrogate father" role with Chan. He reports regularly on his accomplishments—for example, when he won the top prize in a debate competition in which his prison team defeated a team from a prestigious law school in his state. One day, I received a letter from him that contained this moving testimony to the power of service in promoting and consolidating personal transformation among Miller's Children:

> In a prior letter I had mentioned the "Juvenile Deterrent Program" that is being implemented at this facility in an effort to mentor wayward and troubled youths. Well, all the kinks have *finally* been ironed out, and today our first batch of kids showed up for mentorship. There were nine teenagers in all who came up today—ranging from the ages of 16 to 18 years old. To me they just seemed so young, small, and fragile. It gave me another vantage point of how I must have appeared when I came to prison at the age of 17 years old, only 5'6" and only 135 pounds. This event provided me insight from a different perspective, gave me a direct sense of purpose, impact, and import. I noticed as I was striving to help these kids discover their value, my own sense of value was reinforced; all were being affected. This truly was a momentous occurrence. . . . I hope I'm making you proud.

He is. I am.

MIGUEL

Fear and Bravado Give Way to Wisdom

Dade County Jail, Miami, Florida: In August 2014, forty-year-old Miguel S. and I sat in an interview room at the jail where he was being held, awaiting his resentencing hearing. His English is better than my marginal Spanish, so we spoke in my first language rather than his. I asked, "When was the last time you cried?" He answered, "It was two years ago, a couple of weeks after my grandma died. I pulled the sheet over my head in my cell and I cried and cried. No one knew. You're the first person who ever asked about it. If you asked my mother—she was the one that came to the prison to tell me—she would have said I had no feeling about it. I was detached. Other than that, I can't remember the last time I cried." When I asked him how the other guys in the prison thought of him, he reported that when members of the "Thinking of Change" class at the prison and his peers were asked to describe Miguel, they used words like *cold* and *steadfast*. But, he said, "it be just a mask of nothingness. People who never experienced abuse don't understand it."

Miguel's traumatic history is evidenced in his characteristic pattern of "dissociation." He speaks of being a timid child with a "quick temper" growing up—inclined to internalize feelings of all kinds. He speaks of how he "just checked out" when in the presence of his abusive father. As a twelve-year-old, he witnessed the shooting of his friend "Eagle," who was shot in the head accidentally as the result of an altercation taking place across the street from where Miguel and Eagle were walking. "It was a shock to my system," he says, "but it was part of the norm. You heard about it all the time."

When you live in an abusive family and you walk out your front door to a gang-infused urban war zone as Miguel did, "being in touch with your feelings" can seem to be an unaffordable luxury. Numbness is a form of adaptive learning; you learn to survive by disconnecting emotionally. It doesn't mean there are no feelings, just that they are suppressed. But suppressed feelings can be very dangerous: fourteen-year-old Miguel shot and killed a man after an argument outside a bodega late at night escalated to the point of lethal violence. It has taken him more than two decades to develop an understanding of why he did it. *But that was then, and this is now.*

Adolescents—like Miguel in 1990—are prone to melodramatic overreaction. At age fourteen, Miguel was at a point in the development of the human brain when the area of the brain involved in regulating the intensity of sensation (the nucleus accumbens) reaches its peak (it declines after mid-adolescence and into adulthood). As noted in chapter 1, the research of developmental psychologist Laurence Steinberg (and others) demonstrates that in mid-adolescence *everything* feels more intense than it does before or after. Even adolescent rats show the same pattern!

But this is not the only way in which the relative immaturity of teenage brains plays a role in their crimes. Until roughly age fifteen, teenagers have difficulty reading the nonverbal cues offered by human faces. While few adults make mistakes in interpreting facial expression unless they have some sort of brain injury, "normal" adolescents do so regularly—for example, mistaking anger for fear. This fact, too, contributed to the escalation that resulted in Miguel's crime.

More generally, as noted earlier, modern neuroscience points to the role of brain maturation in the quality of human decision making and emotional self-management. It is not until human brains reach their mid-twenties, on average, that brain maturation is complete and the human being is "playing with a full deck." Neuroscientist Frances Jensen captures this well in her book *The Teenage Brain,* most particularly in the chapters titled "Building a Brain" and "Beyond Adolescence: It's Not Over Yet."

Although Miguel was abandoned by his drug-addicted mother, his paternal grandmother, Conchita, served as a mother replacement, so much so that he called her "Mom." Although she herself was often overwhelmed, and was unable to protect Miguel from the abuse dished out by her son, Miguel's father, Miguel believes he was loved unconditionally by her. This was the most positive feature of his life as a child. And I think it is the foundation for his progress toward rehabilitation and transformation during his period of incarceration in the more than twenty years since his crime. My mentor, Urie Bronfenbrenner, used to say that the key to successful child development is having someone in your life who is "crazy about you— irrationally attached to you." Miguel had this kind of positive attachment to Conchita as a surrogate mother, and believing she was crazy about him gave him a place to stand in the emotional universe. This, in turn, allowed the positive experiences he encountered in prison as a young adult to take hold in him.

When Miguel responded to the ten ACE questions, his score was seven. Only 1 percent of American kids face that much adversity. The three adverse experiences he did *not* report pertained to being sexually abused, being physically neglected at home, and having a household member who attempted suicide or was mentally ill. Though Miguel did not report being neglected at home, it is important to note that despite having a positive relationship with his grandmother, who was loving and nurturing, it appears that Miguel grew up in an environment without a sufficient amount of parental guidance and supervision. Conchita was providing for and taking care of numerous other children and additional family members, and consequently she had very little time to attend to Miguel. Often he was left to his own devices, and this culminated in his being allowed to drop out of school at the age of twelve. Thus, it appears as though he actually did experience neglect in childhood; he may be reluctant to publicly or privately acknowledge this because of his strong love and positive regard for Conchita. That said, Miguel's ACE score should probably be recorded as eight, not seven.

I think his answer to the following question is telling: "If we asked one hundred kids from around the country these same ten questions, how many do you think would have a score of seven or more?" He replied, "Fifty out of a hundred"—and seemed stunned that the actual figure is more like one out of a hundred. This is a clear demonstration of how child and adolescent development are "context specific."

When asked about the fathers of other kids he knew growing up, Miguel could think of none that had a resident father. Of course, in his case, having a father in the home meant living with an abusive alcoholic. In what I found to be a shocking and heartbreaking statement, when I asked Miguel about his happiest memory from childhood, he said, "It was the day my father went to prison." Why? Because it ended his vicious physical abuse, he said. As Miguel put it, "That was the happiest day in my life."

When I spoke to him in 2014, with the benefit of a more mature, adult perspective on his behavior as a fourteen-year-old, Miguel said of his crime,

> Now I see it that I was intimidated by that older man, and it was like when my father abused me. My dad would get verbally aggressive, then he would get physically abusive. That man I shot, we had words the day before and it escalated the next day. I been in situations in which I been abused and assaulted. When he advanced on me I pulled my gun and shot him. I believed it was justified then.

He realizes now that it was wrong. *Then* he was a boy, with a boy's brain and insight; *now* he is a man, with a mature brain and a lot of insight. Now Miguel regets his adolescent actions and appreciates that his reaction to the confrontation was wrong. But, given his adolescent issues with emotional regulation and executive function (issues that are compounded by his traumatic abuse history), the dynamics of the confrontation when he was fourteen were overflowing with risk factors for violence, even lethal violence.

A psychological assessment conducted in 1990 indicated that it was difficult to know then how Miguel's development would proceed once he was incarcerated—and, hopefully, received the benefits of education, psychological intervention, reflection, and maturation as he moved through adolescence into adulthood. Without such interventions, Miguel's prognosis was unclear at best. Quoting from the psychologist's report, "Unless some type of specialized placement can be obtained for Miguel, he will be at risk for further reacting in a dangerous manner, either to himself and/or others." His traumatic childhood led to the 1990 psychiatric diagnoses in his records—major depression, hallucinations, suicidality, antisocial personality disorder—and the recommendation that he be committed to a psychiatric hospital.

Had he been offered such a therapeutic "specialized placement" in 1990, Miguel might well have undergone the rehabilitative process in a more speedy and efficient way. But he did not benefit from such a therapeutic placement. Rather, he experienced the much less efficient—but, in his case, nonetheless effective—rehabilitative effects of maturation, reflection, education, and developmental programming available in the prisons in which he has been incarcerated for two-and-a-half decades. At his resentencing hearing, one of the correctional officers from the prison actually took his day off to come and testify on Miguel's behalf.

Miguel himself says insightfully of his life in 1990, "I know the path I was headed down. Prison saved my life. I was on my way to become the person they made me out to be, but I had the chance to become a different person in here." He was a dangerous boy *then;* he's a good man *now.*

DAVID

A Deeply Troubled Kid Becomes a Man Who Can Be Trusted

Hobart Transitional Center, Milwaukee, Wisconsin: I met with David F. for three hours in September 2015. A few days later, I received this message from him:

> Thank you for meeting with me and the others yesterday. After speaking with you, I was left with a very familiar feeling, a sort of weighty meaning-fulness. For me this feeling is associated with my first genuine relationship with the therapist I told you about when I was in the treatment program, Secure Intensive Treatment Program (SITP). He was, in my view, an extraordinary human being, capable of real healing and caring. I get the sense that you are the same kind of person.
>
> I also was reminded of how vitally important your work is to bring light to darkness, so to speak. I have to admit that my experience with the criminal justice system, the intense, negative media, and the living suffering of the victims to my crime has left me somewhat "changed" in a different way. Where once I would have been certain of the vision you so well express in your writing (and life), I'm no longer sure how to hold such conflicting emotional and moral perspectives.... I must tell you that the resolution of that conflict (challenge) seems essential to my ability to live my life.... As you've probably heard from other youth offenders, to hold the truth of the harm I've caused I need a container, or context, or belief system that organizes it. Without it, everything feels ground zero or subject to a relativistic understanding and morality. I discovered my spiritual and moral compass from my crime. Good became the opposite of what led me to commit to that degree of violence. The process has revealed that my narrative of good

or right, of change, largely did not matter to the victims of my crime and the media public. There was no way for me to join or identify with their suffering. I was the man who committed rape and murder. This discordant sense of self and reality flattened my sense of self and life meaning.

Twenty-five years ago, when David was just sixteen, he raped and strangled to death seventeen-year-old Jane P.—a high school classmate whom he had dated briefly until she broke it off. On the day of the murder, he asked if he could borrow her bicycle, planning to steal it. When she balked at handing it over, he was overcome with rage. He tied her up, beat her, raped her, and eventually strangled her to death and disposed of her body in a ravine near his house. As he put it twenty-five years later, "In a fit of rage I slipped the rope around her neck and strangled her." It was a horrible crime in every possible way.

Why did he do it? David says,

> My rage came from a deep-rooted 'denial structure' that had made me selfish, cold, distant, unfeeling and disconnected. Jane bore the burden of this rage because she was the first and only witness to one of my many crimes. I had been stealing and lying and denying wrongdoing since I was eleven years old. But the other crime victims were never present to catch and confront me. Jane's presence made my behavior undeniable. Why didn't I let her go when she pleaded with me? Why didn't I stop before I killed her? I can't say. It's taken me all these years to understand who I was then and why I did what I did.

At the time he killed Jane, David was heavily involved in drugs and had lost his way in the darkness of his thoughts and feelings. Now, twenty-five years later, he has found it. He is a lucid forty-two-year-old man who has become well versed in the law, from his years working as a law clerk in prison. He writes well and speaks with a deliberation borne of deep reflection and suffering—the suffering he caused to Jane and her family and his own pain as he has had to wake up each morning to the fact that he killed "the girl next door." But he does it.

He starts every day with a process of remembering what he did, what it meant, what he has become, and what he owes the world. It's a kind of crusade on his part, this getting up and living a better life *now* to atone for what he did *then*. *Then* he was a teenage boy struggling with the devastating developmental consequences of coping with an ACE score of eight (worse than 999 out of 1,000 kids in America). *Now* he is an amazing man, for whom I have great admiration. Like so many others among Miller's Children, he is living a life of service to others as a legal assistant and enjoying the basic pleasures of human existence.

. . .

Robert W., Muhammad T., Chan L., Miguel S., David F.—each of these individuals illustrates important developmental issues in the lives of teenage killers. This sets the stage for considering the possibilities and limitations of rehabilitation, transformation, and redemption in adulthood for those serving life sentences for their crimes. I will take that on in chapter 4. But first I need to deal with the morality of it all, the right and wrong of sentencing teenage killers. As Paul T. put it:

> What I did was so horrendous and because I hurt so many people I can see why the idea that I have been rehabilitated and could now be trusted to live in the community might seem crazy. And I know that some people think my rehabilitation doesn't matter anyway because what I did was so terrible I don't deserve a second chance at life. I get that. But that's another discussion.

And that discussion—the *moral* discussion—is my topic in the next chapter.

THREE

The Moral Calculus

A LIFE FOR A LIFE?

This chapter goes beyond the scientific issues of developmental analysis to consider the moral issues involved in sentencing—and now resentencing—Miller's Children. It reviews the ins and outs of how religion, ideology, and psychology interact in the complex and difficult decisions that must be made about the future of juvenile killers.

COOK COUNTY COURT, CHICAGO, ILLINOIS: Before I took the stand to testify in the resentencing hearing for Javell Ivory in June 2016 (the *Miller* case with which I began chapter 1), the state introduced into the record statements from the mothers of the two individuals who died in the attack. Obrellia Smith, the mother of the pregnant young woman who died as "collateral damage" in the shooting, read her statement in court:

> I am the mother of Salada Chianti Smith (my nu-nu) who was born on 12–8–1972. She weighed 7 lbs 8 oz. On Sunday, June 22, 1997 she was gunned down and killed in a brutal, senseless drive by shooting, which you Javell Ivory and Darnell Foxx played a part in. Salada was 24 years of age and 6 months pregnant, her baby also died instantly. She left behind her 6 year old child Angela that I have raised. Words can't explain my struggle writing this statement all of these years later. How can I as her mother truly limit myself by detailing within a few pages what her life meant to me? I can't and I won't. But, I will tell you how not having her here has impacted me and my family. Salada's one sibling, my oldest daughter Jamillah never could accept the fact that she was murdered by bullets that ripped her body. She had a nervous breakdown and turned to drugs to deal with her own pain and grief. She was unable to care for neither herself nor her two children. I ended up raising them as well. In 2007, she was found dead of a heroin overdose. I later found a piece of paper written by her saying what colors she wanted to be buried in; both my beautiful daughters taken away by your cowardly actions. Their deaths have created a generation gap to my family. Salad's daughter Angela is

never to know her mom nor her unborn sibling. Angela's future children will never know their maternal grandmother. Jamillah's grandchildren will never know their grandmother. Various milestones in their lives are shaded because they are not a part of them. As for me, true joy and laughter no longer exist. It's extremely hard for me to be part of gatherings with family and friends with their children when mine are no longer there. It's almost too much to bear. To this day, I can still see the visual of her dead body lying in the morgue under a blood-stained sheet. This visual has resulted in me having severe panic attacks. I have several life-threatening health issues. Over the years, I have struggled financially to care and provide for my three grandchildren. We have been aided and lifted up by a loving village of supportive friends. Darnell Foxx and Javell Ivory. I want both of you to know that I am a woman of faith. I never had anything to challenge my faith until Salada was killed. I will never forget your faces when I saw you both for the first time. I can honestly tell you that because of my faith I was able to look at you and not hate you but want you to be held accountable for taking away precious lives. I will never comprehend why you did what you did.

It was a powerful experience to sit in the courtroom and hear Obrellia speak, her voice strong but filled with the emotions of grief and loss, even two decades after her daughter (and unborn grandchild) were killed. She spoke with the special moral authority that comes with such a catastrophic human loss.

THE MORAL CALCULUS OF KILLING

"But if there is any further injury, then you shall appoint as a penalty life for life, eye for eye, tooth for tooth, hand for hand, foot for foot, burn for burn, wound for wound, bruise for bruise. . . ." This Biblical principle is found in Exodus (21–24), one of the five books in what Christians call the Old Testament and Jews call the Torah (or Pentateuch). In the United States, this verse is often used to justify the death penalty, literally a life for a life, but stopping at that phrase. The words that follow, dealing with retributive maiming, are omitted, perhaps in recognition that they belong to a culturally primitive time and place, in which, for example, slavery was an accepted practice.

Even today, however, in countries such as Saudi Arabia that practice a strict version of Islam (which accords great respect to the Bible), the full force and spirit of this primitive prescription for justice can be invoked with state sanction. For example, in 2000, a judge ordered the surgical removal of an offender's eye in retaliation for an attack in which the victim's eye was damaged. In another case, judicially ordered removal of the perpetrator's teeth was the punishment that was deemed to fulfill this moral imperative, this "law of retaliation" (or Qisas, as it is called in Arabic). Chopping off the hands of thieves is widespread. And beheading is the preferred form for implementing death sentences in Saudi Arabia (e.g., 157 in 2015, of which 40 percent were not for murder, as one might expect, but rather for drug offenses).

The underlying principle of a directly proportionate response to crime is thus rooted in the Judeo-Islamic-Christian tradition—or the "Abrahamic tradition" as it is often called, because all three religions trace their roots to the ancient patriarch Abraham. Of course, each of these religions has its softer side as well, a more compassionate side. In Christianity there is Matthew 5:8, which quotes Jesus as saying, "You have heard that it was said, 'Eye for eye and tooth for tooth.' But I tell you not to resist an evil person. If someone slaps you on your right cheek, turn to him the other also. . . ." Life for life and eye for eye, or turn the other cheek? Quite a contrast.

These "soft" and "hard" commands are both found within Christian scripture. The same duality exists in Islam as well, in which virtually every one of the Koran's 114 chapters begins with an homage to compassion ("In the name of God the compassionate and the merciful . . .") and teachings about compassion abound. And it is found throughout the Jewish scriptures and in the centuries of interpretation, elaboration, and teaching that have followed. These teachings are full of messages that pity and compassion for those in distress should create a desire to relieve that suffering—even for the wrongdoer—and that this is part of humanity's kinship with God as the font of mercy. But how does all this play out in the values and "policy positions" of flesh-and-blood people of the Abrahamic faiths?

DEATH FOR TAKING A LIFE?

A 2014 survey conducted by the Public Religion Research Institute revealed significant differences in support for the death penalty versus life in prison with no chance of parole among Americans from different religious traditions. Of course, for our purposes, this question misses the mark on two counts. First, it does not specify the age of the perpetrator. Second, it offers as alternatives neither a sentence with a limited number of years nor the possibility of parole attached to the life sentence. But the survey is useful nonetheless. Among "White Evangelical Protestants," 59 percent favored the death penalty over life without parole (34 percent). Almost as many "White Mainline Protestants" favored the death penalty (52 percent vs. 40 percent). Among "White Catholics," the results were 45 percent and 50 percent, respectively. So much for Matthew 5:8, and the fact that the official position of the Catholic Church is in opposition to the death penalty.

And what about Jews? In the same survey, 33 percent favored the death penalty while 57 percent supported life without parole as an alternative for murderers. Among "Other Non-Christians," the figures were 31 percent for death versus 60 percent for life without parole; and for "Unaffiliated," 44 percent versus 48 percent. Are there any groups that "do better" than the Jews, the non-Christian religious (presumably Buddhists and Hindus, for the most part), and the unaffiliated when it comes to compassion for murderers? Two groups stand out in the survey as having the lowest level of support for the death penalty. Among "Black Protestants," the result was 25 percent for death and 68 percent for life without parole; and among "Hispanic Catholics," 29 percent and 62 percent, respectively.

Of course, in America, blacks and Hispanics are more likely than whites to be connected to someone socially and emotionally who has committed a murder or who has been the victim of murder, according to the federal government's Bureau of Justice Statistics (with both being eight times as likely for African Americans). Perhaps human emotional connection leads them away from Exodus to John 8:7, from "life for life, eye for eye" to "He who is without sin, let him cast the first stone. . . ." And perhaps they have the honesty and humility to echo the centuries-old wisdom: "There but for the grace of God go I."

In the world of Miller's Children, these are not academic questions, not abstract matters of philosophical speculation and theological discourse. They are the bread and butter of day-to-day life in the decades ahead of teenage killers in the wake of their crimes.

SHOULD THERE BE A STATUTE OF LIMITATIONS ON PUNISHMENT?

For juvenile murderers, "death for death" is no longer the issue, because the Supreme Court took the death penalty off the table for juvenile killers when it decided *Roper v. Simmons* in 2005. But "life for life" still is an issue, and the choice between Exodus and Matthew is still *literally* a matter of life and death, for a sentence of life without the possibility of parole means death in prison somewhere down the line.

When it comes to arrest and prosecution, the crime of murder has no "statute of limitations" in America. Some people believe the same should be true for the *punishment* of this crime. For some, this means the death penalty—an eye for an eye. For others, it means a sentence of life without the possibility of parole, and thus eventual death in prison—literally a life for a life, in either case. Resolving these issues is a huge challenge, one that will entail years and years of debate on the moral and philosophical frontier. Or we could all simply move to Norway.

In Norway, the maximum sentence to which criminals can be sentenced is twenty-one years. This applies even to mass murderers like Anders Behring Breivik, who killed seventy-seven people in 2011. After those twenty-one years are served, however, it is possible for a judge to extend the sentence in five-year increments upon application from the prosecutor, and to do so indefinitely. In one sense, this means that Norway *does* have life sentences, but with a big difference. The "default option" is twenty-one years. It takes affirmative action by the state to make a case before a judge for additional incarceration.

This kind of "indeterminate" sentencing could, in theory, lead to life sentences, but in practice (in Norway) that happens extremely rarely. Is this approach better than one that limits the time served, regardless of rehabilitation? I will return to the thorny issue of whether teenage killers (and the community) are better served by determinate sentences or indeterminate sentences in chapter 6. For now, suffice it to say that for *developmental* reasons, I am concerned that sentences for teenage murderers can be either too short—less than the years needed to get them to a mature brain, plus some years of using that mature brain to accomplish fully the goals of rehabilitation and transformation—or too long.

At present in the United States, of course, the system is set up to work in the opposite direction of Norway's. It is the prisoner rather than the prosecutor who has to make the case for release—usually only after serving *decades,* not years, in prison. Why? Because the "default option" is continued incarceration, and parole boards may be loath to release men who committed murder as teenagers, no matter how profoundly they have rehabilitated and positively transformed themselves. This makes for a de facto death penalty for teenagers, "death in prison." Taking a global perspective, American incarceration policies generally are suspect.

To put this in context, of 195 countries around the world recognized as "independent states" by the United Nations, only fifty-four retain the death penalty in law and practice (and up until the *Roper v. Simmons* decision in 2005, the United States was the *only* country authorizing the death penalty for juveniles). For the most part, the United States is the only country outside of Asia and Africa that retains it. According to The Sentencing Project, the United States is the only country still imposing life without the possibility of parole on juveniles.

A recent review of incarceration policies around the world by Nicholas Turner and Jeremy Travis reports that many countries beyond Scandanavia have sentencing policies that put the United States to shame. Portugal was the first country to abolish sentences of life without parole, in 1884. Policies of the International Criminal Court permit the imposition of life sentences, but only for war crimes, crimes against humanity, and genocide. And even in those cases, after thirty years the court will review the sentence to determine whether or not it should be reduced. According to a 2015 *New York Times* op-ed by Turner and Travis, 70 percent of criminals sentenced to prison time in Germany are released after less than two years, and very few serve more than fifteen years.

Writing in 2013, criminologist Bob Cameron put it this way:

> There are essentially five goals of sentencing: retribution, incapacitation, deterrence, restoration, and rehabilitation. For Americans, it would seem, the last of these, rehabilitation, is probably the most controversial. In the United States, for example, rehabilitation is considered a secondary goal, after retribution. Americans want their prisoners punished first and rehabilitated second—and perhaps never restored no matter what. This appeals to a societal sense of justice and fair play that has considerable cultural inertia in our country. Any talk of prioritizing rehabilitation ahead of retribution very typically generates complaints about how doing so will endanger public safety, ignore the needs of crime victims, and—most damning of all—"coddle" criminals. Never mind that certain forms of rehabilitation have been shown through research to reduce the risk of future offending, we want our pound of flesh first and foremost.

It's a strong impulse in America, and it finds expression in America's courtrooms and parole boards, where there is a strong imperative to consider young killers as absolutely and irrevocably damned (and thus doomed). From this perspective, the issue of whether or not a teenage killer is rehabilitated is irrelevant, as we sometimes hear when family and friends of victims speak.

Just as the moral and philosophical issues surrounding life in prison are very personal for teenage killers, the same is true for their victims' families and friends. How do you forgive someone who has taken the life of a loved one? *Should you?* In courts and parole boards across the country, the voices of family members and friends of murder victims are often heard and usually carry a lot of weight in the proceedings.

Christine Buckner is the mother of Joshua Thomas, who was killed in the drive-by shooting committed by Javell Ivory, Darnell Foxx, and the two codefendants in the case recounted in chapter 1. When asked by the press for her thoughts about their future after the resentencing hearing in 2015, she said that she had hoped Javell and Darnell would remain imprisoned for the rest of their lives. These were her words: "The only way I'd forgive them is if my son came back to life. His life was taken away. Why should they run free?"

Why indeed? For a start, there is the fact that these killers were, as the Supreme Court acknowledged, "less guilty by reason of adolescence" when they participated in the killing of Christine Buckner's son. Then there is the fact that forgiving and releasing rehabilitated teenage killers can have immense psychological benefits for the community and society, as well as for the reformed men. Also worth considering is the cost borne by society in continuing to imprison these men long after they have become "safe" for release and capable of contributing to society's well-being. Finally, a case can be made that forgiveness can benefit the family members and loved ones of the victims themselves, if they can follow that path. Getting there allows them to avail themselves of the psychological and spiritual benefits that accrue from the process of forgiveness itself. If they don't walk that path to forgiveness, they can remain mired in the traumatic memories of loss and rage that come from experiencing victimization.

LIVING FORGIVENESS: ONE MAN'S STORY

Portsmith State Prison, Portland, Oregon: I first met Craig Plunkett in 2015. We sat down to dinner on the night before I was to interview an inmate seeking parole for a murder he committed when he was sixteen, an inmate that Craig knew well after years of contact with him (and whose story I will tell at a later point). We met again, eight months later, for breakfast and I learned more about Craig and his path through suffering to redemption. His remarkable story offers insight into the power of forgiveness as a healing force in the world. Craig is a sixty-nine-year-old man on a mission, a holy mission. Seventeen years ago, his twenty-year-old son, Eric, was murdered in his college dorm room. As Craig recounted to me, he was devastated by this violent loss:

> I was so full of hate I could taste it. When they caught the guy who killed Eric I felt a lust for revenge that surprised even me. I wanted the man who killed my beloved son destroyed. That feeling lasted all through the trial and for two years after the killer was convicted and sentenced to death. This hate was frozen until the day I accepted an invitation to speak with a group of inmates at our local state prison as a part of a "victim awareness" program that the prison chaplain ran for guys who had been incarcerated for years as a result of committing murder when they were teenagers. Sitting there with these men who embodied everything I had hated so intensely for such a long time turned out to be the best thing that ever happened to me. Telling my story and listening to their responses was transformative. Their sympathy surprised me. Their insight impressed me. Their empathy overwhelmed me. I left a different man. After I got home I felt like I had to do more. So I volunteered in the prison to help develop and run classes on "forgiveness and compassion." As the years have come and gone I have expanded my work at the prison. Now I think of the men in my class like my sons. And they often say that I am the father they never had but wished they did. When forgiveness replaced hate and a lust for vengeance I began to heal my own pain—and not just the pain of losing my son Eric. I began to heal the pain from my own childhood, from the savage beatings my own father inflicted on me. As a Christian I know that through my work with these prisoners, helping them heal and forgive, and helping other victims find the path to forgiveness, I am closer to God than I have ever been in my whole life.

I spent a day with Craig, at the prison where "his boys" live, and I can attest to the purity of his commitment and his positive impact on the lives of the men he cares for—and who so genuinely care for him. It was inspirational. Craig Plunkett lives in a blessed light. Unfortunately, the family members of other victims are stuck in darkness—the darkness that Craig found his way out of, through the path of forgiveness.

IMPEDIMENTS TO HEALING AND FORGIVENESS

At Dennis D.'s resentencing hearing in Minnesota, his victims' children spoke, twenty-five years after Dennis, then sixteen years old, shot and killed their father and mother, Bob and Mary Thomas. Tim said, "My brother and I found our murdered parents. We have had to live with that all the rest of our lives. If this crime doesn't deserve a life sentence, what does? I consider my brother Sam the third victim of this crime. The loss of my parents was too much for him, and he took his own life fifteen years ago." Another surviving brother, Arnie, said this: "Dennis keeps asking what he can do for us. I can tell him: Be a man and serve out your life sentence. That's what he can do!"

At a hearing in Wisconsin to decide the fate of David F., twenty-two years after his crime, family members of the victim—Martin—spoke. Martin's mother said,

> You think of it over and over and over. I have to imagine the last few minutes of my son's life in an endless loop. And it's a little different every time, but he always dies at the end. If you have to value your child's life in someone else's years, you want as many of those years as possible. It's the same. It's worse at times. It's like it happened yesterday. It's that raw. The only thing to heal the wound to a family's psyche like that is time.

And Martin's father said, "I've lost all faith in the justice system. I'm devastated. Some were getting the death penalty when he committed this horrible crime. He should have been sent to the electric chair."

When Martin's mother said, "The only thing to heal the wound to a family's psyche like this is time," she was sadly wrong. Traumatic memories do *not* spontaneously decay. Time does *not* heal all wounds. Rage and sadness can keep a person afloat in the days, weeks, and even months after a horrible, traumatic experience. But rage and sadness are not enough in the long run. They take a toll of their own, and they generally don't help in dealing with traumatic memories. There has to be a "processing" of those traumatic memories, of the grief, of the rage.

"Trauma-informed cognitive behavioral therapy" can be an important resource in doing the necessary work of processing trauma, as psychologist Ricky Greenwald has found in reviewing decades of research. There are other therapies that work as well—for example, eye movement desensitization and reprocessing (EMDR), which pacifies the overwhelming arousal stimulated by recalling the traumatic event so that the individual and the therapist can process the content of the trauma. Some medications may help, as do the various "mindfulness" disciplines of yoga and meditation. But another important resource is finding a path to forgiveness. As we will see, finding and walking that path to forgiveness has important spiritual, psychological, and physical health benefits.

Thankfully, not all the family members of victims speak with a voice that reflects a frozen attachment to their grief and anger. Some, like Craig Plunkett, speak with the warmth that comes from giving voice to the spirit of forgiveness. After Obrellia Smith spoke at the resentencing hearing for Javell and Darnell, she sat back down near where I sat awaiting my turn to testify. She wept quietly while her granddaughter comforted her. When Obrellia had composed herself a bit, I moved closer and took her hand in sympathy for her loss, and spoke with her briefly. Her pain was excruciating. One source of that pain was her struggle to find the space in her heart and her spirit to forgive the killers of her daughter. When a reporter asked Obrellia for a comment after the hearing, she had this to say: "Whatever will be, will be. Even through tragedy, I believe good will come out of it." I could only marvel at her generosity of spirit. This was Matthew 5:8 at its best.

Like many traumatic memories, Obrellia Smith's recall of her daughter's death had not spontaneously decayed, even though nearly two decades had passed since her daughter had been killed and she was driven to the morgue to identify her bloody body. Trauma is like that. And, like most victims of violence, Obrellia has struggled with both the psychological and the moral issues inherent in murder: "Why did it happen?" and "What does it mean?" What Obrellia said to me next was a clue to one of the impediments she has faced in her efforts to forgive. She told me that when she looked at the two defendants sitting at the attorney's table not ten feet away, she did not see remorse on their faces. Having interviewed one of them, I ventured to tell her that I knew that Javell, at least, *did* feel remorse and regret. And I told her that there were two reasons for the apparent lack of emotional expression on the faces of the two men who had been part of the drive-by shooting that killed her daughter. First, their lawyers had told them not to react emotionally to whatever happened during the hearing. Second, it is a fact that living in prison teaches you to mask your emotions as a matter of day-to-day survival. I hoped that knowing this would ease her path to forgiveness, for her sake as well as for Javell and Darnell's.

After I testified, I left the courtroom reminded acutely of two facts. First, no matter how much compassion and sympathy I feel for the young killers I seek to help, there is a moral and emotional primacy to their victims that must never be minimized or forgotten. Second, the cycles of trauma extend across generations, jumping from family to family through the crimes that the perpetrators commit and the victims they create. One thing I have learned from observing the cycles of trauma is that violence creates a ripple effect across the community that cannot heal without a process of coming to justice, followed by a process of reconciliation and forgiveness.

IS FORGIVENESS THE KEY TO PROCESSING TRAUMATIC MEMORIES?

Obrellia ended her statement in the resentencing hearing for Javell and Darnell this way:

> But, one thing I hope has happened over these many years is that you developed a personal relationship with God and have repented to God to pardon you of your sins. Only he can judge inner heart and give us peace. I will continue to pray for you! Finally, Darnell Foxx and Javell Ivory—I forgive you. Glory to God!

Long the province solely of philosophers and theologians, the study of forgiveness has become a topic for social science research. Psychologist and pastoral counselor Everett Worthington's edited volume *Dimensions of Forgiveness: Psychological Research and Theological Perspectives,* published in 1998, was a milestone in this effort. In it, researchers reviewed social science evidence on the dynamics and power of forgiveness, and the impediments to it, in human efforts to cope with loss, trauma, injustice, and victimization. More recently, in 2015, Loren Toussaint, Everett Worthington, and David Williams have updated this review and expanded its reach. Their work highlights the growing universe of "programmatic" efforts to study and promote forgiveness—for example, Worthington's own "Campaign for Forgiveness Research" at Virginia Commonwealth University, the International Forgiveness Institute at the University of Wisconsin, and the Greater Good Science Center at the University of California, Berkeley. Since the 1998 publication of Worthington's early effort, the number of books about forgiveness has burgeoned. A simple search for books on "forgiveness" on Amazon.com yields more than fifteen thousand entries (most of them "how to" books coming at the topic from a spiritual and/or autobiographical perspective).

Defined as "the act of consciously deciding to let go of resentment or vengeance" by the Greater Good Science Center, forgiveness is not simply an altruistic act or an endeavor that benefits only the one who has caused harm. It does do that, of course, allowing the *motivated and responsible* perpetrator to heal himself after he takes responsibility for the harm he has caused.

John P., who killed two people in a robbery that went bad when one of the victims fought back, articulates this well in a letter to me:

> The only way I could go on living in my skin was to change my life; and that feeling has NEVER left me, though it has grown deeper & more mature as I have grown through the years. I feel deep shame, remorse & regret for what I've done & its impact. That has only grown more intense & painful the healthier & more awake I've become. I felt a NEED very early on to apologize to the victims. But changing my life and helping others do the same strikes me as the only meaningful way I can ever hope to say "I'm sorry." The flip side of that is not changing my life says quite clearly that what I did & their suffering means nothing to me. Nothing could be further from the truth. Early on, these thoughts were focused only on my victims' family, but I later came to see my own family as victims just as much as the survivors of my crime. My aunt calls them "the silent victims." I believe in many ways my family's pain & trauma are equal to the victims' family, but in other ways, my family's is worse in that they have this added layer of shame & guilt that comes with continuing to love & support me through the years. It's complicated stuff, but my point is that when I talk of my victims I include my own loved ones in that definition.

THE BENEFITS OF FORGIVING

Except for perpetrators who either feel justified in the violent act they committed or are devoid of moral sensibility (two exceptions to which I will return in chapter 5), guilt and shame are common impediments to self-improvement and rehabilitation in the lives of Miller's Children. Receiving forgiveness can help remove these impediments and pave the way to both more responsible behavior (in the interest of the community) and improved psychological function and physical well-being (in the interest of the offender, his family, and his loved ones).

In general, however, forgiveness is at least as good for the forgiver as it is for the forgivee. Put simply, engaging in the process of forgiveness generally contributes to a lower level of stress, with all that means for mental and physical health issues like depression, blood pressure, and immune system function. Giving up anger reduces the physiological burden of holding a grudge. For example, people sleep better and have more energy for day-to-day life when they forgive; refusing to forgive is exhausting. Craig Plunkett spoke of this when we talked about his life—how he has great energy that he can direct toward helping others and "spreading the word," now that he has for-given the man who killed his son.

Psychologist Kathleen Lawler and colleagues, reviewing the research evidence and reporting on the results of their own study, found that both as a feature of personality (a "trait") and as a set of specific actions (a "state"), forgiveness leads to better health for the person doing the forgiving, and the principal mechanism for accomplishing this is a reduction in bad feelings ("negative affect"). However, they and others have noted that most of the existing research on forgiveness has focused on responses to "low-level" offenses and, often, hypothetical offenses. Forgiveness is a more complex matter when it comes to actually *losing a loved one* through the violent action of another person. Here, it would seem, forgiveness must not be offered casually or "cheaply."

The old saying that "revenge is a dish best served cold" suggests that the emotional satisfaction of payback increases when it comes after a long process of anticipation, rather than when it is an immediate counterassault that occurs in the heat of the moment. I think the same is true of forgiveness: it should come as the result of a process of reflection and discovery, rather than as a simple and casual response that short-circuits the complex and difficult process of *coming to* the grace of forgiving. As Robert Enright and Richard Fitzgibbons explain in their 2014 book *Forgiveness Therapy: An Empirical Guide for Resolving Anger and Restoring Hope,* getting from rage and hurt to forgiveness requires time and effort—and perhaps professional therapeutic assistance.

I don't take forgiveness lightly, and it would seem that psychological research supports that view. This, I think, is certainly true where teenage killers are concerned. Neither they nor their victims should rush to forgive (and, in fact, most don't), but neither should either party be denied the benefits of forgiveness that is "earned" by the perpetrator over time and "freely given" by the victim with informed consent. However difficult the process may be, however, I am convinced that it is worth it. For victims to deny themselves forever the healing grace of forgiveness is a tragedy, because in doing so they consign themselves to a lifetime of carrying the terrible burden of anger and sadness unabated—as did the family members who lost loved ones to Dennis D. and David F. They deserve more than that. They *need* more than that. And feeling powerless to atone for their murderous actions is a terrible burden for teenage killers to bear as well.

My dictionary defines *remorse* as "deep and painful regret for wrongdoing." From listening to killers for more than two decades, I have come to recognize two principal forms of remorse. The first is regret for what murder has done to the killer's life, what might be called "self-directed" or "egocentric" remorse. I've already told, in chapter 2, how I heard it in the way Robert W. spoke of his deep and painful regret for the murder he committed, but let me say a bit more here. Robert attempted to hang himself while in custody awaiting trial, and to this day he is clearly remorseful and full of regret when talking about what he did. As I reported in chapter 2, he speaks of sitting in detention and fully realizing the "severity of my mistake" and its magnitude, "how I had thrown everything away—no wife and kids . . . nothing but the rest of my life in prison," and that "I have been locked up now four years longer than I was out there in the world! For what? It was so stupid what I did." This is classic self-directed remorse, deep and painful regret for the effect of his crime on *Robert's own life*. The effects of his crime on his victim and his victim's family and friends are not central to it. In my experience, when that comes, it comes later. Is this perhaps somehow parallel to the belief that you must love yourself before you can love others? I think so. Self-remorse is a primitive form of insight, but if it is the *only* form of insight, it has little moral standing.

Much more morally significant is what might be called "other-directed remorse," deep and painful regret for the harm and suffering one has caused others. This is the remorse that opens the door morally to being forgiven, because it demonstrates a recognition of how one's crime has violated and harmed human existence beyond oneself. I think it is one way to initiate the process of rehabilitation. One bit of moral good news in the remorse felt by Robert in the period after his arrest and trial is that he did, in fact, start to go beyond remorse for what he brought on himself and to see how he has harmed others. He bemoaned the fact that his incarceration will mean "no grandchildren for my parents," which was a start toward building the moral foundation for deserving forgiveness. Twenty years later, Robert has achieved a much more complete and profound remorse, an other-directed remorse. He now says, "You know how many people's lives you ruined when you do something like this. It's a ripple effect. There's no taking anything back."

Dennis D. has written eloquently of his own efforts to earn forgiveness:

At some point soon after my arrest, I came to feel deeply and intensely ashamed of and disgusted by the horrific, senseless crimes I committed and the harm I have caused my victims' family, my family and so many others. I was sickened, not just by what I did, but by *what* rather than *who*—I felt I must have become to have been able to commit such a horrible crime.... This was a rock-bottom moment for me that was critically important to starting the rehabilitation and transformation process.... Rehabilitation and transformation necessarily flow from a genuine sense of regret, remorse and recognition of the need to atone and make restitution for the harm one has caused.... There is not a day of my life that I do not think about my victims, and deeply regret that they are no longer here because of my choices and actions. Every choice I make is based, in part, on consideration of what I think they would want me to do. The choices I make are in their "honor." What I mean is that I am trying to respect and honor them; their memory, spirit and legacy, in any and every way that I possibly can.... In the few times that I have interacted with their family, their grief and pain has been undeniable and compelling. I feel it deep in my soul.... It breaks my heart to see their heartache and it sickens me to know that I caused it, but can do nothing to "fix it." I desperately long to ease their suffering in some small way, but that is simply not possible.... There is nothing I can do to help, short of dying.

Dennis and his victims' family have one thing in common: they both need the healing that the giving and receiving of forgiveness would provide in the long run, no matter how painful it would be in the short run. Dennis consciously craves it. His victims' family (at least the ones who spoke at his hearing) don't seem to realize that they need it too. After more than twenty-five years, the time for forgiveness is long overdue, given the efforts Dennis has made to rebuild himself from the ground up, and the way his victims' family are frozen in their grief and rage. In this they are hardly unique. The same could be said for David's victim's family, for Christine Buckner, and for thousands of others traumatized by the actions of teenage killers.

ARE REHABILITATION AND TRANSFORMATION MORALLY IRRELEVANT?

In *Listening to Killers,* I wrote about the processes of rehabilitation and transformation that killers undergo. I return to that topic here in an expanded discussion focusing on teenage killers, because these processes are at the heart of the matter for understanding Miller's Children. *Miller* resentencing hearings involve tough choices beyond the technical concerns of sorting out social history before and after the adolescent's lethal crime. They involve a frightening moral calculus. For some people, there is a transcendent moral issue. There are those who find it morally objectionable that *anyone* who commits a violent crime, particularly a murder, should ever be released. I might add that some people seem to think—incorrectly, as will become abundantly clear—that this is *particularly* true for adolescents who commit murder. Why? Because, from their perspective, it reflects an innate depravity, which is seen as an aggravating rather than a mitigating factor. This is one reason why prosecutors often are so tenacious in opposing resentencing in *Miller* cases (setting aside the issues of ego involved in "winning" versus "losing" in these cases, which I will discuss in chapter 6). It is also often the reason why they show up at parole-board hearings to argue against release for those who have been granted the right to seek it.

For those who see things this way, the prison door should *never* swing open for those who have taken a human life, as Miller's Children have. In the terms of this moral calculus, such acts permanently put the offender outside the realm of normal society, beyond the circle of caring. This kind of moral calculus provides the cultural context for even many "compassionate and humane" judges when they approach sentencing in *Miller* cases. I think it is one reason why they can hear the mitigating stories I and others tell in court—about how some killers have been innocently victimized by profound moral and emotional damage as a result of their upbringing—and *still* reimpose life sentences without parole for troubled young offenders, consigning them to "death in prison."

There is a line of moral argument that the rehabilitation and transformation of young killers is morally irrelevant in deciding their fate, even many years down the line. You can hear it in the testimony of the family members who speak against release in resentencing and parole hearings. But this starts earlier in the process, in the very sentencing of young killers in the first place. This is evident in the dissents to the Supreme Court's majority ruling in *Miller v. Alabama,* in which justices Alito, Scalia, Thomas, and Roberts bemoan the fact that the law of the land is moving in the direction of compassionate and science-based sentencing of teenage killers. They object to the idea that the concept of morality is inextricably linked to cultural evolution, a view that is embedded in the majority opinion in the *Miller v. Alabama* case.

For me, the breakthrough in the shift toward a humane approach to young killers came when the Supreme Court began to bring to bear in its decisions the idea that the definition of "cruel and unusual punishment," of which the Eighth Amendment speaks, is to be understood contextually. *Contextually* here means historically and with an eye toward cultural progress of the sort embodied in the United Nations Convention on the Rights of the Child, which "outlaws" the execution of minors. Although President Bill Clinton signed this convention, it has still not been ratified by the Senate. Nonetheless, it can be understood as a globally negotiated settlement on what it "should" mean to be a child, across cultures and societies. Indeed, the Supreme Court has cited this international convention in its decisions to roll back the severity of legally permissible punishments for minors. The four dissenters in *Miller v. Alabama,* however, see this as a dangerous trend, not an indicator of growing enlightenment.

As Justice Alito observed in his dissent to the *Miller v. Alabama* decision, "The Court long ago abandoned the original meaning of the Eighth Amendment, holding instead that the prohibition of 'cruel and unusual punishment' embodies the 'evolving standards of decency that mark the progress of a maturing society.' *Trop* v. *Dulles,* 356 U.S. 86, 101 (1958)." Of course, Alito deplored that trend, and Justice Scalia agreed, joining Alito in his dissent. Likewise the silent Justice Thomas, who wrote his own dissent, to which Scalia also signed on. And Scalia, Alito, and Thomas joined in a further dissent opinion penned by Justice Roberts.

People of my ilk welcome the trend toward a globalized sense of human rights and standards for the treatment of children and youths, for it signals a move into the better neighborhood of global cultural evolution, where executing minors and incarcerating them for life without the possibility of parole are considered archaic holdovers from a bygone, barbaric era in human history. It moves us toward a cultural and political place where Amnesty International will not be compelled to shame us for our juvenile sentencing policies, as they do now.

Where *is* all this heading? Ironically, perhaps, there are clues in the dissenting opinions offered by Roberts, Alito, Scalia, and Thomas in *Miller v. Alabama.* Roberts wrote this:

Today's holding may be limited to mandatory sentences, but the Court has already announced that discretionary life without parole for juveniles should be "uncommon"—or to use a common synonym, "unusual." Indeed, the

Court's gratuitous prediction appears to be nothing other than an invitation to overturn life without parole sentences imposed by juries and trial judges. If that invitation is widely accepted and such sentences for juvenile offenders do in fact become "uncommon," the Court will have bootstrapped its way to declaring that the Eighth Amendment absolutely prohibits them. This process has no discernible end point.

And Alito wrote the following in his dissent:

It is true that, at least for now, the Court apparently permits a trial judge to make an individualized decision that a particular minor convicted of murder should be sentenced to life without parole, but do not expect this possibility to last very long. The majority goes out of its way to express the view that the imposition of a sentence of life without parole on a "child" (*i.e.*, a murderer under the age of 18) should be uncommon. Having held in *Graham* that a trial judge with discretionary sentencing authority may not impose a sentence of life without parole on a minor who has committed a nonhomicide offense, the Justices in the majority may soon extend that holding to minors who commit murder. We will see.

Alito, Roberts, Scalia, and Thomas *fear* that *Miller v. Alabama* sets the country on a slippery slope to a total ban on life-without-parole sentences for juvenile killers. I *hope* it does. We will see indeed. But a major impediment still stands in the way of this process of cultural evolution, namely the process by which violent youths are subsumed under the category of "absolute evil."

ABSOLUTE EVIL AND MITIGATION

Evil. What is it? Psychological researchers Daniel Saucier and Russell Webster, who have investigated this issue, put it this way in a 2015 study:

In short, the archetype holds that there are people who fulfill egotistical and sadistic tendencies by intentionally inflicting harm on others, and because evil is unmalleable and is the antithesis of order and peace, we cannot reason with or understand evildoers—rather, evildoers should be eliminated from society.

Some people view teenage killers through this lens, as simply "evildoers," as did the family members of Dennis D.'s and David F.'s victims.

In formulating their research, Webster and Saucier built upon the work of Roy Baumeister, who offered a multidimensional conception of "pure evil."

From his perspective, pure evil involves an unprovoked intention to inflict harm on others for pleasure. It involves victims who are innocent. It generally comes from people who are of "the other." It is a stable trait that is related to narcissistic egotism.

To convert their theoretical framework into a reliable questionnaire, Webster and Saucier identified three primary principles that ground the investigation of pure evil. Each has something to contribute to understanding the dynamics at work in the way people and institutions deal with teenage murderers. Here are the three principles:

First, that "trying to understand evil is futile because pure evil is dispositional and will only foster greater empathizing with perpetrators and condoning of their harmful behavior." I hear this often when people discuss Miller's Children. They are highly suspicious of their motives and fear that "understanding" will lead to "excusing." This is such an important issue that I often include in my reports the assertion that "none of this analysis is offered as an excuse for the murders he committed."

Second, that "there is too much evil in the world right now." There is an ongoing moral panic about teenage murders, a panic that ebbs and flows over the decades. In the early 1990s, this moral panic reached a peak with terrifying messages about a coming wave of "super-predators" that was about to inundate America. As the leading proponent of this view, John DiIulio, wrote at that time, these teenage killers were a "new breed" of offenders, "kids that have absolutely no respect for human life and no sense of the future.... These are stone-cold predators!" These words, and the sentiment and thoughts behind them, provided an important impetus for harsh sentencing laws, like the ones that the Supreme Court overturned in *Miller v. Alabama*.

Third, that "mitigating circumstances play little or no role in producing evil behavior." The criminal justice system is built upon the principle of "free will," with the only exception being legal insanity, in which the perpetrator of a crime is either so out of touch with reality that he or she does not know that his or her action is "wrong" or is under the influence of an irresistible compulsion to act. Very few murderers ever meet this narrow definition of insanity (some 0.25 percent—between two and three out of a thousand—of all cases, by one national estimate). Thus, many people seem to believe that the only necessary and appropriate explanation for the actions of teenage murderers is that they "choose" to kill. Mitigating factors are dismissed as excuses, not causes.

Saucier and Webster added a fourth element to their assessment: "general willingness to say that people believe in pure evil." Their final instrument contains twenty-two items assessing a belief in pure evil and twenty-eight items measuring a belief in pure good. Their research demonstrates that the more people endorsed a belief in pure evil, the more likely they were to support aggression as a tool in social relations (not just with respect to the death penalty to deal with criminal behavior, but also with regard to preemptive military aggression to deal with international conflicts). People who espoused this worldview were less likely to credit criminal rehabilitation, policies aimed at racial reconciliation, and social welfare programs. In contrast, people who saw the world through "pure good" eyes opposed the use of social aggression, be it in the form of torture or military aggression, and had a positive view of criminal rehabilitation in prisons (and diplomacy internationally).

Most relevant to our concerns here is that using simulated juries, Saucier and Webster found that people who believe in pure evil demonize perpetrators as "wicked, evil, and threatening" and then respond to them with feelings of justified retribution, namely "greater recommended jail time, opposition to parole, and support for his execution." In fact, the "evil" nature of criminals in the eyes of these beholders *can blind juries and judges to the relevance of mitigating factors.*

I should add here that the legislators who crafted and passed the legal foundations for teenage killers to receive automatic sentences of life without the possibility of parole made the supposed irrelevance of mitigation in the cases of Miller's Children a matter of law. Many states passed these laws in direct response to popularization of the super-predator concept, which turned out to be a myth—adolescent violent crime rates actually declined after the 1990s, rather than taking the pattern of acceleration predicted by those who promoted the concept.

But there is more. In a 2015 report, Webster and Saucier looked at whether the characteristics of particular criminals affected the way people believed they should be treated. Not surprisingly, people recommended more harsh punishment of criminals who were "stereotypically evil" (e.g., descriptions of the criminal as being wicked and threatening). However, the belief in pure evil predicted the harshness of punishment all by itself—even for criminals who were *not* described as stereotypically evil. *That is, this belief predicted the demonization, desire for retribution, and inclination to punish harshly more powerfully than the characteristics of the criminals themselves.* As Webster and Saucier put it, "Thus, some individuals naturally see perpetrators as demons, and retributively punish them, whether or not there is more explicit stereotypic evidence of their evil dispositions."

CAN A JUDGE AND JURY WHO BELIEVE
IN "PURE EVIL" BE TRUSTED?

These findings are very disturbing. In fact, they completely negate the premise that a judge (or a juror or parole-board member, for that matter) is approaching the process of evaluating ostensibly mitigating factors with an open mind (let alone an open heart). *I would go so far as to say that based on Saucier and Webster's research, coming into the courtroom with such a belief in pure evil should be grounds for disqualifying that individual as a juror, a judge, or a parole-board member.* This, to me, is a direct parallel to the fact that jurors can be excluded from juries in death penalty cases if they express moral opposition to capital punishment. For a jury to be "death penalty qualified," it has to be composed of jurors who are morally able to impose a sentence of execution (and this is one reason why Catholics are routinely excluded from such juries if they admit that they subscribe to the Church's "pro-life" teaching against capital punishment). Surely, then, to hear a case fairly, the jury, judge, and the parole board must similarly be "mitigation qualified," in the sense that they are capable of fulfilling their legal obligation to hear and take into account mitigating evidence presented to them. If they are deaf and blind to such evidence, they cannot possibly reach a legally and morally appropriate decision and should be sent home rather than empowered.

Although I have encouraged defense attorneys to litigate the issue, I don't know of any jurisdictions where this is the rule. To be sure, jurors are asked if they have an open mind about a particular case and can be impartial. But if they say "yes," and yet harbor the kind of belief in pure evil studied by Webster and Saucier, they are not telling the truth, the whole truth, and nothing but the truth. Of course, in the case of Miller's Children, the law itself was not "mitigation qualified," because it imposed life-without-parole automatically once guilt had been established, regardless of the life story of the adolescent defendant.

Judges who believe in pure evil should recuse themselves—though, in the American context, this may be a far-fetched idea. It seems that judges generally don't like to be judged. Many years ago, in the course of testifying in a murder trial, I tried to use the judge as an illustration of the point I was making. He quickly interrupted me with the admonishment "Don't try to psychoanalyze me young man!" (At least he referred to me as a "young man," something that doesn't happen much these days.) Thus, it comes as no surprise that when I tried out the idea of judges who believe in absolute evil recusing themselves on some experts in the criminal justice field, one spoke for many when he said, "Recusing the judge who believes in 'pure evil' is an interesting idea. But it'll never happen even if it could somehow be made to work." He did go on to say that "a better approach would be to leave release up to the parole board, assuming the board is composed of people who are like or would listen to you." I retain hope that at least some judges will come around on the matter of pure evil (if not to the point of recusing themselves, at least to the point of having some self-awareness of how their belief in pure evil undermines their ability to see and hear mitigation when it is set before them in court). Of course, the *Miller v. Alabama* ruling has made this essential for any judge making resentencing decisions (as *Tatum v. Arizona* made clear; see chapter 1). As for parole-board members, I will consider them in chapter 6.

THE IMMORALITY OF DEPRIVING TEENAGE KILLERS OF PROGRAMS AND SERVICES

The Supreme Court's *Miller v. Alabama* decision creates this moral question: If young offenders are capable of rehabilitation, must they be given a meaningful opportunity to accomplish and demonstrate such transformation? If so (as I would argue), then what moral obligation does the state have to provide conditions in which youths may develop into healthy and prosocial adults? I certainly have heard a great deal about this from Miller's Children—how they were always put at the bottom of the list when it came time to open opportunities for education or services, if they were deemed eligible to participate at all. The rationale offered by the prison administration was usually something along the lines of "You are never leaving this place, so why should we waste resources on you?"

If the conditions of confinement impede a teenage killer's development and maturation (their "rehabilitation"), are there Constitutional grounds to challenge the policies that give rise to those conditions? Do they fall under the same Eighth Amendment promise of general fairness to those who are being punished by society that resulted in juvenile sentences of life without the possibility of parole being declared "cruel and unusual punishments"? Should the Eighth Amendment provide the basis for insisting that the services provided in state prison systems be adequate and applied fairly? Even to teenage killers? I believe the answer to all these questions is *yes*.

PROPORTIONATE JUSTICE OR COMPASSION?

As I was reading the *Miller v. Alabama* decision, I was struck by this line: "The Alabama Court of Criminal Appeals affirmed [the original sentence of automatic life without the possibility of parole], holding that Miller's *sentence was not overly harsh when compared to his crime* [emphasis added]." Evan Miller had committed a nasty crime—beating a man to death. Of course, prior to *Roper v. Simmons,* the Alabama Court of Criminal Appeals might well have said of a death sentence in his case that it was not "overly harsh when compared with his crime." Now they can't, because the *Roper v. Simmons* decision declared death sentences for juveniles unconstitutional. The execution of juveniles is no longer an option for the trial courts, even if some judges, prosecutors, and citizens who sit on juries—and read newspapers or listen to talk radio—think that it should be, and that it would not be "overly harsh."

But with the juvenile death penalty off the table, we face other questions: *Are* there some teenage killers who should receive life-without-parole sentences on moral grounds? *Are* there crimes so heinous that the perpetrator should never leave prison except in a coffin? Are there what might be called "moral" exceptions to the rule of offering the opportunity for rehabilitation—crimes so heinous that there can be no rehabilitation, no transformation, no reclamation that would justify release? Were the family members who testified against Dennis D. and David F. right?

For them, a belief in absolute evil trumps everything and anything else. For me, this moral exception is a last resort that I refuse to embrace when it comes to adolescent killers. Why? Because I refuse to push them out of my circle of caring, the moral space of my life. And I have been tempted to do so, when sitting across from a young guy who beat a three-year-old child to death because she "disrespected" him; or a guy who raped and killed a defenseless, mentally disabled girl because she "was asking for it and then tried to get away from me"; or a guy who planted a bomb on a crowded street corner after a basketball game with the intention of killing as many people as technically possible, to "show that I can be trusted to act for the cause." I have been tempted viscerally in situations like this, but I have walked myself back from that point because I see it as leading only to a senseless barbarism. Of course, my moral revulsion in these cases is nothing compared to the profound feelings that overwhelm the family members and close friends of murder victims. But I would say to myself, as a hypothetical family member of a victim, that I would need to have a broader understanding and to stand in a better spiritual place than my pain and rage would try to take me.

I have been a "child advocate" for many decades. For the most part, teenage killers are untreated traumatized children, and as such they deserve my compassion, no matter what they have done. I will leave it to others to explain why and how the moral absolutism of a belief in "pure evil" makes sense to them, and how that translates into excommunicating some teenage killers from the human race, pushing them outside our circle of caring. However, there is another, related issue that I think poses a somewhat different question: Are some teenage killers so *developmentally damaged* that they will never recover, no matter how much times passes and how much therapeutic intervention they receive? Although I will return to the latter issue in detail in chapter 5, here I can say that yes, I think there are such exceptions, but they are the infrequent exception to the rule.

THE PSYCHOPATH BRAIN SPEAKS

When I had dinner with James Fallon, to discuss his book *The Psychopath Inside,* he told me something that I found quite disturbing—intellectually and morally. He said that the more he understood the role of genetic vulnerability in producing violent behavior (most notably the *MAOA* "warrior gene" that I discussed in chapter 1), the more he was *against* the death penalty and *for* the sentence of life without the possibility of parole. Why? Because in the case of those born with this genetic vulnerability, he thinks it isn't their fault—they didn't choose to have the risky form of the *MAOA* gene, and they should not be executed for something that was not of their choosing. On the other hand, he argues, the kind of psychological and moral damage they have sustained from the interaction of their genetic vulnerability and their toxic social and family environment leaves them so profoundly harmed that the developmental damage they carry with them *cannot* be remediated. In his view, they cannot be made safe for release and, therefore, must spend the rest of their lives in prison.

For me, the moral bottom line in all but a few, rare cases is to be found in exploring the ins and outs of why and how teenage killers *are* capable of rehabilitation, and thus how and why there is a moral justification for giving them a sentence that recognizes this possibility. I think this will become clearer in the next chapter, where I address two topics: the mystery of *why* teenage killers who have been sentenced to die in prison have any motivation to rehabilitate in the first place, and *how* it is that they accomplish this task once they do marshal their motivational resources to take it on. I will wait until chapter 5 to address the "developmental" exceptions—those individuals who, because of some combination of genetic predisposition and socially and psychologically toxic environments, are thought to be lost causes when it comes to rehabilitation and transformation.

FOUR

Running Away from the Monster

This chapter delves deeply into the processes of change that allow Miller's Children to undergo rehabilitation and transformation. In many cases, at the time of their offenses, the prospects for such dramatic improvements seemed bleak—as evidenced by clinical assessments done at the time of the initial trial. But years into the process, it is indubitably clear that the angry, aggressive, out-of-control teenagers who killed have given way to mature, insightful, and "safe" men.

"HOW HAVE YOU CHANGED in the twenty years you have been in prison?" I asked Dennis D. This is what he wrote:

> I will say that I am not at all opposed to writing to you now in response to that question if you would be interested in me doing so. I will say that your question focuses on "how" we changed, but I encourage you to also think of what seems to me to be an equally important question: "Why we changed!" For me, and in my experience, for many young men who commit homicide, "why" started with shame, disgust, remorse and a desire and need to attempt to atone for what we did. It typically begins as something we do for others— our victims and our own families—more than it is for ourselves. It's the only meaningful way we can ever hope to say "I'm sorry!" It seems it would be a slap in the face of the people we've hurt to NOT change. I COULD NOT continue breaking the hearts of my loved ones. I had to give them something to hold onto; some reason to feel "proud" (or at least not ashamed) of me. In truth, the shame and disgust I felt about what I did was so intense that I knew I MUST change to be able to continue living in my skin. I had to "get as far away from that MONSTER as I possibly could!!" I could go on, but I think that will give you a sense of what I'm talking about. I've heard & seen many variations of these motivations throughout the years. It is no coincidence that of the first 18 prison hospice volunteers 15 of us had committed homicides. Almost all of us spoke of seeing hospice as a means to atone or make amends for our crimes. This is a statement as much about the

individuals as it is about hospice in my view. I think many people think people who commit homicides—and perhaps any crimes—are cold, callous, evil people, rather than broken people. I think people think we don't care about what we did or who we hurt & that the crime means nothing to us at best, or it is a badge of honor at worst. I think helping people understand that change is critically important to many of us who commit such horrible crimes is an important part of the story.

I agree. While Dennis is particularly articulate in explaining why and how he did it, he is by no means unique in what he has done since he joined the ranks of teenage killers at age sixteen—and the tribe of kids lost to life without parole two years later, when he was convicted and sentenced more than twenty years ago. And his kind of rehabilitation and transformation is not a new phenomenon.

RECOVERING FROM THE CRIME
OF THE CENTURY

In May 1924, two Chicago youths, nineteen-year-old Nathan Leopold and eighteen-year-old Richard Loeb, kidnapped and murdered fourteen-year-old Robert Franks. Rich, intelligent, and well educated, the two adolescents hatched the plot to demonstrate how smart, cunning, and above the laws of society they were. However, they blundered and were soon caught—because, among other reasons, one of the boys inadvertently left his eyeglasses at the site where they dumped the body.

The case attracted enormous public attention. After all, the perpetrators and the victim came from wealthy and prominent Chicago families. Antisemitism was widespread, and all three boys came from Jewish families (although the victim's family had converted, and Loeb's mother was Catholic). Also, the young killers were involved in a homosexual relationship: Leopold was clearly in love with Loeb (although it is hard to know how exactly, if at all, Loeb reciprocated the affection, there being the suggestion that he mostly used his sexual attractiveness to Leopold as the basis for manipulating him). All in all, it was what we today would call a high-visibility case. Thus, the press of the time, which was perhaps even more prone to hyperbole than ours today, took to calling it "The Crime of the Century."

Leopold and Loeb were convicted, and, given the heinousness of the crime, the prosecutor asked for the death penalty. The boys' families were able to pay for a state-of-the-art defense, complete with several psychological expert witnesses. Their reports are preserved, and I have read some of them. I should note that much of the material seems quite solid by today's standards. For example, Dr. William White said this about the Richard Loeb and Nathan Leopold he evaluated for the court:

> Richard lied about all sorts of things. . . . He was continually building up all sorts of artificial situations until he himself says that he found it difficult to distinguish between what was true and what was not true. . . . He considers himself the master criminal mind, controlling a band of criminals. Nathan's pathology began in early childhood. His classmates at the Douglas School had teased him relentlessly; his estrangement from his peers had begun when he was seven or eight years old and had continued through his time at the Harvard School and into the present. Nathan had always been a lonely unhappy child, ever the outsider: and to protect himself from further pain and hurt, he had retreated into an inner world where emotions counted for nothing and intellect was all. Nathan, like Richard, was trapped inside a world of fantasy. . . . Nathan and Richard complemented each other. Richard needed Nathan's applause and admiration in order to confirm his sense of his own self. But Nathan also needed Richard to play a role. . . . It was a bizarre confluence of two personalities, each of which satisfied the need of the other. Nathan would never on his own initiative have murdered Bobby Franks. . . . I cannot see how Nathan would have entered into it at all alone because he had no criminalistic tendencies in any sense as Richard did, and I don't believe Richard would have ever functioned to this extent all by himself, so these two boys with their peculiarly interdigitated personalities come into this emotional compact with the Franks homicide as a result. . . . Richard's outstanding feature was his infantilism. I mean by that these infantile emotional characteristics. That is the outstanding feature of his mental condition. He is still a little child emotionally. . . . Nathan also is the host of a relatively infantile emotional aspect of his personality . . . but he has reacted by a defense mechanism, which has produced the final picture of marked disordered personality make-up in the direction of developing feelings of superiority, which places him very largely out of contact with any adequate appreciation of his relations to others.

Well said.

In addition to the psychological experts, the boys' wealthy families retained as their lead attorney the world-famous Clarence Darrow, who presented a *twelve-hour* plea for the boys' lives. The judge was persuaded, and Leopold and

Loeb were spared the gallows, sentenced instead to "life in prison plus ninety-nine years"—effectively a sentence of life without the possibility of parole.

The Rest of the Story

Leopold and Loeb were sent to Stateville Prison in Illinois to serve out their sentences. I have visited Stateville more than once to conduct interviews for *Miller* cases, and from time to time I receive letters from inmates there asking for my help (many of the state's juvenile lifers are housed there). The original 1925 building stands. It evokes Louis XIV's Palace of Versailles, except that it has been extended in the rear by an ugly addition, from both sides of which extend high, gray concrete walls quite different from the lovely "wings" of the French king's palace.

Out front is a small entrance building through which visitors to the prison pass. Despite the grandeur of the original main building, it's a grim place. The first time I visited, the facility was on lockdown because an inmate had attacked his cellmate and gouged out one of his eyes. As Peter A. told me when I interviewed him, "After being here for twenty-four years, I can tell you this prison has a long history as a barbaric place."

Thus, it is not surprising that Leopold and Loeb had to contend with prison violence at Stateville. In 1936, Richard Loeb was killed by another inmate, in a grisly attack with a razor that occurred in the shower. Nathan Leopold rushed to his beloved's side as he died in the prison infirmary. The details of the murder were unclear (some say obscured deliberately by prison authorities), but the attack appears to have been the result of a sordid affair that involved protection payments to other inmates and sexual assault. End of story—or at least that part of the story, because Leopold lived for many years afterward.

Given the diabolical nature of his crime in 1924, the severity of his offense in committing the absolute evil of murdering a defenseless fourteen-year-old boy, and the psychologically devastating evaluation of him provided by Dr. White at the trial ("marked disordered personality" and "still a little child emotionally"), what could have been expected for Nathan Leopold's future as a human being coming of age in prison? What might be the prognosis? At the time of his arrest and trial, his prospects for rehabilitation might have appeared bleak indeed, and anyone who offered a positive and hopeful prediction for his future would have been suspected of naive optimism, or of providing duplicitous testimony, paid for by his wealthy parents to "get him off."

However, despite the sentence of life plus ninety-nine years, Leopold was paroled in 1958 and lived on as a free man, continuing a decent and humane life until his death in 1971. It would appear that the convergence of three factors made this possible. First, the wealth of Leopold's family meant that, in addition to the expert legal representation during his trial (which spared his life), he continued to be represented by competent and motivated attorneys in the years of his incarceration. Second, he became a model prisoner and underwent a process of rehabilitation and transformation. He followed the rules, and went beyond that to work at improving conditions at the prison. This included enhancing educational programs that benefited other inmates, working in the library, and volunteering in the prison hospital. Third, he matured. His adolescent brain developed into an adult brain, and his "executive function" and "emotional regulation" improved.

He eventually wrote a memoir, *Life Plus 99 Years,* that was published in 1958. That same year, he was paroled (after numerous failed attempts engineered by his lawyers) and moved to Puerto Rico (apparently to get as far away from Chicago as he could and still meet the condition of his parole that he remain in the United States). There, he led what appears to have been an exemplary life. He married and contributed to the community as a medical assistant and educator. His sponsor was the Brethren Service Commission, which welcomed him, supported him, and, as Leopold put it, "gave me so much more than that, the companionship, the acceptance, the love which would have rendered a violation of parole almost impossible." In 1971, at the age of sixty-six, Leopold died of a heart attack.

In 2015, Victory Gardens Theater in Chicago staged a production of John Logan's play *Never the Sinner,* which chronicles the Leopold and Loeb case. I was asked to be on a panel discussing the case by the theater's management (as part of a continuing-education series tied to their productions). One of the panelists was Jason Nargis, a librarian at Northwestern University who curates the university's Leopold and Loeb collection. He shared a document found in the archives that included a report by Leopold's probation officer, who visited him in Puerto Rico. It seems that to the end of his days, Leopold expressed love for his partner in crime, Richard Loeb: he had a portrait of his lifelong love above the fireplace in his home in Puerto Rico. When it comes to teenage killers, some things change, but some things remain the same.

Faced with a "death-in-prison sentence," with no possibility of eventual parole, how do some young killers change for the better? As we will see, most young killers who actively rehabilitate themselves do so through education, therapy, transformative contemplation, and inspirational spiritual development. But we can't discount the process by which some simply seem to get "tired" as they age and are forced into grudging self-awareness. In the 1994 film *The Shawshank Redemption,* Red Redding (the character played by Morgan Freeman) appears before the parole board after serving forty years in prison for a murder committed when he was a youth. Asked if he has been rehabilitated, Red responds this way:

> Not a day goes by I don't feel regret, and not because I'm here or because you think I should. I look back on myself the way I was . . . stupid kid who did that terrible crime . . . wish I could talk sense to him. Tell him how things are. But I can't. That kid's long gone, this old man is all that's left, and I have to live with that. . . . Rehabilitated? That's a bullshit word, so you can just go on ahead and stamp that form there, sonny, and stop wasting my damn time. Truth is, I don't give a shit.

While Red's case is fictional, it does reflect an important truth, widely known in the corrections field, namely "progressive aging." Researchers across time and place have found that the rate of criminal violence declines with age (and not just in prisons, but in society outside prisons as well). Indeed, one expert, Mark Cunningham, refers to this as "one of the most robust and accepted tenets in criminology."

However, according to researchers Grant Harris, Marnie Rice, Vernon Quinsey, and Catherine Cormier, the story is not quite so simple. Their work has focused on the development of a screening approach called the "Violence Risk Appraisal Guide" (and a companion work focused on sexual offenses, the "Sex Offender Risk Appraisal Guide"). In a 2014 study led by Rice, they report that among sex offenders, age alone does not predict recidivism well at all. This may be due to the special dynamics of sexual offending (in contrast to "regular" violence), wherein the core identity issues may be less likely to "automatically" resolve with aging.

Prison disciplinary problems generally decrease as inmates get older, regardless of how the prison context treats them, according to the classic study conducted by Travis Hirschi and Michael Gottfredson, published in 1983 and replicated in studies since then. Another report documents that "kids" in their twenties commit ten times the infractions of "geezers" in their sixties. This improvement shows up also as a decline in personality problems—for example, a negative correlation between time served and high scores on a widely used personality assessment, the MMPI scale: older men had better scores because psychological problems decrease over time. Studies using the California Psychological Inventory profiles of inmates report the same finding: inmates who have been incarcerated for a long time reflect better social and psychological adjustment. What is more, inmates who have served long sentences express more prosocial attitudes toward the criminal justice system than short-termers. Some of this may be attributable to the fact that as men get older, their commitment to conventional "masculinity" declines, resulting in greater emotional intelligence and greater appreciation for nonviolent conflict resolution. This is the conclusion of a program of research conducted by psychologist Matthew Jakupcak and colleagues.

WHAT ABOUT ANTISOCIAL PERSONALITY DISORDER?

As I have written before (in my 2015 book *Listening to Killers*), I am skeptical of conventional diagnoses from clinical psychology and psychiatry. Most of the time, I think, they do not really explain much of anything. Rather, they tend to be a label for an observation, perhaps a snapshot of troubled thoughts, feelings, and behavior. For example, if a child demonstrates a chronic pattern of aggression, bad behavior, acting out, and violating the rights of others, that child can be diagnosed with "conduct disorder." But do we really know any more about that child by virtue of attaching this label?

As I noted in my 1999 book *Lost Boys,* a research report issued by the agency that oversaw the New York State youth prisons concluded that 85 percent of the boys being detained had conduct disorder. The question, of course, is this: *How else* do you get yourself sent to a youth prison except by demonstrating "a chronic pattern of aggression, bad behavior, acting out, and violating the rights of others"? To me, it's a bit like saying that a study shows that 85 percent of the players on a high school football team are athletes. Of course they are! The more interesting question about incarcerated youths is *Why are the other 15 percent there?* And many other important questions remain to be addressed:

How do boys develop conduct disorder? Is it a homogeneous group? Are there multiple pathways to arrive at this pattern of behavior? Can it improve? If so, under what conditions does it improve? And so on and so on.

If the pattern of thinking, feeling, and (mis)behaving that elicits a label of "conduct disorder" persists into adulthood, it is likely that the diagnostic label will switch to the adult diagnosis of "antisocial personality disorder." And if there is one diagnosis that marks an inmate as a lost cause from the point of view of prosecutors and parole boards, it is antisocial personality disorder. Guys who get this label are generally thought to be incorrigibly evil in their behavior and hopeless with respect to their prognosis going forward. When faced with this label, parole boards and juries are likely to decide that the person "accused" of this label and "diagnosed" with this condition is truly a lost cause.

Yet even this dreaded diagnosis declines in severity, or even subsides, as men age—even when comparing forty-five-year-olds with men in their twenties. Of course, in most of these studies, age and length of incarceration are themselves correlated, so it is not always clear how much of the effect is attributable to aging, and how much to the cumulative effects of incarceration (setting aside the methodological problem that there is a correlation between the length of the sentence and the severity of the crime). In any case, I believe that even teenagers who appear to be on the verge of receiving the dreaded diagnosis of antisocial personality disorder when they turn eighteen, because of their history of adolescent conduct disorder, should *never* receive life-without-parole sentences. It is simply impossible to be sure they will not recover, will not find a path to rehabilitation and transformation. This is not to say they will take that path (as we will see in chapter 5), but only that no one who commits a murder as a teenager should be forever denied the possibility of that journey.

EMERGING ADULTHOOD

Red's comments to the parole board in *The Shawshank Redemption* are a valid picture of the long-term prospects for at least some adolescent killers. But is it necessary to wait thirty, forty, fifty, or more years to see that effect? While the research on progressive aging does point to an important process that applies to many young killers, it is not the whole story. While aging can and does generate perspective and insight, I believe that the process can be accelerated when it is stimulated deliberately by interventions to provoke and sustain improved decision making (executive function) and management of emotions (emotional or "affective" regulation). Therefore, I think it is crucial to focus on the years between adolescence (when the murders with which we are concerned here occurred) and the adulthood into which these killers have grown (typically in their mid-thirties). This twenty-year period can be, and often is, very potent in producing insight, impulse control, and a general lessening of the forces that generate violent behavior in the first place, if for no other reason than that many of the important measures of brain maturation appear to coalesce by age twenty-five. Thus, whereas most fifteen-year-olds are not playing with a "full deck" when it comes to brain development, most twenty-five-year-olds are, and they can make use of that mature brain in the *next* ten years to become rehabilitated and transformed.

Psychologists are starting to direct their research attention to what developmental psychologist Jeffrey Arnet called "emerging adulthood" in his 2014 book of that name (offering what he calls "a theory of development from the late teens through the twenties"). He cites a wide range of evidence to support the view that "emerging adulthood is a distinct period demographically, subjectively, and in terms of identity explorations." Arnet reports that when asked if they have "reached adulthood," nearly 60 percent of those eighteen to twenty-five years old answer, "In some respects yes, but in some respects no." Moreover, various forms of risk-taking behavior (unprotected sex, most types of substance abuse, and risky driving behavior) peak not in adolescence, but in this period of emerging adulthood. What are some of the dimensions in which maturation takes place in ways that are relevant to understanding how and why some young killers "get better"?

Kathryn Monahan and colleagues reported on a study of how individual variability in the development of psychosocial maturity is associated with desistance from antisocial behavior among juvenile offenders as they moved from adolescence to early adulthood (ages fourteen to twenty-five). They document how psychosocial maturity continues to develop from adolescence into the mid-twenties. They found different developmental patterns of maturation when contrasting those who desist from and those who persist in antisocial behavior. As would be expected, the more the delinquents exhibited psychological maturation, the more likely they were to desist from committing further delinquent acts.

That very process is one of the foundations for the hope expressed in the *Miller v. Alabama* decision: with maturity comes improved social behavior.

Dustin Albert and colleagues have found similar results. When kids were posed a set of "strategic planning" tasks, by age seventeen they had mastered "easy" problems, but *not until the early twenties* were they routinely mastering the "hardest" problems. The study found that it was improved memory and impulse control that accounted for the superior performance at later ages, and that these improvements in functioning were correlated with brain development in the regions that are employed in dealing with these tasks and solving these problems.

Perhaps they are not children, these young killers, but for the most part they are not adults (boys rather than men; girls rather than women). As a developmental psychologist with forty years of professional experience, and as a seventy-year-old man with grown kids in their thirties and forties, I do see them as boys and girls, lost boys and girls. Some of them, the younger ones, really are just kids, no matter how the legal system tries to define them as adults. And they demonstrate a capacity for bouncing back from what and who they were as teenagers to become good men (and women, although the number of women among Miller's Children is very small; I have worked on such cases, but there aren't enough for me to speak with confidence about them).

RESILIENCE IN ACTION

One way to conceptualize the rehabilitation of teenage killers, this "bouncing back from what and who they were as teenagers," is to see it as a form of resilience. I see it in how they move from the dark days of their adolescence, when they committed a murder and were thrown into the abyss of prison, into the light in adulthood. Examining what researchers like Emmy Werner have identified as common foundations for resilience sheds some light on how they do this (see box 2).

Actively Trying to Cope with Stress

The guys I know who demonstrate resilience often speak of how they took it upon themselves to get better, to become someone better than they were as teenage killers. For example, Karl A. has demonstrated an active stance in relation to his life situation, both before and after he was involved in a murder at age seventeen. He speaks of several points in his life when he might

BOX 2. RESILIENCE FACTORS

- Actively trying to cope with stress (rather than just reacting)
- Cognitive competence (at least an average level of intelligence)
- Experiences of self-efficacy and a corresponding self-confidence and positive self-esteem
- Temperamental characteristics that favor active coping attempts and positive relationships with others (e.g., activity, goal orientation, and sociability) rather than passive withdrawal
- A stable emotional relationship with at least one parent or other reference person
- An open, supportive educational climate that encourages constructive coping with problems
- Social support from persons outside the family

have avoided being sucked into "life on the streets." He says that when it was time to go to high school, he tried to get out of his neighborhood and attend a better school in a safer part of town. This required him to falsify his address so he could meet the residency requirements for the better school. To do this, he went from house to house in that safer neighborhood, looking for someone who would give him a document he could use to prove that he lived in that neighborhood (finally finding "an old white lady who gave me a gas bill I could use"). As Karl puts it, "I tried to escape!" Once he got into that safer high school, he thought he had "made it." He was involved in sports there and had a part-time job. But then his mother forced him to "come back home," and Karl ended up back in the high school in his home neighborhood. That meant he was back in the "war zone" where his mother's choice of residence placed him.

Karl is a good person whose active efforts to find a positive path for himself were overwhelmed by the social toxicity of his neighborhood and high school. He joined the dominant gang in his neighborhood as a matter of "geography and protection," but he says that his gang affiliation was not crucial to him until he was incarcerated, when it became more important for his protection. However, once he became old enough and had a position of respect, he disaffiliated himself from the gang ("dropped the flag"). Cultivating a spiritual orientation to his life has proved invaluable in creating and sustaining these changes. He displays at age forty-one the same "active" approach to stress that he did as a teenager, only now he has the resources and opportunities he needs to live the "safe" life denied him as a seventeen-year-old.

Cognitive Competence

The most successful of Miller's Children are of average or above-average intelligence and are able to direct their intelligence to the task of figuring things out and taking advantage of the opportunities available to them. Those who fall below this standard often struggle.

Test reports for Larry F. in 1991, when he was fifteen years old (and approximately a year before the murder for which he was sentenced), indicate marginal intellectual resources—with a tested verbal IQ of 78 and a Full Scale IQ of 72, which put him in the bottom 3 percent of the American population for his age. But when Larry was assessed before that, at age eleven, his overall IQ was 84, which put him in the "low average range" (in contrast to his score four years later, which suggested intellectual disability). As a side note, this discrepancy speaks to the role of disruptive emotional factors in tested intellectual development. It is worth noting that the school psychologist concluded his 1991 report with this recommendation: "Continuation of placement and the possibility of counseling to provide Larry with an outlet to explore his feelings will be discussed." It would appear that no counseling took place, and a year later he killed sixteen-year-old Betty Lawrence.

Larry had been assigned to Special Education (which was extremely onerous to him). The school psychologist reported that

> Larry yearns to be in general education and fit in with all others, but currently he does not possess the internal resources to attempt this. Larry presents himself as a "cool" and detached adolescent, yet this is just a denial of his true feelings and serves as a defense mechanism to protect him from the anxiety he is experiencing.

Larry suffered from the double whammy of being intellectually limited and emotionally overwhelmed by his life situation (including the stigma of being placed in a Special Education program).

When I met Larry twenty-five years later, he was still struggling, having made little progress in becoming the kind of rehabilitated and transformed person who could safely be released into the world. In contrast, many of his peers displayed average or above-average intellectual ability and were able to use that intellect as a tool in service to rehabilitation and transformation. It's worth noting here that Larry's case highlights one of the most troubling issues in sentencing and release, namely that those individuals who are held to be least *culpable* because of their intellectual limitations (as codified in the Supreme Court's 2002 *Atkins v. Virginia* ruling that outlawed the execution of mentally disabled perpetrators) may also be least amenable to rehabilitation because of those same mental disabilities.

Self-Efficacy, Self-Confidence, and Positive Self-Esteem

Replacing shame with pride is a big challenge for Miller's Children, since shame is one of the common ingredients in the toxic psychological and social brew that leads to aggression, according to the research of psychiatrist James Gilligan. The combination of negative definition of self offered first by family and schools and then by the courts and public opinion—for example, being labeled a "monster"—is a big nut to crack. When guys can find positive things to do—be it as a hospice volunteer, a law clerk, a plumber, or a certified yoga instructor, for example—they can create a positive sense of themselves that is restorative and transformational.

Peter A. has served twenty-five years in prison for the murder he committed when he was sixteen. Given his extended family's strong identification with the Crips gang and the neighborhood in which he lived, it was natural for Peter to be drawn into the gang-dominated life, with all its adverse consequences. He took that path, and it was the dominant fact of his adolescence (before he was arrested) and early adulthood (while he was incarcerated), until he "woke up" and saw the need to take a different path. This is the path that led to a prosocial transformation from gangbanger to the businessman and family man he is today (despite his ongoing incarceration).

Peter has sustained a long-term relationship with a woman on the outside, and they plan to marry when (if) he is released as a result of his upcoming resentencing hearing. He maintains a strong connection with the son he barely knew when he went to prison. Peter and his fiancée have developed several businesses that demonstrate Peter's entrepreneurial orientation, for example a "gift basket" business and a real estate project (PA Property Management). And he has a job offer (as a livery driver) awaiting him if he's released. And he has founded an organization designed to help inner-city youths avoid the criminal path that he took—"Men Against Guns." He says of his motivation for this, "I see my old self in the young guys on the street and I want to help them avoid what I have gone through."

The evidence of Peter's prosocial behavior in the period after 2010 attests to this rehabilitation, including his 2011 official affidavit disaffiliating himself from the gang that had been a significant part of his life for more than fifteen years. He says, "In prison I spend every day reading and studying because I believe one day I will get out of this place and I want to be ready." He also reports that "even as a sixteen-year-old, I knew I had to do something else and all that comes with it." Although he was unable to extricate himself at that point in his life (he says that at the time of his arrest he was exploring options for enrolling in a trade school), he has, as an adult in prison, taken that alternative path.

Temperamental Characteristics That Favor Active Coping and Positive Relationships with Others

Temperamental variations are an important influence on human development in general. They certainly play a role in the rehabilitation of teenage killers—as they do in the developmental issues that originally put them in a position to murder someone. Of special importance is how some of Miller's Children find ways to "tame" their temperamental vulnerabilities as they move from adolescence to adulthood.

Quinton P. was diagnosed early on with "attention-deficit/hyperactivity disorder" (ADHD). And as noted in the evaluation by a Dr. Thomas in 2005, "Consequently, his ability to refrain from acting on his impulses, and thereby conform his conduct to the requirements of law, was weakened by these ADHD-related cognitive and emotional vulnerabilities." The underlying roots of such a diagnosis are unclear (namely the degree to which it reflects a basic temperamental condition or a response to traumatic and inconsistent child rearing). Nonetheless, the fact that he received such a diagnosis indicates that his relations with the social world of school, peers, family, and community were colored by this overall disposition. Both the reports of others and Quinton's own report indicate that he engaged in a lot of "bad behavior" that elicited harsh punishment and led to some of the torture he experienced at the hands of his stepfather (and mother). Rather than controlling his "bad behavior," this torture only served to exacerbate it. Thus, while it seems likely that Quinton's temperament contributed to the diagnosis of ADHD, there was likely a strong environmental contribution to his processing of information and his behavior in social situations like school. This is true in most such diagnoses.

Research conducted by R. James Blair and colleagues has shown that the diagnosis of conduct disorder (a chronic pattern of aggression, bad behavior, acting out, and violating the rights of others) in most cases arises out of "anxious reaction" to difficult family situations, not out of some genetic disposition to "callousness." Similarly, ADHD can reflect the child's response to stress and trauma, a response that can be heightened by temperamental vulnerabilities. Conversely, elements of temperament can change as brain maturation goes forward in concert with changed environmental conditions and human volition. The "malleability" of even adult brains in the face of changed circumstances and choices made is clear, as neuroscientist Norman Doidge demonstrates in his book *The Brain That Changes Itself.* Children differ temperamentally in how and to what degree they will react to particular experiences growing up. This includes being "easy to soothe" versus "difficult to soothe," as well as "impulsive" versus "reflective." It incorporates being "highly emotionally reactive" versus "emotionally disconnected." These traits can carry over into adolescence and adulthood, and thus affect prospects for resilience. Some infants are judged to be "easy," others "difficult." Research indicates that only a small minority (10 percent in the classic study conducted by Alexander Thomas and Stella Chess) of "easy babies" have significant difficulties by the time they are in elementary school, while for "difficult babies" the figure is more like 80 percent. But things can change in adulthood, as they have in Quinton's case. Through years of meditation and reflection, he has been able to shift his temperament away from the hyperactivity and difficulty paying attention that plagued his childhood and adolescence. Now he is a calm and reflective man, and that bodes well for his further rehabilitation and transformation.

A Stable Emotional Relationship with at Least One Parent or Other Reference Person

If a teenage killer can retain the unconditional love of a stable parent or parental figure, it can make a huge difference, because that person provides a social and emotional anchor in the world outside prison. This anchor can help keep a teenage killer from getting lost in the darkness and despair of prison life. When Robert W. (whose story I told in chapter 2) went to trial in 1994 for a drug-related murder, his parents sat in the front row of the courtroom every day, as did one of his former teachers and his high school football coach. A petition was sent to the judge by people in Robert's hometown, asking that mercy be shown in sentencing him. However, the law at the time tied the judge's hands, and Robert received the mandatory life-without-parole sentence stipulated for a teenage killer. For more than twenty-one years, Robert's parents have stood by him in every way they could. Even his emotionally distant father—who had never said "I love you" to his son until the sentencing hearing, as far as Robert could recall—has been there for him in ways that he was not before Robert was arrested. Robert's mother, who was a positive influence on his life throughout childhood and continued to be supportive even during his adolescent delinquent phase, has given him ongoing support. She even started a small business in the hope that her son would have a place to work and something valuable to inherit when he was released (which came to pass in 2016, as recounted in chapter 2).

An Open, Supportive Educational Climate That Encourages Constructive Coping

Education is a key element of rehabilitation and transformation for teenage killers. It often starts with a GED and then moves to college-level courses (in the increasingly rare event that cash-strapped prison systems offer them). But of equal—and sometimes greater—importance is whether or not a teenage killer embarks upon a program of *self-directed* education and study.

Ever since Donald Z. got through the turbulent decade between age sixteen, when he killed a man, and his mid-twenties, his record of participation in self-betterment programs in prison has been exemplary. These include programs such as "Life Skills," which improved his anger management. He has had some positive relationships that served a mentoring function (e.g., helping teach the "Life Skills" program after he completed the course). And he has been engaged in productive activity that required him to learn technical skills. For example, after completing the "Environmental Services" course at the prison, he now works as an environmental services technician, helping regular prison staff maintain the heating and cooling systems. But most importantly, he has undergone an intense process of education, reflection, and spiritual development.

Donald's records and the observations of numerous individuals (including correctional staff who are prepared to testify on his behalf) speak to his development. Donald received his GED, hopes to attend college, and reads for pleasure and education (which he did not do as a teenager). For example, he says his favorite book is an inspirational text titled *Not Easily Broken,* which offers an exploration of resilience. This, plus his educational activities as a serious student and practitioner of Islam, have increased his understanding of self and the social dynamics of his life. With his growing insight and self-awareness, Donald even began to have an appreciation for the level of victimization he had experienced. This processing of his early experience has led him to a mature position with respect to his parents. He says of his mother,

> Forgiving her took a long time. It really helped when in 2009 she admitted that she "wasn't the greatest parent." I told her, "All I wanted you to do is understand that what I really needed was my parents." My father was the reason she was so down—the crack cocaine and the violence that he brought her to. But she was addicted to him.

As a result of all the work he has done on himself, Donald has reached a good place in his life. Having arrived there, he is now prepared to go out into the world as a free man. Of course, he will need help and support to make a successful transition to "the world." After all, he went to prison before he had a chance to engage in the normal transitional experiences that take a boy from being a teenager to being a young adult. But he is now safe.

Social Support from Persons outside the Family

Having someone inside the prison system who cares matters a great deal. I often hear about these "angels"—be they therapists, counselors, inmate mentors, spiritual guides, or teachers—and the role they have played in a guy's ability to get on (and then stay on) track and to focus on rehabilitation and transformation. Dennis D., for example, wrote to me about the mentors—in person and in print—that have supported and guided him over his decades in prison:

> When I came to prison, a Catholic priest took an interest in me so I started attending Catholic services and singing in the choir, but not because I was particularly interested in or moved by Catholicism. I was there for the community.... In 1998, Kornfield's book "A Path with Heart" jumped off a book shelf at me and ultimately led me to check out a Buddhist Study Group at the prison I was at . . . and I've never looked back since. Spirituality is a creation of God and knows no limits, in my opinion. So, I see myself as a spiritual person rather than a religious person and I don't know that even identifying myself as "Buddhist" fits. I started a Buddhist Study Group that "coincidentally" had

its first meeting on my birthday. I attend Buddhist and meditation groups on Sun, Mon and Wed. I meditate every day. I read "Buddhist" texts. Presently I am reading Thich Nhat Hanh's "Heart of the Buddha's Teachings," Rodney Smith's "Awakening," and Noah Levine's "Refuge Recovery" (applying Buddhist principles to addiction recovery). "A Path with Heart" is one that I always have nearby and return to often. I also read a lot of Pema Chodron's stuff. It has been an interesting blossoming of my spiritual life since 1998, but it all started with that priest who took an interest in me and became my guide to a world full of mentors.

RESILIENCE AND POST-TRAUMATIC GROWTH

Resilience is a many-splendored thing, and it flourishes in some Miller's Children eventually, even when their early efforts to do well in life are thwarted by an unsupportive and hostile environment. Most of the rehabilitated teenage killers I have met have found their way to this gateway and passed through it to a kind of spiritual "promised land." But they have done so by coming through the valley of darkness, being fully "broken" by what they did and who they were—and eventually coming back from the darkness into the light. Psychologists Richard Tedeschi and Lawrence Calhoun have termed this journey "post-traumatic growth."

Post-traumatic growth goes beyond resilience—the "bouncing back" that is common for 85–90 percent of those affected by a single traumatic event (like witnessing the 9/11 attacks firsthand or being robbed at gunpoint). Tedeschi and Calhoun are talking about what happens after a person has been "rocked to their core"—broken down, perhaps to the point of a clinical diagnosis of post-traumatic stress disorder or some other serious mental health problems.

When I attend mass, sitting in my regular pew in Madonna della Strada Chapel on the campus of Loyola University Chicago, the words in the Catholic liturgy that move me most, every time I say them, are these: "Lord, I am not worthy that you should enter under my roof, but only say the word and my soul shall be healed." This confession of sin and inadequacy, of brokenness followed by the promise of redemption and healing sustains me—in my work and in my life. If these words mean so much to me in living my life "on the outside," how much more do they offer for guys living—and perhaps dying—"on the inside," for murders committed when they were teenagers?

These words offer solace and hope, and they can also offer an important clue to the process of rehabilitation and transformation that is at the heart of the story of Miller's Children, at the heart of post-traumatic growth.

According to the work of Tedeschi and Calhoun, the rebuilding of self that can come *after* hitting rock bottom, after being unworthy "that you should enter under my roof," includes five dimensions:

- Appreciation of life
- Relationships with others
- New possibilities in life
- Personal strength
- Spiritual change

They estimate that from one-half to two-thirds of people who are broken by trauma demonstrate post-traumatic growth. I count most of the successes achieved by Miller's Children among them. Why do some experience this post-traumatic growth while others do not? Research is just starting to address this important question, but there are some indicators. Tedeschi and Calhoun report that "openness to experience" and "extraversion" are predictive. Eric Dunn and colleagues have added to this by identifying the possibility of genetic variations that can enhance the potential for such post-traumatic growth (e.g., the *RGS2* gene that is implicated in fear-related disorders generally).

THE CASE OF JEFFREY M.

Jeffrey M. was arrested in 1999 for a murder committed when he was seventeen. Like many of the guys in his situation, he had issues with violent behavior early in his prison "career"—in 1999 and 2000, when he was still an adolescent. When I spoke to him about this in 2016, he said, "When I was in county jail I was told you had to respond when tested. This guy stole my radio and I had to fight to get it back." However, as time passed he found a way to move to a more positive approach. "Later there were some older guys in prison who were inspiring. Other than that, I just didn't want to be that person anymore. I never was a violent person wanting to hurt people. I just had hope." According to correctional-facility files, his record has been good and has consistently improved since 2000, and he has not had any serious infractions for many years. The tattoos on his body chronicle this: they include the words *humble, family, forgiven, blessed,* and *not easily broken.*

Jeffrey speaks of how he has developed a mature understanding of himself and his life as a teenager. This kind of insight is exactly the possibility that even most very troubled adolescents carry within them, if given the opportunity to become more "emotionally intelligent" through education, reflection, and the processes of neurobiological maturation. This is, of course, one of the foundational principles contained in the Supreme Court's decision in *Miller v. Alabama.* As Jeffrey put it,

> I was searching for something to change me and the way I'm thinking. Growing up I was influenced by negativity. When I was growing up, the drug dealers were the people who had money. They were the ones I could go to for money and nice clothes, so I decided when I was ten that I would become a drug dealer too.

Indeed, Jeffrey's behavior in the murder appears to have been linked to the kind of "impulsive" and "stupid" behavior often demonstrated by adolescents in general when in crisis, particularly in the presence of peers—an "audience." He says of his adolescent crime, "I just went along with the group. I was like a sheep. I didn't have the inner strength to say 'no.' I am different now." As an adaptation to his chronically violent social environment, Jeffrey suppressed or extinguished some of the inhibitions against acting violently that might operate in other individuals with less violently traumatic experiences (and that might well have prevailed in Jeffrey had he not grown up in a "war zone"). This "psychological" phenomenon must be seen in light of the broader accumulation of risk factors and absence of developmental assets in his life—and the social toxicity of his environment, as defined by the impact of racism and the Southern culture of honor that became embedded in the thinking of his ancestors and was passed down to him. The net effect of all these factors was to reduce his capacity for prosocial and skillful executive function and emotional regulation in the social world beyond the family.

That's what makes him one of Miller's Children. He committed a murder at age seventeen—as part of a bungled attempt to rob a drug dealer in his neighborhood who was thought to be carrying a large amount of cash—but in the many years since then he has become a man, and a good one at that.

In developmental psychology, much has been made of the role played by early attachment relationships in shaping the course and form of attachments later in life. For example, as research conducted by Geraldine Downey and colleagues has shown, children who have insecure attachments to parents early in life may develop a pattern of "rejection sensitivity" that extends into adulthood. This has been found to help explain some of the domestic violence committed against women by men whose fear of abandonment stimulates an aggressive response—sometimes even a murderous response.

By the same token, one of the ways in which Miller's Children find psychological traction in their effort to rehabilitate and transform themselves is by rethinking and reprocessing key relationships in their lives—most often with their mothers, but sometimes with their fathers—and forming and sustaining new relationships that offer them a chance to reinvent themselves relationally. Jeffrey M. is an example. Despite being involved in a murder when he was seventeen, Jeffrey is not "generically violent" and incapable of intimate relationships. His crime and the life that led up to it do not seem to reflect a "malignant heart"—an immutable habit of violent, antisocial thought and behavior—or to warrant the psychiatric diagnosis of antisocial personality disorder.

I find evidence for this in his attachment to his adult son, Jeffrey Jr., to whom he is devoted—and who has led a successful life in counterpoint to his father's failed adolescence. It is also evident in Jeffrey's attitude toward his mother, who struggled with substance abuse and being the victim of domestic violence at the hands of Jeffrey's father, up to and including the day when Jeffrey was arrested and sentenced to life without parole. More than twenty years later, he appreciates that his mother has "cleaned up her act."

When asked to describe his mother, Jeffrey says, "She is a very strong individual. Even with her limitations and her addiction she never abandoned me. Despite her troubles." This statement indicates *both* that Jeffrey does not "accuse" his mother of rejecting him (despite her chronically neglectful parenting of him and his sister) *and* that he demonstrates a generosity of spirit where she is concerned. Learning how to let go of anger toward the people who let them down—and, in a sense, put them on the road to a life-without-parole sentence in the first place—is an important resource for Miller's Children. If truth be told, it's important for all of us.

One of the principal conclusions I have drawn from my more than two decades as a psychological expert witness in murder cases is that a good working hypothesis in approaching most killers is that they are untreated traumatized children inhabiting and controlling the minds and hearts of scary teenagers and men. Why are they so scary? Because young children are the most violent people among us! Psychologists Richard Tremblay and Daniel Nagin make this point when he observes that about 90 percent of two-year-old boys (and 80 percent of two-year-old girls) engage in "violent" behavior—hitting, biting, kicking and the like—but we don't see this clearly because they are so physically weak. What would happen, they ask, if tomorrow all the two-year-olds in the world woke up and were six feet tall and weighed two hundred pounds? His answer: by the end of that day most parents, babysitters, and early-childhood educators would be maimed or dead. I have met six-foot-tall, two-hundred-pound toddlers in prisons across America. If they have been traumatized, they are dangerous—to themselves and others.

Carl O. was sexually abused as a young child, and his traumatization had never been dealt with effectively. Having been so traumatized, what Carl needed was high-quality therapeutic support to deal with the ongoing psychological effects of his victimization. He did not receive that support. He reports it this way:

> I will say that between my teacher and my parents there was discussion about the availability of some kind of counseling for me. I lived in a small town (then 2000 people). The group was going to be in the neighboring town of Johnsonville, but I was told I was likely going to be the only boy involved in that group. I was terrified of the idea of talking about the abuse with anyone, much less a bunch of girls I didn't know. I declined and that was the end of it.

But of course it wasn't. We now understand that traumatic memories don't spontaneously decay. They can remain vivid and powerful many years (even decades) after the trauma that gives rise to them.

Even when immediate professional therapeutic intervention is available and experienced, what is required, more generally, is the "natural" therapy of education, reflection, and spiritual growth over a period of years. Carl has accomplished this, as is evident in his mature rendering of how he has made peace with his parents about their "failure" in helping him when he was a child (and even a teenager). He reports:

> Years later, in 2005 or 2006, my mother came to visit me in prison & we spoke of the abuse and its impact on my life. She said she felt like she had completely failed me as a child, because she sent me to the abuser (trusting her friend), and failing to get me help afterwards. She had a lot of pain, grief and guilt around the issue still then. Thanks to treatment I got in prison, I was able to come to some peace with the abuse and its impact on my life years earlier, so I was able to relieve my mom some, I think, by telling her that I don't see it that way, it wasn't her fault and it no longer controls or imprisons me, it's just regrettable historical facts.

Carl sits in prison serving a life sentence but has the wisdom to say that the trauma he experienced "no longer controls or imprisons me." Like many others, he is cobbling together a program of recovery from the limited resources available to him in prison, his own spiritual explorations and reflections, and the maturity that comes along with these efforts. But the most efficient way to get to that point is access to high-quality therapeutic intervention.

GETTING THERAPY

There are multiple components to the process of change, once the commitment to change is made. One is the experience of therapy. Most of the therapy available in prisons has been in the form of "behavioral" programs aimed at reducing negative behavior—that is, behavior that is risky and dangerous. However, according to a review conducted by psychologist Ian Barron and colleagues, there is little evidence that such efforts sustain long-term behavioral change. Why? The problem with such approaches is that they typically don't deal with the underlying developmental dynamics that give rise to and sustain the problematic behavior to which they are addressed.

What is at the core of those underlying developmental dynamics? The answer is what Bessel van der Kolk, Robert Pynoos, Dante Cicchetti, and their colleagues have called "developmental trauma." This recognition has given rise to and support for "trauma-informed" interventions. When it comes to treatment programs for teenage killers, my go-to resource is psychotherapist/criminologist Kathleen Heide. She has spent decades applying her intelligence, training, insight, and compassion to the question "What kind of programs are needed for teenage killers if they are to become rehabilitated and transformed?" When I posed this question to her in 2016, this is how she responded:

In brief, I think intensive evidence-based treatment is critical, especially related to trauma. I agree maturation is a key component, so sentences that take youths past their mid-twenties make sense, provided meaningful treatment is provided to them while they are incarcerated. Otherwise the time in prison is likely to be destructive to their psychological, emotional, and moral development. During incarceration, contact with prosocial individuals from the outset is imperative. Hopefully, some of these people will be family members committed to the youths' rehabilitation and re-entry into society. Finally, aftercare that is targeted to the individual's special needs, and those of his family if he will return to them, is essential.

From my experience today, we miss the boat because we do not intervene immediately. Many youth arrested for murder today are subjected to protracted pre-incarceration periods awaiting trial. During this period, which may last several years, no treatment is provided; their psychological and emotional needs are not addressed. Accordingly, when they finally are sentenced, they are often hardened and resistant to therapy even if it later becomes available to them, which in most cases, it does not.

I recently had a case on resentencing where the records indicated that the youth at the time of the killing was very upset, contrite, and remorseful. It took several years before he went to trial. During that time, the boy's story about his life circumstances and the criminal incident changed. The new version, which I read in the pre-trial records and the trial transcript, was not corroborated and to me was not credible. When I saw him years later, he took no responsibility for his homicidal behavior, experienced no guilt, and was devoid of any feeling. He had many callous unemotional traits, which I doubt were present at the time of the incident more than ten years earlier. I felt very sad after evaluating him. It was quite clear that this young man could have been helped soon after the incident occurred. At the time of my evaluation, I clearly saw him as a risk to society, as he had come to see himself as the victim and felt completely justified in his homicidal behavior.

Heide points to the Capital and Serious Violent Offender Program in Giddens, Texas, as a model. Other efforts along these lines exist—group-focused programs that have shown promise when used in secure facilities to help adolescents behave better by dealing with the unresolved trauma that so often feeds their bad behavior. Let me mention some examples of structured psychotherapy for adolescents.

Responding to Chronic Stress (SPARCS) focuses on efforts to promote positive consciousness among traumatized adolescents—including improved self-concept, meaning-making, and regulation of emotions.

Trauma and Affect Regulation (TARGET) quickly (in the first week) produced significant decreases in problems such as depression, making of threats, and staff interventions to impose restraint on juvenile detainees, effects that eventually included reduced recidivism.

The Sanctuary Program focuses on using trauma-informed group therapy to enhance emotional regulation and to deal with loss, thereby building the institutional capacity to serve as a "therapeutic community."

The Risk-Sophistication-Treatment Inventory offers an important resource in determining what a youth will need in the way of intervention. Grisso and Kavanaugh cite its "Treatment Amenability scale" as an important resource that can help in deciding how likely a youth is to make productive use of efforts aimed at rehabilitation. A tool like "Youth Level of Services/Case Management" can also be useful in figuring out how to match intervention plans with the need for, and probable effectiveness of, intervention associated with a particular youth's criminal behavior.

As even a cursory look at the demographics of young killers reveals, many of them (maybe most of them) come to prison not just with what might be called "individual" trauma (e.g., child abuse and interpersonal peer assault) but from environments that produced "collective" trauma—the domestic war zones in which community violence flows from the presence and actions of gangs and other systematic sources of violence. For this reason, as Heide notes, trauma-informed recovery programs for violent youths are essential. Some such efforts draw from the experience of dealing with kids from war zones. For example, the Children and War Foundation's "Teaching Recovery Techniques" program (TRT) uses a cognitive-behavioral approach. It offers five to seven weekly sessions in a kind of psychological first aid for children growing up in war zones. TRT offers instruction on how to deal with some of the day-to-day disruptions caused by unprocessed trauma (e.g., intrusive memories, avoidance of evocative stimuli, and overwhelming arousal) and the questions of meaningfulness that often accompany these "symptoms," such as feelings of loss. In one small-scale study, Perrin Smith and colleagues found that despite being a short-term intervention, the program did have some observable effects. When used with adolescent detainees, the program was associated with reduced distress when prompted to think about traumatic events and with a reduced number of aggressive incidents reported by staff members who monitored behavior in the facility. And beyond such formal "programs" is a recognition of the importance of surrounding adolescents with what have been called "developmental assets."

BUILDING UPON DEVELOPMENTAL ASSETS

When I interview guys in prison, seeking to illuminate their developmental pathway, one of the things I am looking for is the degree to which they experienced "developmental assets" growing up. Developmental assets are the positive counterpart to "risk factors" in development. Of the "40 Developmental Assets" described by the Search Institute (see chapter 1), American youths, on average, report having seventeen. Many of the young killers I have interviewed report very few. However, some report significant numbers of developmental assets, and often they fall into two categories that serve these individuals well later, after they are in prison and make the commitment to change of which Dennis D. spoke. Eric G., whom we met in chapter 1, is a good example.

Eric was charged with murder at age sixteen and has spent twenty-six years in prison. According to his responses during our interview, Eric experienced thirteen of the forty assets growing up. The assets that he identified fall mostly into two categories, his family (e.g., "I receive a lot of support from my family members" and "My parents encourage me to do well") and internal positive attributes (e.g., "I am good at making and keeping friends" and "I believe that I have control over things that happen to me"). The fact that his self-identified assets pertain predominantly to his personal characteristics, values, and morals and to his familial relationships bodes well for his rehabilitation. With appropriate support and access to prosocial environments, it is likely that these assets will continue to develop and ensure Eric's positive reintegration into society. Eric is not an inherently "bad" person who rejected positive support and guidance. Rather, he is a good person with a strong and supportive family who became misguided during adolescence and went down a dark and dangerous path that led to his committing a murder.

It seems to me that Eric's sense of morality and social responsibility, in addition to his intelligence and creativity, could enable him to have a significant positive impact on society. As long as he continues on this trajectory, and continues to have access to prosocial institutions while avoiding the negative influences he was exposed to as an adolescent (which he now vehemently rejects), this positive trajectory is likely. Evidence of this potential can be seen in his adoption of and commitment to his religious beliefs, as well as his efforts to mentor younger inmates, helping guide them on a better path that rejects criminal behavior and violence and focuses on how to improve society.

In prisons like the one to which Eric was sent for the first ten years of his sentence, there are not many opportunities for prosocial engagement. Nonetheless, Eric has tried to make the most of his time while incarcerated, and to make a positive impact on the world and on the lives of others. This commitment is especially impressive, considering the fact that Eric was sentenced to life without the possibility of parole, and therefore had no "extrinsic" motivation to engage in self-improvement efforts.

Others in this situation could be overcome by despair and helplessness, and could find themselves seemingly wasting their life. Eric, however, rejected that option and chose to make the most of the limited opportunities that were available to him. With this in mind, it is my belief that he would continue to do so if released.

Looking at his responses to the 40 Developmental Assets questionnaire, it is clear that the thirty-three assets he did *not* report experiencing were mostly supportive aspects of the community context in which he was growing up. These include items like "I receive support from three or more nonparental adults," "My neighbors encourage and support me," "I feel safe at home, at school, and in my neighborhood," "My best friends model responsible behavior," "I go out with friends 'with nothing special to do' two or fewer nights per week," and "I feel valued by adults in the community."

What emerges is the negativity of the "war zone," the kind of neighborhood (as noted earlier) in which 60 percent of ten-year-old "conduct disorder" cases become seriously violent delinquents (versus the 15 percent in more positive, supportive neighborhoods). Eric often "editorialized" in his responses as we went through the list of the 40 Developmental Assets. For example, when he came to the item "I tell the truth even when it is not easy," he responded, "Back then? No!" And to the item "I feel good about myself," he said, "I never felt that back then." The point is that Eric *now* has a mature perspective on who he was and what he did *then* when it comes to external and internal developmental assets. When I asked him to redo the 40 Developmental Assets checklist from the perspective of his life now, though still in prison, he identified thirty-three assets as ones he believes he has now.

When young guys go to prison for murders committed as teenagers, they face many challenges in pursuing a path that leads to rehabilitation. One is the social pressures to engage in negative behavior. While this pressure is most intense when prison life is controlled by gangs and racial group animosities (as it typically is in most prisons), it exists for everyone, certainly every young guy. Being free of that pressure and coercion to "be bad and do bad," as one guy put it, is a gift that can facilitate the process of rehabilitation by providing the social space to do and be good.

Brian N. killed another teenager when he was sixteen, and he received a mandatory life-without-parole sentence. After a resentencing hearing twenty years later, he was released from prison. When I asked if there were any things that didn't happen, but could have, that would have sabotaged his recovery, he told me this:

> When I got to prison I was taken under the wing of a group of white guys who were from Toledo, like I was. They told me that if I followed the rules they would have my back, would protect me. "What rules?" I asked. "Stay with your own race. Pay all your debts. Always have company when you approach a guard. Mandatory working out. Mandatory going out on the yard whenever you can." All of this was for protection of the group. But they also gave me "permission" to participate in the programs the prison offered (education and rehabilitation) and they didn't ask me to do illegal things—like being the one carrying the knife for the group. This allowed me to work my way down from Level 4 to Level 3 in the prison and thus take part in the programs that eventually got me out. Without their support I wouldn't have been able to do that.

CONSCIOUSNESS RULES

Social structures, therapeutic interventions, brain and personality maturation—all these elements of the rehabilitative process are important. They are important mostly because they lead to a shift in consciousness, a shift away the "war zone mentality," the ego-driven yearning for dominance, the ready acceptance of violence as a currency of human interaction, the shamed identity, the behavioral and emotional sequelae of trauma, and all the other habits of the mind and heart that led teenage killers into acts of lethal violence in the first place. It is the shift in consciousness that matters most. Why? Because it leads to the process of rehabilitation and transformation that is at the heart of the story for Miller's Children, and "changed consciousness" is the core issue.

Many years ago, when I was a graduate student at Cornell University, my mentor, Urie Bronfenbrenner, told me an important story about the power of consciousness in human behavior and development. I will summarize it as follows. In the now defunct Soviet Union, psychology was embedded in the Communist vision of transformation. They called it "making the new Soviet Man." As a Russian colleague put it to Urie, "You are trying to understand Man as he is while we are trying to understand how to make him what he should be." As a result, Soviet psychologists did a lot of work on what is called "classical conditioning," a concept developed by Ivan Pavlov in his famous studies of dogs in which he linked a natural response (salivating in response to presentation of meat) with a researcher-chosen stimulus (the ringing of a bell); the result was that dogs "learned" to salivate when they heard the bell. This, Soviet psychology believed, was a model for creating that "new Soviet Man" to which Communist ideology aspired. Decades of research sought to fine tune this model with human beings (not just the animals with which it was pioneered and, in fact, is still used in Russia, in the United States, and around the world).

In one study, conducted in East Germany (before the Soviet empire fell and East and West Germany were reunited as one country), researchers set out to classically condition a behavior among elementary school children in five locations. A footnote in the report indicated that the results revealed that the experiment worked as expected in all but one of the schools. Why not in that one? It turned out that the janitor in the school was taking a night class in psychology in which he learned about classical conditioning and told the children about what he had learned. The result? By having the knowledge of what was being done and how they were *supposed* to react, the children "decided" to be immune to the experiment, to resist the classical-conditioning paradigm. It's been nearly half a century since Urie shared this story, but it is often on my mind, because for me it represents one of my core conclusions about human behavior and development, namely that "consciousness rules."

What can stand up against the brutality and depersonalization of prison life? In a primitive sense, there really are only two forces powerful enough to meet this criterion. One is ideological fanaticism and the other is religious belief. This was the conclusion drawn by psychoanalyst Bruno Bettelheim as he sat in a Nazi concentration camp in 1938–39 and observed who among his fellow inmates retained their humanity, and who succumbed to the barbarism invited and imposed by the Nazis. Bettelheim concluded that it was the Communists and the ultra-religious who succeeded. Only they could say to themselves (and at least implicitly to their Nazi captors): "You cannot touch me because I am connected to something more powerful and enduring than you." In the case of the Communists, it was Marxism-Leninism, which they believed would consign the Nazis to the proverbial "dustbin of history" (to use Leon Trotsky's language). For the ultra-religious, it was their God who would keep them spiritually safe in the face of the temptation to surrender to despair and dehumanization. Of course, looking back on it, Communism was not a good long-term bet, because it ended up in the dustbin of history with the fall of the Soviet Union and the turn to capitalism in China, leaving the latter country with the authoritarianism of Communism but not its egalitarianism. The ultra-religious, on the other hand, are still very much in business, the world over.

HOW TO LIVE WITH A DEATH SENTENCE

A long prison sentence, particularly a "death in prison" sentence like the ones imposed upon Miller's Children, presents a staggering psychological and metaphysical challenge to any human being, but particularly to a young human being. In one sense, however, it "merely" brings into the sharpest possible focus that challenge that each of us mortals faces: living well in every moment, with the awareness that death will come eventually. It is in this sense that receiving a sentence of life without parole from a judge is akin to receiving a terminal medical diagnosis from a doctor.

As a study summarized by Guida Zanni reports, "Patients . . . may react in 1 of 5 possible ways to the diagnosis: denial ('It must be a mistake'); despair or depression ('Nothing will help'); anger ('I do not deserve this'); acute anxiety ('I am a nervous wreck'); or fighting determination ('I will beat this')." Many individuals display a combination of these reactions. The same is true of adolescents receiving their "terminal" sentence. One inmate said, "I am innocent." Another said, "I am going to kill myself." A third said, "Someone is going to pay for this!" A fourth said, "I can't sleep at night I am so afraid of what's going to happen to me." A fifth said, "I am going to beat this!"

But this is not the whole story, either for patients receiving a terminal medical diagnosis or for young defendants receiving a life-without-parole, eventual-death-in-prison sentence. In the case of terminal medical diagnoses, many patients find meaning in their condition. In some studies, as many as 90 percent of patients with life-threatening diseases report being affected positively in some way. These positive adaptations include a greater appreciation of life, changes in priorities, improved interpersonal relationships, and greater spirituality. It is common for values to shift from material success to friendships and family. I observe some of the same changes in Miller's Children: when you have nothing left ahead except existing as a human *doing* time, you can choose to embrace life as a human *being*.

HOPE

What is powerful enough to stand up to the incredible weight of guilt, shame, demoralization, and suffering that so many young killers feel as they come to terms with what they have done, and what they face as a result? As we will see, the ultimate answer to this question is "spirituality" (not simply "religion"). Why is this crucial? Because gaining a glimmer of the divine gives the prisoner a positive place to stand in the universe, when the material world around them offers dehumanization, despair, and the temptations of nihilism. It gives them dignity when there is only humiliation. It gives them purpose when there is only the aimlessness of days in confinement. It gives them hope when there is only darkness.

You can hear that hope in David F.'s thoughtful message, two years after he was released and two weeks after we met for lunch, sent as I was on my way to the prison in which he had spent twenty years:

> Perhaps I can help you with the next phase of your life's work. I'm hopeful it fulfills Dostoevsky's last words in *Crime and Punishment,* in which Raskolnikov, awakening from his madness, first realized love: "But that is the beginning of a new story—the story of the gradual renewal of a man, the story of his gradual regeneration, of his passing from one world into another, of his initiation into a new unknown life. That might be the subject of a new story, but our present story is ended."

David is making a new life out of the fabric of hope, and the way he is living his life does inspire me to continue my quest on behalf of men like him.

Researcher Richard Jessor refers to the role of religious experiences as the basis for "a personal control against problem behavior" in youth. Other researchers (e.g., Shortz and Worthington in their 1994 study) found that "spiritually based" coping activities (e.g., "trusting God for protection and turning to him for guidance") were most significantly related to positive coping behaviors (e.g., "positive focus" and "interpersonal support"). Looking across all this research, we see that religion is protective to the degree that it embraces and communicates messages of love and inclusiveness (rather than judgmental rejection and emotional brutalization) and involves youths in a loving community of peers. This premise provides a logical bridge to larger issues of the potential role of *spirituality* in the transformation of teenage killers. I focus on spirituality rather than religion for two reasons. First, the spiritual component of religion is the key force. I say this without diminishing the importance of the social structures that support spirituality. Religions will offer this ideally, of course, but in practice they often contain toxic messages of shame that undermine the spiritual messages of affirmation. Second, the American constitutional framework separates church and state, and for this reason state-supported facilities cannot direct inmates into "religious" programs (but they can encourage spiritually enhancing practices such as meditation and reflection).

Setting aside the various religious issues that emerge out of the spiritual experience, the core existential issue, particularly for those with traumatic experiences that are common to incarcerated men who killed in adolescence, is the question of "meaning." In a study published in 2006, Bessel van der Kolk and colleagues asked incoming psychiatric patients, "Have you given up all hope of finding meaning in your life?" Among those who experienced major trauma prior to age five, 74 percent answered "yes." Among those who experienced major trauma after age twenty, the figure was "only" 10 percent. After asking thousands of adults this question, I conclude that the baseline for the general population is something on the order of 1 percent.

SPIRITUAL LIFE BEYOND RELIGION

Prisons are places where frequent instances of brutality are overlaid on chronic systems of brutality. This is an impediment to spiritual development, even as it promotes formal religious rhetoric and practice. But what is spiritual development? I particularly like this definition, offered by Peter Benson and colleagues in a 2008 study:

> The process of growing the intrinsic human capacity for self-transcendence, in which the self is embedded in something greater than the self, including the sacred ... the developmental "engine" that propels the search for connectedness, meaning, purpose, and contribution ... shaped both within and outside of religious traditions, beliefs, and practices.

My colleagues Fred Bryant, Stuart Hart, and Katherine McDowell and I reviewed a broad range of studies and found research linking spirituality and religious involvement among adults to resilience in the face of stress and adversity, protective avoidance of risky behaviors, higher levels of subjective life quality, and lower risk of psychopathology. All of these can and do contribute to the rehabilitation of teenage killers as they move into and through adulthood in prison. But at the pinnacle of this mountain of research is the capacity to attend to and appreciate positive experience, what Fred terms "savoring." One form of savoring that is especially relevant to inner spiritual experience is the process of *marveling,* through which, as Fred understands it, individuals experience awe and wonder in response to a sublime or humbling external stimulus that embodies great majesty, power, rarity, or mystery.

Is this possible in a prison, where inmates are usually cut off from nature, live in bland physical environments, and experience a very restricted range of experiences? After all, psychologist Kirk Schneider has identified the following conditions that interfere with awe-based awakening: poverty and deprivation, haste, closed-mindedness, and preoccupation with money, status, or consumerism. I find that so many inmates are "hungry," not just physically, but psychically as well. On the other hand, Schneider finds that "awakening to awe" requires that certain conditions be met, including the capacity to subsist, to slow down, to savor the moment, and to focus on what one loves, and time to reflect and contemplate in natural settings both alone and with others. *If* an inmate chooses to follow the monk's path rather than the savage's road, prison *can* offer support for this way of wisdom. I hear that in the insightful words of Warren T., a year after a resentencing hearing resulted in his release:

> Although I obtained my "freedom" I must tell you that the resolution of that conflict (challenge) seems essential to my ability to live my life. And, where once prison gave me the space to process and reflect on deeper issues,

I have not been able to find space for that out here. As you've probably heard from other youth offenders, to hold the truth of the harm I've caused I need a container, or context, or belief system that organizes it. Without it, everything feels ground zero or subject to a relativistic understanding and morality. I discovered my spiritual and moral compass from my crime.

One definition of *trauma* is an event from which you never recover, which changes you forever. Committing a murder at age sixteen, as Warren did, is such an event, and he, like the rest of his tribe of lost boys, will spend the rest of his life running away from the monster and becoming the best man he can be—as a spiritual being, struggling to find his way outside the confines of the monastery that he made of the prison he was sentenced to almost three decades ago.

FIVE

———

Are There Exceptions?

This chapter addresses perhaps the most troublesome issue I have faced in my work with Miller's Children—the question of whether some teenage killers really do meet the criterion for life without the possibility of parole that the Supreme Court laid out for us—"the rarest of juvenile offenders, those whose crimes reflect permanent incorrigibility." For these boys and men, rehabilitation and transformation would constitute a miracle.

HANOVER STATE PRISON, BERKSHIRE, MASSACHUSETTS: After I met with a group of "juvenile lifers" at the prison they call home, Bobby S. approached me, file folder in hand. "Dr. Garbarino," he said politely, "would you take a look at my file and let me know what you think?" I took the file with me and had a chance to read it—all fifty-eight pages, single spaced—on the plane flying home. It began with the crime he committed in 1992, when he was sixteen, and continued until 2013, when he was evaluated by a psychologist who had interviewed him, done some psychological testing, and reviewed Bobby's twenty-plus years of prison records.

The report did an amazing job of addressing a series of questions relevant to Bobby's case, most notably, "Were Bobby's psychological difficulties and personality fixed at age 16? Was he untreatable, and did his condition become worse over the years as the chief psychologist for the prosecution postulated in 1992?" That prosecution psychologist had diagnosed Bobby with a "personality disorder" and probably didn't label it "antisocial personality disorder" only because of Bobby's age at the time (official diagnostic guidelines require that a person be at least eighteen years of age to receive this diagnosis, since it is conceptualized as the "adult" version of child and adolescent conduct disorder). Given that perspective, it is not surprising that this psychologist wrote in his report that "the underlying pathology which is apparent from this young man's behavior is likely to become more severe as he ages" and that "this person is not amenable to treatment or rehabilitation."

As it turned out, nothing could be further from the truth. Now, more than twenty years later, Bobby is a well-functioning moral agent, stable psychologically, and demonstrating insight into the origins of his developmental issues and the role of family dynamics in pushing him off course as a teenager. The prosecution psychologist missed many important features of Bobby as an individual (including the significance of his young brain) and of his family situation—what was later understood to be "persistent emotional abuse in the form of obsessive concern about and control of his behavior and appearance, harsh judgement as well as episodic verbal and physical abuse by his mother," as one subsequent evaluation put it.

What is more, Bobby was a smart kid, with a tested IQ of 130. His intellect equipped him to take advantage of the therapeutic opportunities offered in prison, and he was sent there at a time before budget problems and a shift in incarceration policy from rehabilitation to punishment. Thus, he got started on the road to recovery before some of the programs that Bobby and others of his age and condition made use of in the 1990s were terminated due to budget cuts to the correctional system's programs. Within just a few years, an evaluation of him noted that he was "demonstrating increased progress, including more openness about his own issues, support with peers, and making use of information presented in the group. He was making progress with respect to development of empathy, and was able to grasp the desolation that he caused his victim's family and friends." This is hardly what you would expect from someone with an untreatable personality disorder.

Twenty years after the crime, Bobby was given a thorough evaluation. Among other things, it showed that when assessed using the standard measure for identifying psychopaths/sociopaths (the Hare Psychopathy Checklist), he scored "notably below generally accepted cutoff points." And on the "Structured Interview of Reported Symptoms," Bobby "was very high in acknowledging common foibles and everyday problems that are experienced by most individuals—meaning he showed very low defensiveness." On a measure of "risk," Bobby had zero out of ten items indicating "lack of insight, negative attitudes, active symptoms of major mental illness, impulsivity and unresponsiveness to treatment." His overall risk-for-violence score on the Hare checklist was 6 out of a possible 40 (I will describe the checklist later in this chapter), meaning a "low risk for violence." By age thirty-seven,

Bobby had become a lovely man—cooperative, caring, insightful, and compassionate.

At the time of his crime twenty-one years earlier, Bobby *did* show signs of an identity crisis, including severe immaturity and confusion about his short-term and long-term goals. He was overwhelmed at times by worry and nervousness, fears and anxiety. Moreover, he appeared self-occupied and prone to ruminate about feelings of inferiority, inadequacy, and not being safe. As the final evaluator noted in her report, "a number of these characteristics are not uncommon in many adolescents." And that, of course, is the point of this recounting of Bobby S.'s story and indeed of this entire book: *You can't make definitive and permanent judgments about teenagers who kill because they are unfinished, and how they finish depends on what they do and experience in the future, as their brains and personalities mature, as they become part of an adult social network.*

As the 2012 evaluation of Bobby S. concluded,

> It is my opinion that Bobby is likely to make a better-than-average adjustment in the community and to make positive contributions to others. He already has a substantial and positive support group with his family as well as long-term friends, including those who worked successfully with him in the prison system and who have become highly successful themselves in the community.

That is certainly the man I met. But not every kid who commits a murder as a teenager can and will undergo such a nearly miraculous process of rehabilitation and transformation. There are exceptions.

THE SAD CASE OF ALONZO P.

Sanson State Prison, San Diego, California: Alonzo P. was convicted of a particularly gruesome murder when he was sixteen years old. He and a friend abducted a male prostitute they had encountered on the street, took him to an abandoned warehouse, and tortured him. The vicious assault culminated in Alonzo putting a gun into the man's anus and firing the bullet that killed him. Speaking with Alonzo eighteen years later, it is difficult to determine how much of the emotional disturbance he reports from childhood, adolescence, and adulthood is the result of innate temperamental predispositions, and how much is the result of coping with unreported and unacknowledged adverse experiences as a child. In our interview, he spoke often about feeling emotionally disconnected or angry. In comparing himself to his brother Lawrence, Alonzo said, "He was reserved and timid, I was outgoing and bad. He felt it was best to deal with life's problems internally, but I always thought it was better to act out." He said of a time when his father showed up at his mother's house: "My dad came over and he was drunk. He got into a fight and my uncles beat him up." When asked how he felt about that, Alonzo replied, "It was fun." There appear to have been many instances in which Alonzo's response to what would normally be considered "emotionally charged events" was disconnected. One highly significant feature of this disconnection is the report (in a 1997 assessment, when Alonzo was fifteen) that he engaged in cruelty to animals. The report indicates that Alonzo told the evaluator at the youth detention center where he was being held for a minor assault charge that he had been engaged in cruelty to animals since he was twelve years old. The evaluator's notes include this: "dogs, cats, and squirrels. He kills them—runs over with car, shot them, threw off building, put them in the oven and microwave. Out of anger and for fun." When asked about this in our interview nineteen years later, he reported that he did so out of "wanting to feel power" and because they were "something insignificant ... not human." This is a very disturbing admission, and it speaks to how damaged Alonzo was by the combination of his temperamental vulnerability and his adverse childhood—with an ACE score of eight adverse childhood experiences. Despite my compassion for him, I thought then that the prospects of his ever being rehabilitated were dim, perhaps because he had never been "habilitated" in the first place.

IS EVERYONE ELIGIBLE?

Can every young killer be rehabilitated and transformed? Are some so emotionally and morally damaged that for them to get better and become emotionally and morally whole would constitute a miracle? While as a spiritual being and a Christian I am bound to believe in miracles as a matter of faith, as a developmental psychologist I am bound to believe in probabilities and statistics as a matter of science. The malleability of brains in response to altered life circumstances—even in adulthood—justifies the hope that even extremely damaged teenagers can recover and become "safe" for release into the community. But the existence of what might be called "developmental exceptions" to the general rule of rehabilitation and transformation in the lives of teenage killers argues for caution in this matter in general, as it did in particular in the case of Alonzo P. Understanding these developmental exceptions is the goal of this chapter.

THE CONSEQUENCES OF PROFOUND
AND PERVASIVE TRAUMA

I believe that the first and most common developmental exception is found among individuals who have been so profoundly traumatized as children that they don't—perhaps can't—recover from the damage they sustained. Researchers Eldra Solomon and Kathleen Heide provide a foundation for this view in their efforts to differentiate among three kinds of trauma: single incidents (Type I), multiple incidents resulting from chronic exposure to traumatic events (Type II), and severe and pervasive trauma during the early years of life (Type III). They say of the Type III trauma experienced in early childhood by individuals like Alonzo P. that it "is more extreme. It results from multiple and pervasive violent events beginning at an early age and continuing for years. Typically, the child was the victim of multiple perpetrators, and one or more close relatives. . . . Generally, force is used and the abuse has a sadistic quality."

When Solomon and Heide examined twenty-three possible long-term effects of the three types of trauma, they found that only two were typically found among Type I cases. These were "full, detailed memory" and "PTSD symptoms" (PTSD being the official diagnosis used to encompass the common effects of traumatic experiences, including intrusive memories, avoidance of triggering stimuli, and negative changes in thinking and mood). In Type II cases, full, detailed memory began to deteriorate and four additional effects were commonly observed: "poor self-esteem/self-concept," "interpersonal distrust," "feelings of shame," and "dependency." Finally, for Type III trauma, there was no detailed memory, but the total number of symptoms was twenty-two! Collectively, they form the ultimate picture of what a massively damaged human being looks like:

- PTSD symptoms
- Denial

- Repression
- Emotional numbing
- Poor self-esteem/self-concept
- Interpersonal distrust
- Superficial relationships
- High anxiety
- Chronic depression
- Suicidality
- Feelings of shame
- Foreshortened sense of the future
- Dependency
- Rage
- Affective dysregulation
- Self-injury
- Eating disturbance
- Substance abuse
- Narcissism
- Impulsivity
- Identity confusion
- Dissociative symptoms

Many of these are precisely the issues found in Alonzo P.'s history.

About the only long-term effect *not* typically found in Type III that is found in Type I (and, to some degree, in Type II) is full, detailed memory. As Solomon and Heide note, this alone is a major social problem. In Type I and Type II cases, the person can recount the traumatic incident(s) and thus be recognized as a victim, whereas individuals who experience Type III trauma are often not even identified as victims. They are likely to receive a misdiagnosis based on the long-term effects of their trauma, including dissociation and habitual coping tactics, which frequently mean that they cannot remember and provide a full and detailed account of their experiences. Thus, *the effects obscure the cause*. Josiah M. provides a sad example of this.

THE CASE OF JOSIAH M.

Greenville State Prison, Portland, Maine: Josiah M. killed two other teens when he was seventeen. All three were homeless, living in an urban squatter camp under a highway overpass. Police reports say that Josiah got into an argument over a sleeping bag and the conflict escalated, leading to the murder, in which he stabbed both men repeatedly. When I interviewed him nineteen years later, he couldn't report much about his childhood, except to say that it was bad. He did have more to report about his early adolescence, including the time he spent as a prostitute. When I asked him how he felt about being a sex worker during adolescence, he said, "I was so detached, I could have read a novel while it was being done to me." His dissociation was pervasive and intense, perhaps providing the basis for the "delusional state" reported by the police who arrested him.

The long list of potential consequences in Type III trauma cases means that the mental health professionals who assess people like Josiah often assign them a similarly long list of diagnoses. With some twenty-two symptoms to draw upon, it is not surprising that different clinicians focus on different clusters of them, and this produces a variety of diagnoses. It is reminiscent of the parable of the blind men asked to describe an elephant. One feels only a leg and thus concludes he is encountering a tree trunk. Another feels only the tail and concludes what is before him is a rope. Another feels only the elephant's trunk and reports that he has encountered a snake. The "elephant in the room" in Josiah's case is his multiple and extraordinary adaptations to the extraordinary adversity he experienced in childhood and adolescence. The developmental damage he incurred was so pervasive and profound that it has manifested as multiple (and sometimes contradictory) effects, and hence multiple clinicians have drawn different diagnostic conclusions.

A review of Josiah's records indicates these diagnoses: attention deficit hyperactivity disorder; conduct disorder; antisocial personality disorder; schizoaffective disorder, bipolar type; and bipolar disorder type 2. However, a review of the reports of his behavior and thinking made by a variety of observers suggests that he could have (and perhaps should have) been diagnosed with additional problems and issues. These include pediatric early-onset bipolar disorder. Josiah is not the champ in this regard, however. When I reviewed the records of thirty-two-year-old Tim L., I found evidence of eleven separate diagnoses! He, too, was best understood as a case of Type III trauma.

The panoply of problems found among Type III trauma victims arise in part from the fact that a cognitively overwhelming experience may stimulate conditions in which the process required to "understand" the experience has harmful side effects itself. That is, in coping with a traumatic event, children like Josiah in his first years of life may be forced into patterns of behavior, thought, and emotion that are themselves "abnormal," compared with patterns prior to the event or patterns characteristic of children who have not experienced such psychological devastation.

Like most Type III trauma victims, Josiah cannot present a coherent narrative of much of his childhood victimization or of his behavior while an adolescent and young adult. He does report some memories from early childhood (e.g., "my mom slapping me across the face and making my nose bleed" and "my dad sitting by my bed when I had nightmares and night terrors" and "my mom putting her bra and high heels on me and sending me in to wake up my father"), but it is only after many, many years of reflection that he has formed *any* consistent narrative account of his childhood. When asked about negative memories of his father, he reports, "I don't know."

His chronic mental health problems and acting out can be traced to his adaptation to the extreme adversity of severe physical, sexual, and psychological maltreatment during childhood—most notably parental rejection. When I posed the ACE questions to him, his score was eight—meaning he had experienced more adversity than 999 out of 1,000 kids in America. The formal and informal systems of child protection that should have cared for him had failed him—from his extended family's failure to protect him from his parents, to the failure of the leadership in multiple institutional settings to protect him from the predatory sexual behavior of other residents and from staff members.

My review of Josiah's social history and my interview with him lead me to believe that in addition to the Type III trauma he experienced in the first three years of life, he experienced significant psychological maltreatment at the hands of his parents and parent-surrogates throughout his childhood and adolescence. His mother's "psychological unavailability" was severe. The fact that he was terrorized, isolated, ignored, corrupted, degraded, and rejected in childhood is clear. He was sexually and physically abused. For example, he speaks of being sexually molested at age nine and says, "I had to walk around with that in my head." All these forms of psychological maltreatment were costly to Josiah's development. Instead of providing some developmental compensation for his early Type III trauma, they compounded the damage, and that may be crucial to understanding why he is an exception to the rule of rehabilitation and transformation I find so often in Miller's Children. This becomes clear when we review the multiple dimensions of the psychological maltreatment he experienced:

Rejecting—One of his earliest memories as a child is of his parents sending him away from home (to his aunt) and refusing to care for him. His emerging identity as a transgendered person was rejected as well. He says, "I never really felt like I was a member of my family. My mother wanted girls, so when she had girls she didn't need me anymore."

Isolating—He was cut off from potentially positive family interaction by his parents, such as when they "kidnapped" him from relatives who were actively caring for him as an infant and young child.

Ignoring—His mother was often psychologically unavailable to him.

Terrorizing—He was threatened with violent attack by his mother as a form of discipline. He reports that when he was fifteen, his mother tried to choke him to death.

Corrupting—He witnessed substance abuse in his family and its consequences in chronically out-of-control behavior.

Degrading—He was tied to the bed for long periods when he was a child. As punishment, at one point, he was dressed in a bra and pink lacy panties and forced to stand in the front yard of the house.

Who would have possessed the resilience necessary to overcome this fundamental assault on the process of becoming a functioning human being? Certainly not Josiah.

THE CENTRALITY OF EARLY ATTACHMENT

What we know about the nature of Josiah's attachment relationship with his mother certainly suggests that it is was not the "secure" attachment that research demonstrates is crucial for normal social and emotional development. How could it be for a Type III trauma victim? Instead, it is likely that he developed a seriously anxious, ambivalent, and insecure relationship with her. According to the Mayo Clinic,

> A child with reactive attachment disorder is typically neglected, abused or orphaned. Reactive attachment disorder develops because the child's basic needs for comfort, affection and nurturing aren't met and loving, caring attachments with others are never established. This may permanently change the child's growing brain, hurting the ability to establish future relationships. . . . Reactive attachment disorder is a lifelong condition, but with treatment children can develop more stable and healthy relationships.

This suggests that if Josiah had been exposed to high-quality therapeutic interventions early in life, rather than pervasive psychological maltreatment, he might have been able to remediate his attachment issues. But there is more to Josiah's attachment issues than "reactive attachment disorder."

Research among delinquent kids like Josiah has found that they are likely to have attachment issues. This should come as no surprise, since "secure attachment" is one of the building blocks of successful human development. When asked for "the word that comes to mind when I say 'mother,'" Josiah responded, "Fucking bitch." This too is unsurprising, in light of a study by Marlene Moretti and colleagues, published in 2004, which reported that delinquent boys were more likely to demonstrate "dismissive/avoidant" attachment problems in contrast to "preoccupied" attachment problems: 31 percent of delinquent boys and 6 percent of delinquent girls demonstrated dismissive/avoidant, compared to 40 percent of girls and 15 percent of boys demonstrating preoccupied attachment issues.

I think this is one reason why the process of transformation and rehabilitation so much depends, for many males, on first finding a way to *feel* the connection to their mothers (and, to some degree, their fathers) and then to process that feeling to the point of forgiveness and reconciliation. There is nothing worse developmentally than to be rejected by your mother, and so "getting her back" is often a crucial step in recovery from the issues that push teenagers (particularly male teenagers) into violence. I have been told by more than one adolescent killer that the only good thing to come of being charged with the crime was that it led to his mother coming back into his life psychologically, and retrieving the sense of being cared for by her that had been lost somewhere in childhood or early adolescence.

The process is usually not simple and easy. For example, later in our interview, Josiah elaborated on his attachment issues and offered as mature and forgiving an interpretation of his mother as is possible for him, saying, "Don't get me wrong, I love my mother. She brought me into the world. She's about as good at being a mom as I am at being accepted." That is not full recovery from disrupted attachment relations with his mother, but it is a start.

IS REPAIR POSSIBLE FOR ALONZO AND JOSIAH?

As with Alonzo P., I wondered whether Josiah's moral and emotional damage would be, or even *could be,* repaired. Seventeen years had passed since Alonzo killed a young man by shooting him in the anus after torturing him for hours; and two years had passed since Alonzo killed two men in prison over drugs. Nineteen years had passed since the murders Josiah committed, and he had been involved in multiple violent encounters in prison. Could these men be healed? Could they be rehabilitated? Could they be transformed? Time had passed, but I could not help but think that the answer is no.

While I am rarely inclined to hopelessness, the severity of the damage to Josiah and Alonzo as human beings pushed me in that direction. But maybe they will experience a miracle, and this possibility is precisely why I believe that *no teenager should be sentenced without the possibility of parole.* New scientific hope is to be found in a study documenting that adolescent psychopaths can be treated successfully if sufficient time, energy, and focus are brought to bear.

The starting point is the observation of neuropsychologist Kent Kiehl and Judge Morris Hoffman that "the received wisdom has been that psychopathy is untreatable, based on study after study that seemed to show that the behaviors of psychopaths could not be improved by any traditional, or even nontraditional, forms of therapy." Some studies even show that therapy—most notably group therapy—makes psychopaths worse. Why? Because they use the group process to hone their appreciation for the vulnerabilities of others and their skill in manipulation.

In contrast, an approach developed by Michael Caldwell and colleagues, labeled "decompression treatment," offers intense and intensive *one-on-one intervention*—several hours a day for at least six months—that focuses on "the slow and methodical rebuilding of the social connections that are absent in psychopaths," as Kiehl and Hoffman put it. This approach appears to succeed with juveniles (but not necessarily with adults, although in principle the neuroscience of brain malleability in adulthood suggests that perhaps it could, if offered intensely enough over a long enough period). Recidivism in those convicted of violent offenses was reduced by half (from 36 percent for traditional approaches to 18 percent for the decompression model). However, in their follow-up analyses, Caldwell and colleagues found that the effects for violent juveniles were confined to those scoring in the moderate range on the measure of psychopathy; the treatment was not effective for the most severely psychopathic among the teens (i.e., those scoring more than 31 out of 40 on Hare's scale of psychopathy).

What about teenagers whose thinking and feeling at the time of their crimes was not an aberration brought on by severe and prolonged trauma but rather a fundamental element of who they *are,* by virtue of the brains they brought with them into childhood and adolescence? Let us consider such a case.

CRAZY BRAIN

Vale State Prison, Charleston, South Carolina: Johnny H. killed his twin sister the day after their thirteenth birthday, in 1999. He stabbed her to death backstage in the auditorium of the middle school they attended together. Why? When I spoke with Johnny seventeen years later, he told me that he had to kill his sister because she knew that he was planning to embark on a "career" as a serial killer, and he was afraid that she might tell on him, thus thwarting his plans for an extended killing spree. He reported to me that prior to killing his sister, he had been studying serial killers for more than two years—watching every movie he could get his hands on that portrayed serial killers, such as *Natural Born Killers*—and believed it was his "destiny." One thing he learned from his "research" was that serial killers mostly used knives, so that was why he stabbed his sister rather than shooting her. He got caught after this first murder, he told me, because he carelessly left behind his eyeglasses at the scene of the crime (a lapse that, of course, made me think of Leopold and Loeb, whose case I chronicled in chapter 4) and, when he returned to retrieve them, left bloody fingerprints. Those were later used to identify him after he aroused the suspicion of police when they interviewed him. When I asked him what would have happened if they hadn't caught him, he replied, "I would have kept killing until they did, of course."

Johnny the boy was a killer. What about Johnny the man? According to the records made available to me, Johnny did not receive *any* clinical diagnoses prior to committing the crime that had brought him to prison with a life-without-parole sentence. However, in the years since he was arrested, tried, convicted, and sentenced, he has received multiple diagnoses by the various clinicians who have assessed him. These diagnoses include schizophrenia, paranoid type; obsessive-compulsive disorder; psychotic disorder; mild depression; obsessive-compulsive behaviors; and delusional thinking. In our interview, Johnny reported that he has also received diagnoses of conduct disorder, general anxiety disorder, narcissistic personality disorder, and delusional disorder.

But perhaps the most telling and explanatory diagnosis of all was offered by a psychiatrist who examined Johnny shortly before our interview. He concluded that Johnny had begun to experience a gradual decline in psychological functioning beginning in the summer of 1998, which escalated through the year-and-a-half leading up to the murder in 1999. In short, Johnny was experiencing the general trajectory of adolescent-onset psychosis, and it culminated in the psychotic episode in which he killed his sister. What does Johnny think of this now? He says that of all the diagnoses he has received over the years, the one that he thinks fits him best is delusional disorder. "I agree with that," he says.

Johnny's tested IQ in middle school was 132 (which put him in the top 3 percent of kids his age). During his period of incarceration, he has maintained a high grade point average (3.9) in the eight college-level correspondence courses he completed. Thus, it is clear that the less-than-average intellectual development that figures significantly in those who do not demonstrate resilience in the face of adversity is not an issue in Johnny's case. However, unlike other Miller's Children, he has not been able to bring his above-average intelligence to bear on the process of rehabilitation and transformation. He talks a good game, however.

Johnny's intellectual sophistication was evident when he offered me his self-analysis: "I can become fixated on an idea, but now I know how to reality test. Becoming a serial killer was a delusion, I know that now." He quoted from the standard psychiatric reference, the *Diagnostic and Statistical Manual of Mental Disorders (DSM),* acknowledging that "it was a 'firmly held false belief.'" While admitting that he would have continued killing had he not been caught, he believes that eventually he would have given it up, saying, "I would have gone in a different direction. The serial-killer fixation was waning.

Previously it was exciting and satisfying as I struggled to find meaning in life, but it was losing its allure. I would have fallen apart eventually." Wow.

STILL CRAZY AFTER ALL THESE YEARS?

When I met him, Johnny was thirty years old. There were reports in his records that as Johnny passed from a troubled and volatile adolescence (starting with the "psychotic episode" at the time of the crime) to a more prosocial and stable young adulthood in the prison system, his thinking ("executive function") and feelings ("emotional regulation") improved substantially, and with that improvement in thinking and feeling his conduct has comported more and more with the requirements of a prosocial and "safe" life. The same psychiatrist who described Johnny's adolescent-onset schizophrenia and delusional behavior looked at the thirty-year-old Johnny and said he "demonstrates multiple current strengths and assets that demonstrate he is a good candidate for rehabilitation."

That may be, but he certainly was not there yet, seventeen years after killing his sister. Whatever progress he will make in the future, he faces an uphill battle, in part because of the social toxicity of the culture with which he has infused his consciousness and identity. As he now acknowledges, as a thirteen-year-old entering into adolescent-onset schizophrenia, Johnny was caught up in a delusion. However, the *content* of delusional thinking does not exist in a cultural vacuum. After all, Johnny had easy access to a plethora of "serial killer movies" and grew up in a religious community that emphasized the reality of Hell and preached an impending apocalypse. But if Johnny was suffering from emerging schizophrenia, wasn't he disconnected from the larger culture and cut off from reality? Much as this might make intuitive sense, it turns out there is more to the story.

Consider this amazing finding from a three-country study, led by anthropologist Tanya Luhrmann, of the content of auditory hallucinations ("hearing voices") among schizophrenics. Luhrmann and her team found that in the United States, violent imagery permeates the thinking of these "crazy people" who are thought to be "out of touch with reality." But in Ghana, most of the "voices" were perceived as largely positive conversations with God; and in India, the voices mostly were critical of the person's housekeeping style ("Clean your house!"). In the United States, 70 percent of the voices heard by schizophrenics told them to hurt themselves or others (compared to only 20 percent in India and 10 percent in Ghana).

While this study was confined to schizophrenics, it seems only a small extension to recognize how our culture of violence permeates the consciousness of even those of us who are not "certifiable." For example, early in 2017, the Republican-led U.S. Congress passed, and President Trump signed, legislation overturning an Obama-administration rule that prevented people with serious mental illness from purchasing and owning guns. Explaining his opposition to the restriction and the need to overturn it, the House Judiciary Committee's chairman, Republican Bob Goodlatte, said: "It assumes that simply because an individual suffers from a mental condition, that individual is unfit to exercise his or her Second Amendment rights." This follows on 2013 state legislation in Iowa that affirmed the legal right of blind people to carry guns in public. Gun issues seem to be where cultural craziness meets political cravenness in a culture of violence. Is it any wonder that when Americans go crazy, they are likely to be motivated to commit acts of violence?

In Johnny's case, this general cultural phenomenon was compounded by the content of his media diet. The food for thought in that media diet included some of the most violent, disturbed, and disturbing movies ever made, such as Johnny's favorite, *Natural Born Killers.* He also liked *X-Men,* because it was about fighting against the "people who don't accept mutants." The implication is clear that Johnny identifies with the mutants. As he said, "I always knew I was different." Tellingly, his favorite TV shows *now* include *Supernatural* ("It's so realistic") and *Criminal Minds* ("That show is popular among normal people," he explained). Of murdering his sister, he reports, "It was something I had to do. It was on my schedule, on the list—do it then go back to class." What a state he was in at that point in his life!

It appears that Johnny came to adolescence with severe issues regarding emotional regulation as well as executive function. His emotional regulation issues included "cutting," which is commonly understood to be a primitive attempt at emotional regulation in children and youths because it uses the release of endorphins to reduce emotional suffering. However, the principal problems Johnny had with emotional regulation took the form of obsessive and compulsive traits, leading to a diagnosis of obsessive-compulsive disorder by a clinician assigned to evaluate him after he committed the murder. He had various obsessions and compulsions regarding what he ate and wore, as well as "ritualized" checking on the house's back door and the stove's knobs, according to his parents' statements in the wake of his crime. Today, he reports, this checking is under better control, though he makes "to do" lists that he reviews obsessively. But he is far, far away from being "cured" and thus "safe." I believe he is entitled to a sentence that permits parole at some point in the future, even though I doubt he will ever reach the point where he would be safe.

NOT CRAZY AFTER ALL THESE YEARS

Bartlett State Prison, San Francisco, California: Despite the "monstrous" nature of his crime, Xavier Y. was not a monster, but rather a troubled four-teen-year-old boy in a state of psychiatric crisis when he stabbed his father to death in 2002. According to the records made available, Xavier had received clinical diagnoses prior to committing the crime—most notably depression. He had begun to experience a precipitous decline in psychological function-ing in the spring of 2001. This included frequent suicidal thoughts—"every couple of days," he says (e.g., thinking about killing himself by burning char-coal in an enclosed space and reviewing various types of rope with which to hang himself, and composing possible suicide notes to leave for his parents: "Sorry. I love you"). These thoughts were coupled with several practice runs (such as putting a plastic bag over his head, saying, "I tried it. If I liked it I would go through with it, but I didn't like it") and an actual attempt that landed him in the hospital. This series of crises escalated over several months, and it culminated with him killing his father, then making another attempt to take his own life later that day.

Could anyone have foreseen, immediately after the murder, that there was realistic hope for Xavier? I could see a path, if he received appropriate and effective intervention in prison and thereby became more prosocial and sta-ble in his young adulthood. If that happened, his executive function and emotional regulation might improve substantially, and with that improve-ment in thinking and feeling his conduct could gradually meet the require-ments of a "safe" life. Looking back on it fourteen years later, his crime seems much more clearly linked to a mental health crisis, a crisis that could be "fixed," than to an irremediably disturbed mind and heart. Adolescents are prone to melodramatic overreaction, and Xavier's fascination with violent video games had fed his emotional problems. Research has documented that such games can suppress empathy in "normal" youths; their effects on troubled youths like Xavier may well be more extreme. The game to which Xavier devoted himself includes the use of a military-style knife to kill enemies. This fed Xavier's preexisting fascination with these weapons, including a collection of some twenty knives, most of which were bought for him by his parents. He readily identified "when my depression started" as his worst memory (before the murder, of course).

Xavier was seen at a local counseling center in the months preceding the day he killed his father. The therapist at the center concluded that he was suffering from depression, and psychotropic medications were prescribed to treat it. There are reasonable grounds to consider that those medications may themselves have exacerbated the mental health crisis that led to the murder. One of the antidepressants prescribed to him, Prozac, has been linked to suicidal thoughts and agitation in adolescents taking the drug to deal with depression and is suspected to be linked to homicidal thoughts as well. In fact, in a 2011 case in Canada, a judge ruled that Prozac was *the cause* of a fifteen-year-old boy's fatal stabbing of his best friend. In any case, things looked very bleak in 2002. But by the time I saw Xavier in 2015, he had made tremendous progress. His maturing and detoxified brain equipped him to take advantage of the therapeutic experiences offered by the prison in which he had been incarcerated for more than a decade, and by all accounts, unlike Johnny H., he was "cured."

Despite the grotesque crime he committed as a teenager, perhaps Xavier is a crucial counterexample to the pessimism that pervades clinical assessments of "crazy" adolescent killers. I have told his story here as much to remind myself to keep hope alive as to keep that hope alive in my readers.

SOCIAL TOXICITY POISONS TEENAGE BRAINS

It seems clear that unlike Xavier, Johnny was sucked into pornographic and extremely violent media images to a point where, I fear, he will never escape. In understanding both boys, however, I believe that the place to start is the general finding that the effect of violent televised images on aggressive behavior is as big as the effect of secondhand smoke on lung cancer—accounting for only about 15 percent of the common variation between these two variables. As alluded to above, research conducted by Laura Stockdale and colleagues on violent video games indicates that playing "first-person shooter" games suppresses empathy, which is understood as one of the factors that prevents violent behavior. All this is in the "normal range" for American kids (bizarre as that may seem from a historical and cross-cultural perspective). After all, normal teenagers are likely to have difficulty accurately assessing the emotions of others—and their own. This is well established in research on adolescent brain development (as we saw in chapter 1). However, Johnny's ingestion of violent images went well beyond the normal diet of thirteen-year-olds and was augmented by ingesting hard-core pornography as well.

We must remember that Johnny's exposure to socially toxic cultural influences was occurring during a period in human brain development when the area of the brain involved in regulating the intensity of sensation (the nucleus accumbens) reaches its peak (declining after mid-adolescence and into adulthood). As noted earlier in this book, the research of developmental psychologists like Laurence Steinberg and neuroscientists like Frances Jensen (and others) demonstrates that in mid-adolescence *everything* feels more intense that it does before or after. It is little wonder, then, that the twelve-year-old Johnny became pathologically engrossed in the violent and sexual images that entered his head via videos. His list of favorite films and TV shows from that period of his life reads like a "who's who" of killing (from *American Psycho* to *Silence of the Lambs*).

Johnny's pornography habit illustrates this as well. Modern neuroscience research on the impact of pornography on the brain—as reported in Norman Doidge's book *The Brain That Changes Itself*—shows that even in adulthood, the brain is sufficiently malleable that a diet of pornographic viewing can rewire its response to sexual stimuli. This produces an effect in which "normal" sexual stimuli take a backseat to the "abnormal" sexual stimuli provided by hard-core pornography. For an adolescent brain like Johnny's—which is, if anything, *more* malleable because of its status as a developing organ—the effect of ingesting large doses of pornography would be expected to be even more severely perverse. And for a boy like Johnny, plagued by obsessive and compulsive traits, entering the world of violent and pornographic media images spelled disaster.

Johnny's obsession with violence came to fruition in his fixation on the idea of himself as a "serial killer in training." One of the risks associated with full Internet access for kids is that it gives them access to unlimited information, some of which they are not well equipped to process, even when they are, like Johnny, highly intelligent. In his case, this included access to "diagnostic" information about the traits associated with being a serial killer. As he reports, "I had two—lots of pornography and spending a lot of time alone. Once I identified with being a serial killer, after that it all went to hell. I began training to be what I was 'destined' to be." This "training" included the fact that he "tried to eliminate any emotions I had . . . to expose myself to intense things and 'manage' my reactions." He reports that at his trial, his attorney *advised* him to manage his emotions and "remain stoic." It is possible this contributed to the impression that he was a stone-cold killer, an adult monster who would never be safe to live among "normal" citizens, rather than the troubled boy he was (and, in most modern societies other than the United States, would have been seen as).

All of this fed, and fed upon, the pattern of paranoid and delusional thinking that was arising in Johnny's mind as he moved from being a twelve-year-old boy to being the (barely) thirteen-year-old teenager who killed his sister. Indeed, a psychiatric assessment concluded that the thoughts and behaviors Johnny increasingly demonstrated in the year leading up to the murder "are highly consistent with the general progression of decompensation among adolescents who experience a first psychotic episode." They are also indicative of the difficult process of moving from the immature brain of a child toward the mature brain of an adult. For example, Johnny reports that he "didn't appreciate the magnitude of the crime" he committed a day after his thirteenth birthday. The part of the brain most involved in rational thought and reality testing—the frontal lobe—is immature in adolescents generally, and this is one reason why they are notorious for doing "stupid" things.

Even as he began his slide into the "dark side" of human experience, Johnny did live amid a generally positive social environment, as indicated by his experience with what the Search Institute has called the "40 Developmental Assets" (see chapter 1). According to his responses during our interview, Johnny experienced twenty-five of the forty assets growing up (compared with the national average of seventeen). What is more, when paired with his ACE score of zero adverse experiences, his relatively high number of developmental assets suggests that his murderous behavior arose not from the kind of massive developmental damage found in the life of Josiah M. and Alonzo P., but rather from the working of a "crazy" brain immersed in a socially toxic cultural environment. He displayed a kind of "asset resistance" to the positive influences in his life.

Of particular concern to me, when I sat with Johnny in 2016, was that he told me he has transferred his obsessive impulse to heavy metal music (which has displaced his earlier "obsession" with rap music). There is also his continuing interest in criminal violence (e.g., his fascination with *Criminal Minds*). A clinical assessment had recently cited this as evidence of "future dangerousness." Johnny dismissed this assessment. That, I think, is a problem. Given his history, it would seem that for Johnny to be immersed in the violent imagery common in heavy metal and the monstrous violence portrayed in TV shows like *Criminal Minds* is akin to a person recovering from a severe drinking problem hanging out in bars with his long-standing drinking buddies. I believe that to change his brain in a more positive direction (and thus increase its safety as a force in Johnny's life), he would have to forgo this social toxin in favor of more "wholesome" cultural content in every domain. But he chooses not to do so.

CAN JOHNNY GET BETTER? WILL HE?

Will Johnny "get better," to the point that we could be confident that he is rehabilitated, as others among the tribe of Miller's Children have been? Xavier did. Paul T. did, too. Paul was clearly in a state of psychiatric crisis when he killed his sister and two of his friends twenty-seven year ago. But through excellent psychiatric care, the support of other inmates, and his own intelligent search for stability and inner peace, Paul is "well" now. I *want* to believe that Johnny can and will get to that point—but, based on what he said and did when I met him in 2016, I am doubtful. Nonetheless, he is one of Miller's Children, in the sense that he is entitled to a resentencing hearing by order of the U.S. Supreme Court. He may be an exception to the rule of rehabilitation that provides one of the foundations for the *Miller v. Alabama* ruling, but his adolescence alone should have been enough to exempt him from receiving an automatic sentence of life without the possibility of parole.

Had the court that sentenced him in 2001 been operating under the guidelines of the post–*Miller v. Alabama* legal framework, a good case could and should have been made that Johnny was a possible candidate for eventual parole as he matured, was educated, and reaped the benefits of being involved in psychosocial interventions, including psychotherapy (and perhaps medication). Such an understanding of his possible rehabilitation might have been reflected in a sentence that permitted parole after his maturation and development could be observed and evaluated fully. But what if Johnny had been more than "crazy" when he killed his sister? What if he had been a true psychopath?

PSYCHOPATH BRAIN

Ralston State Prison, Atlanta, Georgia: Samuel X. started life thirty-two years ago as an abused child. But over the years that culminated in his first murder (at seventeen), he became a true psychopath. Rather than undergoing a process of rehabilitation and positive transformation in the decade after he entered the criminal justice system and was sentenced to life without parole, he underwent a process of increasing disconnection from the emotional and moral dimensions of "normal life." Whatever he was when he came to prison in 1984, he was a psychopath when I interviewed him in 2015.

According to the records, a prison psychologist in 1987 diagnosed Samuel with "antisocial personality." He started down this path at an early age. Samuel's family of origin was so toxic that each of the six children (Samuel and his five siblings) fled their home when young. Samuel ran away at twelve and hitchhiked on his own for two years. As he puts it, "Since I was twelve, I was never a member of my family." As one relative put it, "He was raised by the state." His father was actively abusive, physically and emotionally, while his mother was withdrawn and psychologically unavailable. He experienced a series of detentions in the years after leaving home, and he ended up in the adult correctional system at age seventeen when he murdered a man who had picked him up as he was hitchhiking from Athens to Atlanta, Georgia.

Samuel was twenty years old at the time of his diagnosis of antisocial personality disorder. He had been sentenced to adult prison a couple of years earlier. As he reports of that experience: "It was great being in adult prison. I always had older friends. They taught me a lot." As I see it, what they taught Samuel compounded the moral and emotional damage he had experienced in his family, and pushed him over the edge into psychopathy. However, it is imperative to recognize that while other young inmates (some of whom I have introduced in earlier chapters) might have fought against and rejected the negative influence of these older friends, Samuel embraced them and what they taught him.

One prison psychologist made this observation of Samuel: "He has very little insight into his behavior." In my interview with Samuel, he repeatedly spoke of how clueless he had been about himself until well into young adulthood. The crucial diagnosis of antisocial personality disorder speaks of "callous disregard for the feelings of others." In Samuel's case (as in so many others), I consider this the result of a long history of dissociating himself from emotions as a way of coping with his traumatic family experiences. Samuel speaks of how the abuse he suffered at home was a "family secret" that he carried with him into the world. But I believe that his emotional callousness was not inevitable. Rather, it is the consequence of his vulnerability to the toxic effects of abuse and his corresponding survival response to chronic psychological trauma in childhood and adolescence.

Fifteen years after he entered prison for the murder committed when he was seventeen, Samuel convinced the director of a mental health program in the prison that he was ready to live in a special unit with its own garden and dormitory. Six months later, he murdered another inmate and one of the staff and buried them under the unit's rose garden, feeling no remorse about what he had done. It's a cautionary tale. Is the young psychopath Samuel a classic example of the "irreparable corruption" and "sophistication–maturity" that the Supreme Court said were the necessary data to justify life-without-parole sentences for juveniles? As Thomas Grisso and Antoinette Kavanaugh have pointed out in their review of *Miller* issues, measures of psychopathy are not likely to provide incontrovertible evidence. They cite two lines of research in support of this point.

First, measures of psychopathic traits during adolescence do not provide a good estimate of enduring and unchangeable "traits" when applied on a case-by-case basis. Psychologists differentiate between *states* and *traits*. The former are situational responses (like being angry after being insulted), whereas the latter reflect long-term dispositions (like being impulsive). States can lead to changes in traits if they occur repeatedly, the situation that gives rise to the response is enduring, and the individual is temperamentally prone to incorporate the state into their repertoire of traits.

Second, when used to predict future behavior of adolescents, these measures result in a lot of "false positives": they incorrectly identify kids as having a psychopathic personality disorder who, in adulthood, display a non-psychopathic personality (and its accompanying behavior). Robert Zagar points out that the Hare assessment approach is correct only 75 percent of the time (in contrast to his own more complex and more "objective" algorithm that is correct in predicting future violence some 95 percent of the time). Additionally, as Grisso and Kavanaugh note, measures of psychopathy seem particularly compromised when used with the racial and ethnic minorities who comprise the bulk of the cases that fall within the *Miller v. Alabama* decision (some 70–80 percent, according to their data). These valid critiques notwithstanding, the important work of understanding guys like Samuel remains, and it requires a deeper look at the range of issues in detection and intervention that arise the minute someone is suspected of demonstrating his kind of "moral insanity."

BAD HABITS OF HEART AND MIND

The first version of the *DSM,* published in 1952, included a set of diagnoses under the heading *sociopathic personality disturbance.* In 1968, the term of choice became *antisocial personality.* In 1980, it became *psychopathy,* defined in terms of a focus on violation of social norms (and not on issues of emotional disconnection). Since 1990, the organizing term in the *DSM* has been *antisocial personality disorder.* It's a complicated and fascinating story. Perhaps the best short (fifty-two pages) review is the 2011 article by Kiehl and Hoffman quoted above. They address with exquisite precision the crucial matters when it comes to the morally insane: Who are they? Where do they come from? What do they do? How much do they cost society? And how do we deal with them?

As I see it, one way to differentiate between the terms *psychopath* and *sociopath* is to say that sociopaths demonstrate a really bad habit of aggressively antisocial behavior (and usually an absence of remorse about how they victimize people), hence the historical use of the term *moral insanity.* However, their behavior often reflects the particular culture and environment in which they have been raised. They acquire ways of thinking and values that lead to and validate criminal behavior. Sociopaths, for example, may be gang members and members of criminal syndicates. These individuals engage in criminal and violent behavior as part of a lifestyle "choice." However, they do not lack a fundamental connection to other human beings. They may well be loving parents, devoted children, committed spouses, and loyal friends, *so long as you are inside their circle of caring.* But if you are outside that circle, you have no claim on them morally or emotionally. One young sociopath said this to me when referring to the state of his moral relationships: "I would do *anything* to protect the people I cared about. If they weren't in my circle I wouldn't pee on them if they were on fire."

Of course, the discussion of where to draw the moral lines is always infused with cultural assumptions of what is "real" and what is "normal" when it comes to moral behavior. American founding fathers George Washington and Thomas Jefferson (to name but two) were slave owners. Were they sociopaths? The French philosopher René Descartes tortured dogs in an attempt to prove a philosophical point—nailing a dog to a barn door and eviscerating it, then proclaiming that the sounds it made were nothing different from the grinding of gears in a mechanical device.

This is why I have long believed that *the* moral issue in most situations is precisely where an individual (and a society) draws the boundaries of the circle of caring. It's one of the central tensions in the Judeo-Christian-Islamic traditions: Am I my brother's keeper? Who is and who is not included in the injunction to "love thy neighbor as oneself"? Who decides who is deservedly killed, when scripture says that to kill one human life unjustly is like killing the whole world? My point is that sociopaths generally draw their circles of caring smaller than what is considered normal in their societies, their time, and their place. Most of us are somewhere between sociopaths and the Dalai Lama. Within their circle of caring, sociopaths can have "normal" emotional attachments and compassion. Not so psychopaths.

Psychopaths are individuals who have some underlying and fundamental lack of empathy and conscience. They have no circle of caring: they are "completely rational but morally insane," to use Kiehl and Hoffman's words. But they may not necessarily engage in *criminal* behavior. Indeed, some might even be called "prosocial psychopaths," and they are found disproportionately in occupations where ruthlessness and callousness can be useful in achieving success legally. Some corporate businessmen who amass great wealth at the expense of stockholders and the public, for example, clearly display many psychopathic traits. They are what Paul Babiak and Robert Hare have called "snakes in suits."

When antisocial psychopaths and non-psychopathic sociopaths are caught committing a crime, they go to prison, where they are classified as cases of antisocial personality disorder (ASPD). But according to Kiehl and Hoffman, "ASPD is present in 65%–85% of the incarcerated population while psychopathy is present in only 15%–25% of that population. Psychopathy is present in 20%–30% of those who have ASPD." This is why I prefer to differentiate between psychopaths and sociopaths. I think it is a crucial distinction for purposes of sentencing and intervention (and not just for Miller's

Children), regardless of the fact that both groups are likely to receive the "official" label of antisocial personality disorder.

Where do these two groups, psychopaths and sociopaths, come from? As always, the interaction between "nature" and "nurture" is complex and is best captured by an ecological maxim: When the question is "Does X cause Y?" the best scientific answer is usually "It depends." Robert Hare puts it this way in his book *Without Conscience:* in both these groups, "biological endowment—the raw materials that environmental, social, and learning experiences fashion into a unique individual—provides a poor basis for socialization and conscience formation." Of course, the genetic transmission of these vulnerabilities usually works hand-in-glove with the inadequate parenting offered by the biological parents of these children. For example, in one case, a mitigation specialist summed up a defendant's social history by saying she was "born of psychopaths and raised by sociopaths."

Studies reviewed by Kiehl and Hoffman suggest that about 96 percent of psychopaths are "caught" by the criminal justice system, which means that some 4 percent of psychopaths live their lives outside of prison, in the world, and these are mostly the ones raised in solidly prosocial families and communities, with effective parents—people like James Fallon (see chapter 1). As already noted, given the state of current models for psychological/psychiatric nomenclature, if they are seen clinically in the criminal justice system, both sociopaths and psychopaths are likely to receive a diagnosis of antisocial personality disorder. I think it is best to see such a diagnosis as really just a *label* for the pattern of thoughts, feelings, and behaviors they have demonstrated, starting in childhood or adolescence—when it is called "conduct disorder"— and continuing into adulthood.

By definition, teenage killers cannot be diagnosed with antisocial personality disorder; the official diagnostic criteria developed and promulgated by the American Psychiatric Association (which publishes the *DSM*) require that a person be at least eighteen years of age before that diagnosis can be made legitimately. But if Miller's Children come to prison with a history of conduct disorder in adolescence and continue to behave badly once they cross the line into legal adulthood, they are likely to end up with the official stamp of disapproval that comes with a diagnosis of antisocial personality disorder. In a sense, this is prima facie evidence that they are therefore sociopaths. With that diagnosis may come the allied—but, as we have seen, *false*—presumption that they are psychopaths. However, being labeled a sociopath is not the whole story.

Psychologist Robert Hare literally "wrote the book" about psychopaths, which I quoted above—*Without Conscience: The Disturbing World of the Psychopaths among Us.* Published in 1999, it spells out the hallmarks of psychopathy and provided the basis for the Hare Psychopathy Checklist, the screening questionnaire that has become a part of standard practice in the field of inmate assessment. This checklist is designed to bring into focus the defining characteristics of the psychopath, namely *selfish and unfeeling victimization of other people* and *an unstable and antisocial lifestyle,* especially among inmate populations. It seeks to identify twenty manifestations of these two underlying aspects of character and personality, a list that evokes what I learned about Samuel X., both from the official records and from the words he spoke to me:

- Glib and superficial charm
- Grandiose (exaggeratedly high) estimation of self
- Need for stimulation
- Pathological lying
- Cunning and manipulativeness
- Lack of remorse or guilt
- Shallow affect (superficial emotional responsiveness)
- Callousness and lack of empathy
- Parasitic lifestyle
- Poor behavioral controls
- Sexual promiscuity
- Early behavior problems
- Lack of realistic long-term goals
- Impulsivity
- Irresponsibility
- Failure to accept responsibility for own actions
- Many short-term marital relationships
- Juvenile delinquency
- Revocation of conditional release
- Criminal versatility

One problem is that the person doing the assessment uses the clinician's "structured professional judgment" to score each item as 0, 1, or 2 (corresponding to how strongly and clearly it appears to be present). This can lead to bias, of course (and error, according to Robert Zagar's research). In any case, those who receive a score of 30 or more (out of a possible 40) are defined as psychopaths—which, as Kiehl and Hoffman note (importantly) excludes most cases of antisocial personality disorder, unless they also exhibit the emotional and interpersonal characteristics of the truly "morally insane" psychopaths.

Among the general population, the average Hare score is about 7; among inmates it is 22. This is not surprising for several reasons, among them the fact that some of the Hare items (e.g., juvenile delinquency) are essentially tautological for inmates, because they measure the very reasons such persons are in prison, being assessed via the Hare checklist, in the first place. In addition, the level of adversity among incarcerated criminals is much higher than in the general public to start with, given the empirical links between child-hood adversity and the odds of juvenile delinquency and later criminal behavior. For example (as noted in chapter 1), a study of Florida juvenile offenders conducted by Michael Baglivio and colleagues found that nearly 38 percent (30 percent of the males and 45 percent of the females) reported five or more ACEs, compared with just 7 percent (or 10 percent in other studies) in the general population. And a study conducted by James Reavis and colleagues found that the ACE scores of offenders convicted of crimes including child abuse, domestic violence, sexual offenses, and stalking were four times higher than those of the general population.

The "psychopath vs. non-psychopath" comparison among incarcerated populations is thus taking place in a specialized context of individuals who, as a group, have very high levels of adversity in common. Many of the characteristics included in the Hare assessment match up with the developmental consequences of Type III trauma, of course, which speaks in part to the origins of psychopathy itself. Hare has made it clear that, as a general rule, he believes that psychopaths are not *simply* the product of early trauma, regardless of initial vulnerability. Research conducted by Hare and colleagues suggests that *at least among incarcerated populations,* the family backgrounds of psychopaths and non-psychopaths do not differ significantly.

As always, the core issue in biology is context. Some are born with brains that are primed to turn away from "normal" patterns of thinking and feeling unless they are nurtured in especially positive families and communities, rather than socially and psychologically toxic ones. When they are placed in toxic environments, both the vulnerable brains and the non-vulnerable brains are prone to develop patterns of antisocial behavior that lead down the pathway to prison.

But where do these brains come from in the first place? Some researchers believe that psychopath brains are simply a genetic anomaly that exists in all human populations—a long-ago mutation that stuck around because those who have it are able to reproduce successfully before they are detected and neutralized. Cultures differ in what they do with these people once they are detected. For example, the traditional response of the Arctic Inuit was to set such people adrift on ice floes so that they might die and not "infect" the larger community. America incarcerates them—unless they are prosocial enough to turn their nefarious skills to noncriminal success in business, politics, and other fields. But *simple* genetic explanations may not be the whole story. The emerging field of epigenetics offers another causal explanation.

EPIGENETICS, FOR BETTER OR FOR WORSE

The core idea of epigenetics is that genetic material is just the starting point for human development. The conventional scientific understanding is now that environmental influences interact with genetic material to produce traits, behaviors, and characteristics in a manner and to a degree that is much more powerful than previously thought. However, conventional science typically stops at social, psychological, nutritional, and "physical" aspects of the environment.

Thus, for example, the "heritability coefficient" of a trait (i.e., the degree to which that trait is inheritable) is not a fixed value, but rather a variable. If the question is "What is the heritability coefficient of a trait?" the answer is, once again, "It depends." It depends on the psychological and social environment into which that genetic material is deposited—like being born into my 1950s family and community, rather than the 1980s family and community in which Alonzo P. grew up.

Recent advances in the study of epigenetics have even led to a rethinking of the previously discredited "Lamarckian" hypothesis, namely that when traits change during an organism's lifetime, those changes can be passed on to the next generation by changing the genetic material that is inherited by offspring. This phenomenon has been documented in rats, for example. Parental rats who were conditioned to fear a previously neutral odor passed on this fear to their offspring, without any opportunity for this to be communicated other than genetically. And it has been found in people as well. For example, a study conducted by Natan Kellermann concluded that Holocaust survivors transmitted a genetic vulnerability to trauma to their offspring. Some Native Americans have embraced this research as a possible key to understanding how what their ancestors experienced—starting with a 90 percent die-off of the indigenous North and South American populations within a generation of initial contact with the European invaders and continuing through centuries of cultural and social destruction—shaped who they are as a people today.

The Lamarckian model of evolution rings true when you look at the social history of many teenage killers, particularly the most sociopathic among them—at the intergenerational patterns in which trauma begets trauma begets trauma in an escalating pattern, particularly among those who are least able to undergo rehabilitation and transformation. I find that these intergenerational reports help me retain a compassionate stance in my interaction with teenage killers and the men they become. I see where they came from, and it helps me focus on how they got there. As a social worker once told me after reviewing the social history of eighteen-year-old Zack, who met a young woman on the Internet and then, after they met in person, stabbed her ninety-two times and said he would like to do it again, "He was raised by an extended family of psychopaths and sociopaths."

And thus, when I am tempted to judge and blame the abusive and neglectful parents who started these killers on their path to a dark place, I look at where *they* came from and how *they* got to the dark place from which their murderous offspring arose. As it turned out, the psychopaths and sociopaths who raised Zack were themselves raised by psychopaths and sociopaths. Sometimes it is small comfort, but it is often the only comfort to be had—this humbling awareness of the pathology being passed along, across generations. It is a rationale for suspending moral judgment on young killers, despite the need to control their dangerous behavior.

Although individuals differ in their resilience in the face of trauma, it is important to note that when the nature of the trauma is severe and prolonged enough, the casualty rate reaches virtually 100 percent (if all forms of dysfunction are included). For example, a World War II study of American soldiers reported by Dave Grossman revealed that after sixty days of continuous combat, the rate of psychiatric "casualty" reached 98 percent (and those who did not break down were characterized as having psychopathic personality profiles). Similarly, we can recall the study in Chicago conducted by Patrick Tolan and colleagues (cited in chapter 2), which revealed that among abused children living in the most violent and impoverished neighborhoods and who were also exposed to racism, 100 percent exhibited significant psychiatric and/or academic problems between the ages of thirteen and fifteen.

A NOTE ON THE ROLE OF RELIGION IN CRAZINESS

A lot is said (and written) about religion by guys in prison. As I pointed out in chapter 4, I believe that spiritual development is a crucial resource in the process of rehabilitation and transformation. However, some of what is said and written in prison regarding religion—whether it is about "finding Jesus" or "coming to Allah"—is nothing more than BS, simply designed to curry favor or manipulate the recipient. Some of it reflects outright delusion. For example, Thomas W. said this when I asked him about why he legally changed his name (as I reported in my book *Listening to Killers*):

> That's right. I don't use that name anymore. I changed it, for religious reasons. My true name is "Glorious Warrior." You can call me that. I'm a Buddhist. I started studying and reading when I came here. This was years ago, and I learned a lot about Buddhism from this book they had in the library. The more I learned, the more I realized that Christianity was not enough for me. I needed more, so I became a Buddhist, 'cause I am a deep spiritual being. Buddhists believe in reincarnation, you know. That's coming back again and again after you die, each time as a more powerful person. Me, I been coming back a long time, so I'm a teacher now, like Jesus was, only better, 'cause I'm Buddha too. That's why I changed my name to Glorious Warrior, 'cause I am like Jesus and Buddha put together, but I am tougher than they were. That's why I'm better.

When I asked him to elaborate on how he traveled this path, his response was disturbing:

> OK, it doesn't really matter now, because of who I am now, you know? I killed some people back before I realized who I really am. It doesn't matter just like all the shit I went through when I was a kid. It doesn't matter, 'cause it was before I saw the truth about myself, that I was reincarnated. That's when I changed my name to who I really am.

It's worth pointing out that he followed this declaration by asking me if I could get him some drugs, and when I told him that I couldn't he lost interest in me and our conversation.

While "Glorious Warrior" is an extreme case to be sure, he is not unique. "Jailhouse conversion" is common—whether it be a form of manipulation, a delusion, or sincere—and it involves virtually every religious tradition, whether Christian, Muslim, Buddhist, or you name it (although I must say that the closest thing I have personally encountered to a Jewish jailhouse conversion was the man who had embraced occult Judaism and was studying Hebrew).

WHOSE SON ARE YOU?

Are there individuals who are destined to be profoundly morally damaged— "morally insane"—regardless of the way they are treated and how they are raised? Are there individuals who are born with the kind of "crazy brain" that leads them down the path of psychopathy? Are there men who never do the work of rehabilitation and transformation but instead just try to con their way through to "work the system," perhaps by posing as religious men? Are there guys who remain mired in delusion? I have to say yes to each of these questions. But admitting that is, for me, the last resort rather than the first. All too often, prior to the *Miller v. Alabama* decision in 2012, it was the first resort in the criminal justice system in America. What is more, it is *still* all too often the first rather than the last resort, once these lost boys cross the *legal* line from being seventeen-year-old juveniles to being eighteen-year-old adults.

Damaged as he was, and horrified as I was about the way he thought, felt, and acted, I could not expel Alonzo P. from my circle of caring and my sense that he could have become a different man if he had had a different life as a boy. As I left the room in which he and I had been talking for the past three hours, I put my hand on his shoulder and said the most reassuring words I could think of: "If you had been my son, you wouldn't be here." I like to think that if I had raised him and had contributed my genetic input to his brain, he would have been a different person. I like to think so. I need to think so. I could not continue to do what I do without that bit of hope.

When it comes to psychopaths, *hopelessness* has been the watchword. For example, a classic study conducted by Vernon Quinsey and colleagues found that group treatment for psychopaths made them *worse*—apparently because they treated the program as an opportunity to hone their manipulation skills. This parallels results from adolescent treatment programs, as reviewed by Thomas Dishion and colleagues in 1999: numerous studies have found that the more the process of adolescent groups is turned over to the kids themselves, the more the most negative teens are likely to take over the social process and make other kids worse. More than thirty years ago, Ronald Feldman and colleagues found that even if only 30 percent of an adolescent treatment group are offering negativity, it is enough to turn the other 70 percent in a negative direction. This is one reason why the "decompression treatment" noted earlier is successful with adolescents on the verge of full-blown psychopathy—it relies on intensive one-on-one rather than diluted group sessions. This offers some light at the end of the tunnel—at least where juveniles are concerned. The net result is that the "exceptions" will become more and more rare as our understanding improves of who psychopaths and sociopaths are, where they come from developmentally, and how to intervene in their lives effectively.

SIX

Translating Hope into Law
and Practice

To be hopeful in bad times is not just foolishly romantic. It is based upon the fact that human history is a history not only of cruelty, but also of compassion, sacrifice, courage, kindness.

What we choose to emphasize in this complex history will determine our lives. If we see only the worst, it destroys our capacity to do something. If we remember those times and places—and there are so many—where people have behaved magnificently, this gives us the energy to act, and at least the possibility of sending this spinning top of a world in a different direction.

And if we do act, in however small a way, we don't have to wait for some grand utopian future. The future is an infinite succession of presents, and to live now as we think human beings should live, in defiance of all that is bad around us, is itself a marvelous victory.

HOWARD ZINN

This concluding chapter lays out a series of issues in law and practice that arise from my experiences conducting developmental analyses of Miller's Children. These include everything from breakdowns in the parole-board system in some states to the persistence of an unforgiving, punitive approach to criminal justice for juveniles. But there are encouraging signs, foundations for hope.

MUCH OF MY PROFESSIONAL LIFE has been lived as an effort to understand the dark side of human experience—war, abuse, racism, poverty, and violence—and to shed light on that darkness, particularly as it affects the development of children and adolescents. In 2008, I even published a book titled *Children and the Dark Side of Human Experience*. But nothing in my past has meant as much to me as entering the world of Miller's Children. Why? Because that world is filled, first and foremost, with stories of hope amid despair, of moral and psychological recovery in the face of developmental insult and damage.

Prior to the Supreme Court's ruling in *Miller v. Alabama* (and the follow-up decisions in *Montgomery v. Louisiana* and *Tatum v. Arizona*), while many of Miller's Children were motivated to pursue a sacred path of rehabilitation and transformation, many others were truly hopeless by any conventional standard, and some were plagued by anger and despair at being consigned to this condition. Their sentences of life without the possibility of parole constituted a terminal diagnosis of their inhumanity. For many, this did not abate until the Supreme Court's rulings in favor of their humanity. Into their darkness came a ray of hope and a sense that they would experience a new kind of justice. Many of them were moved to hope. I was too.

In a strange way this work has been profoundly *refreshing*—emotionally, scientifically, and spiritually. As I enter my eighth decade of life, I am profoundly grateful for that refreshment. But there remains much to do for Miller's Children, and for the teenage killers who come after them. There are significant challenges to be met, the first of which is determining "developmentally appropriate" sentencing policies and decisions for teenagers who kill.

DEVELOPMENTALLY APPROPRIATE
SENTENCING DECISIONS

The more time I have spent with Miller's Children, the more I am haunted by these questions: Would they have undergone the process of rehabilitation and transformation if they had not been sentenced to life without the possibility of parole? Was it the utter hopelessness of their situation that provided the psychological climate in which they changed as they did? Would they have done as much if they knew in advance that there was a possibility of light at the end of the tunnel for them—ten, twenty, or even thirty years down the road?

I think of my dear John Christianson when I wrestle with these questions. I have known John since 1993, when he was barely fourteen years old, because I served as an expert witness in his murder case. I have written about John before, in both my 1999 book *Lost Boys* and my 2015 book *Listening to Killers*. I want to repeat here some of what I wrote about him in the latter book, to set the stage for my answers to these questions that sometimes keep me up at night.

John was thirteen years old on March 6, 1993, when he killed seventeen-year-old Mannie Richards, who, along with some of his friends, was threatening John and another boy as they walked home from school in Camden, Oregon. On May 25 of that year, the judge in the case ruled that John would be tried as an adult. A press report presented what happened in court this way:

John Christianson is the youngest child to face trial as an adult in county history, officials said. But the boy's lawyer contends Christianson shouldn't be treated as an adult. "He's completely frightened," she said. "He thinks his life is over." Christianson began to cry when the judge made his ruling. Christianson also is charged with two counts of first-degree assault, unlawful possession of a firearm, second-degree assault, brandishing a weapon and two counts of felony harassment. The charges were filed in response to the Richards shooting near Camden City Park, and an encounter the night before when Christianson is accused of threatening other youths with the same rifle he used the next day to kill Richards. The boy will be held in the county jail pending arraignment and a trial. A deputy prosecutor was pleased with the judge's ruling and hopes it will send a message to others. "We hope that the impact will be through the school systems and law enforcement that juveniles with guns aren't being treated as youngsters," she said. "If the message passes that the penalties are severe, it will impact their behavior."

I met John later that year in the county jail, as he awaited trial. Interviewing him with me was Claire Bedard, who had conducted many of the interviews upon which I drew for my book *Lost Boys*. That meeting with John was the start of a relationship with him that has lasted more than two decades. John's young life was full of trauma and loss. His mother was a drug addict who came in and out of his life. His father was in prison. He was raised mostly by his maternal grandparents, but from time to time spent vacations with his mother and her boyfriend in Los Angeles, where he was drawn into the world of gangs and drugs.

It's a long story of confusion, sadness, anger, and escalating problems in school and with his peers that culminated in the events that landed him in jail, facing trial for murder. But there was something profoundly appealing about John. Maybe it was his earnest hunger for connection and guidance as he spoke of how he was influenced by the Christian preacher who visited him (and convinced him that he should accept punishment for his sins) and the adult murderer in the next cell (who drew him further into the dark side of life with his tales of sexual violence). Maybe it was the fact that his hands reminded me of my own son, Josh. Whatever it was, I was hooked, and so was Claire. John pled guilty to second-degree murder and received a sentence of twelve years in an adult prison—albeit in the juvenile wing of that prison until he turned eighteen.

John and I corresponded over the years, and I was able to visit him a few times when my professional travel or vacations took me to the Pacific Northwest. He once sent me a Father's Day card in which he talked about "growing up in the land of the lost." When he graduated as valedictorian of the high school he attended within the prison, Claire and I were there to cheer him on. But his graduation present from the criminal justice system was that he went directly from there to the dark world of the adult wing in that same prison. He told me of all that he learned spending his adolescence in prison.

Like many kids who have been abandoned by their parents, John was haunted by their ghosts. All John knew about his biological father was that he was Mexican, and the only Mexicans John socialized with before he went to prison were the boys he met when he visited with his mother in Los Angeles, who happened to be gangbangers. I don't think it is coincidental that he became a leader of the Mexican gang in prison. By all accounts he was good at it, a natural leader.

Soon after he began his sentence, John's grandmother died, and he grieved the loss of the woman who had been more of a mother to him than his mother ever was. To his credit, John's grandfather, Ron, stuck by him over the years even though he was only his grandmother's second husband, and not biologically related to John. Ron visited John as often as he could and half hoped, half believed that the goodness in his grandson would prevail over the moral and emotional damage that he brought with him into the prison. He knew that John's damaged sense of self was reinforced and amplified by his experiences in prison, year after year as an incarcerated adolescent, until he was integrated into the ranks of the adult inmates. But still Ron hoped for a good outcome.

I shared that hope, but over the years, when I visited John and when we spoke on the phone or exchanged letters, I felt and saw his hardening identity as a criminal. He had a sense of this himself, often remarking that the norms and ethics of life in prison were very different from the norms and ethics of life on the outside. He learned how to fight, how to lie, how to intimidate, how to manipulate, how to protect himself from exploitation, and how to exploit others. What he *didn't* learn was how to live successfully in the outside world or even to live with himself in prison. Research by psychologist Craig Haney confirms that in this, John was like many adolescents who receive lengthy sentences, particularly lengthy sentences in adult prison: they become "institutionalized."

As he approached the end of his twelve-year sentence, John spoke of his dreams of making a good life for himself, outside "in the world." But more and more, as the release date approached, it became clear that his terms of reference—money, cars, thrills, and sex—doomed him. After his release, being a felon made it hard for him to find a job. When he did get one, it was with a business owned by his girlfriend (with whom he had a child). When that relationship ended, he was out of a job and at loose ends; before long he was working as a bodyguard for a drug dealer.

He was arrested and ended up back in prison. Eventually, we lost contact as he disappeared into the penal system and the "lifestyle" it represented. He told me in one of our last conversations that this way of living was familiar to him. He knew the rules. He knew how to make his way there. Having come of age in prison, he was so thoroughly "prisonized," as Haney uses that term, that he was more "at home" back there than he had been in the outside world after his release.

I always wondered how John's life might have been different if the criminal justice system had treated him as the kid he was in 1993, rather than the adult it believed him to be, the "danger to the community" the judge called him in court when he transferred John's case to adult criminal court. What if that judge hadn't moved John out of the juvenile system, where he might have had a better chance to forge a different path? Confronted with a thirteen-year-old boy, as I was in 1993, you have to wonder, "What if . . .?"

After all, adolescence is the time when issues of "identity formation" become salient. The work of James Marcia built upon the groundbreaking theory of Erik Erikson in this regard. Marcia elaborated on Erikson's idea that the challenge of adolescence is "identity vs. role confusion." As Marcia saw it, there were multiple alternative paths for teenagers with regard to identity issues. He posited that the key in adolescence is the degree to which there is an exploration of identity issues, followed by commitment to an identity as defined by all the domains that make up a human existence—from vocation and religion to ethnicity and gender roles. Most specifically, he focused on four alternative paths for adolescents:

Identity diffusion—when the adolescent doesn't know enough to answer the fundamental question "Who am I?"

Identity foreclosure—when the adolescent prematurely decides who he or she is, conforming to the expectations of others without undergoing a complete process of identity exploration

Identity moratorium—when the adolescent is exploring alternatives but has not made a commitment yet

Identity achievement—when the adolescent has gone through a full process of exploration, reached a conclusion, and made a commitment to his or her answer to the question "Who am I?"

It had seemed to me that John's experiences in prison robbed him of the opportunity to "do it right" when it came to the process that would lead to a positive, prosocial identity. He didn't have the necessary luxury of that process. Instead, he was rushed into the foreclosed position that he was "a criminal."

In late April 2014, out of the blue, I received a long letter from John. It read, in part,

> Jim:
> It has taken me years to sit down and write you this letter. And even now the words fail me. There is so much I want to talk to you and Claire about, so many things I want to tell you. I miss the both of you. I miss our connection, our love and the sense of family we had together. It's very hard for me to write this letter. I feel so much shame, for sitting here in prison once again at 31 years old, and for allowing my life to turn out this way.... But through it all I am still filled with hope. This is not how my story will end.... Your lost son is still a work in progress. The journey continues ...
> With Love,
>
> *John Christianson*

The words "still a work in progress" encouraged me. It sounded like he was undergoing a remedial process of identity formation, and in this he sounded like many of the young men in their thirties whom I knew as Miller's Children. I wrote back to John, reaffirming my care for him and asking for more information. He wrote back quickly, describing how he had severed his ties with the gang. He told me that he had moved into a special unit in the prison reserved for men who have cut themselves off from their gangs. He did this, he wrote, in order to create enough social and psychological space to do the rehabilitation and transformation work that must be done to redirect that "journey" of which he spoke. In my follow-up letter, I promised to visit him and kept the door open for him to become something more than my "lost son." I was able to hope for John again and offer what support I could. Time would tell. There were no guarantees, but there was hope . . . again.

I saw John in 2016. It was a happy reunion, and we continue to exchange letters. He says he is on the right track this time, as a man in his mid-thirties (he had been in his mid-twenties during his short-lived release from prison). What troubles me is this question: *Was John's initial sentence—of twelve years, when he was only thirteen at the time—either too long or too short?* Was it too long, in the sense that had he been sent to a juvenile detention facility with an intensive program of therapy and resocialization, he might have "recovered" by the time he left adolescence, as Kathleen Heide's analysis of treatment programs (see chapter 4) would predict? Such an experience could have prevented identity foreclosure as a "criminal" and promoted a more normal period of exploration and crisis that might have led to the positive identity he was now seeking in his mid-thirties. Or was the sentence too short to provide the "hitting rock bottom" that seems to be essential for the deep process of rehabilitation and transformation to take root? Was it too short to permit the kind of post-traumatic growth that Richard Tedeschi and Lawrence Calhoun have studied (also discussed in chapter 4)?

Criminologists Heide, Norair Khachatryan, and their colleagues have undertaken a long-term follow-up study of teenage killers that sheds light on this issue. They looked at the post-release behavior of forty-eight "juvenile homicide offenders" (which included teenagers convicted of attempted homicide, as well as those who actually killed someone). The average time they followed up with these individuals was almost thirty-one years. Follow-up data indicated that nearly 90 percent of the released offenders had been rearrested—some as soon as months later, others in a matter of years (eighteen years in one case). What is more, most of those rearrests (70 percent) were for violent crimes. Discouraging news.

But it is critically important to report that the average time that the juvenile homicide offenders served in prison was eight years. This means that few served time beyond the point at which they had experienced the brain maturation that comes in our mid-twenties, and almost none served long enough after brain maturation to have the decade of personal growth that leads to the kind of rehabilitation and transformation I have observed in so many of Miller's Children. Moreover, Heide and colleagues found that those who served six or fewer years were more likely to be rearrested than those who served seven or more years—80 percent versus 50 percent—and were six times more likely to be arrested for violent crimes.

This brings us back to John. I believe that because he wasn't given the juvenile option, he didn't have a real chance to take advantage of the therapeutic resources that might have been available to him as a teenager, resources that might well have turned his malleable development in a positive direction. Had he been treated as the kid he was, he might well have been guided along a developmental pathway quite different from the one he took when locked up in a prison. I can only speculate about this, of course. But there is research to ground this speculation, research that demonstrates teenagers can change for the better when exposed to high-quality psychosocial interventions.

John is bright, but at thirteen he carried a lot of unprocessed psychological baggage (e.g., maternal and paternal abandonment, traumatic experiences, attention issues that compromised his success in school). He had a lot of work to do. However, when the juvenile detention route was blocked, the alternative was a sentence of "only" twelve years in an adult prison, where he didn't get the therapeutic intervention he needed (and might well have gotten in a juvenile detention facility). How did John respond to that? I think he decided—whether consciously or not—that he could "wait it out." But in so doing, he only got worse rather than better, as an inmate in an adult prison with a fixed term that would not even take him to the point of brain maturity.

Thus, when he was released in 2006, John was still much the same troubled kid he had been when he was arrested as a thirteen-year-old in 1993, with all his issues of decision making and emotional management still in play, *plus* the issues of being "prisonized" that arose from spending most of his adolescence, and the transition to adulthood, incarcerated. I believe that his demons were intact and ready to overcome what Abraham Lincoln famously called "the better angels of our nature." He said he wanted to "be good," and at some level I think he really did. But he was unprepared to act on this, not ready to live a positive, prosocial life on the outside.

For me, one important warning sign was when John said that his goal was to buy a Cadillac Escalade (which he did, somehow). Unlike so many of Miller's Children, who have recognized superficial materialism as a false god, John was still full of "attachments" to cars, money, power, and all the other temptations of the flesh and the spirit that brought him down, and back to prison, within three years of being released.

When he wrote to me from prison in 2014, he was again saying all the "right things." And when I spent an afternoon with him in the visiting room of his current prison residence in 2016, he repeated those good things to me, offering them with conviction. I certainly want to believe him, and at some level I do believe him. But again, I am left to wonder if he would have been better served by a longer prison sentence for the murder (second-degree murder, to be sure) that he committed in 1994. The twelve-year sentence meant that he was released when he was twenty-five years old, precisely the age at which neuroscience research tells us he was, for the first time, dealing with life from the stronger position of having a mature brain—playing with a full deck, so to speak.

In this respect, John was different from most of the Miller's Children I have written about in earlier chapters. Unlike them, he had not had a substantial period of time when he could confront his demons—maternal abandonment, paternal absence, drug abuse, anger management issues, confronting racism as a Mexican-American kid in a very white community—with the advantage of an adult brain and the opportunity to make use of that mature brain in figuring out life in general, and his life in particular. And as noted above, he had not experienced the rock bottom that seems to be the prerequisite for post-traumatic growth. Maybe he has now. Time will tell, as John is due to be released again in a few years.

I cannot help but wonder if teenage murders should receive *either* juvenile detention with intensive therapeutic intervention *or* life sentences, *but always with the possibility of parole in the years immediately after brain maturation is likely to be complete, and thus as the prospects for post-traumatic growth increase during the individual's mid-twenties and early thirties.*

I find that I look at and listen to teenage killers differently now than I might have before I began this work. Recently, I sat with sixteen-year-old Antonio R., whose lawyers were fighting the prosecution's efforts to have him moved from juvenile to adult court. In the past, I might have taken it as a matter of faith that he (and society) would be better off retaining him in juvenile court rather than exposing him to the adult system in court and in prison. I would have seen it as fundamentally a human rights issue, and that would have been that. But now I found myself having doubts.

The study of recidivism among teenage killers conducted by Khachatryan, Heide, and colleagues was very much on my mind as I sat with Antonio and tried to imagine who and what he would be if he stayed in the juvenile system and therefore was released at age twenty-five (when the legal foundation for a juvenile sentence would run out). Antonio's responses to my questions—and to those of the ACE and 40 Developmental Assets questionnaires—troubled me. His self-report put his ACE score at zero and his number of developmental assets at thirty-seven! And although I told him that the worst thing he could do was tell me something untrue that could be shown to be untrue, he denied being present in the same city at the time of the crime (a gang-related murder), even though there was compelling evidence from many sources that he was there and shot the victim six times—evidence that included his Facebook postings. He expressed no remorse and seemed cavalier about the whole matter. His records indicated a long history of troubled and troubling behavior in school before he dropped out at age fourteen. In a prior assessment done by a probation officer for a delinquency charge when Antonio was fifteen, everything he (and his mother) said seemed equally cavalier and rosy.

I couldn't tell if he was "simply" lying or if he was even more troubled and dissociated than he appeared to be, and I hoped that an evaluation by a child psychiatrist would help clarify this matter. In any case, I felt torn about whether Antonio was a good candidate for juvenile court (and thus a maximum of nine years, leading to his release at age twenty-five) or if he should be moved to adult court, where he could receive a twenty-year sentence (which would take him nine years past the "magic" age of twenty-five, when he would have the benefit of a mature brain for dealing with his feelings, his identity, and his place in the world). In the latter scenario, he might well travel the path that so many of Miller's Children have traveled.

But how to decide which option was most appropriate? Perhaps the best approach would be the screening algorithm developed by psychologist Robert Zagar (described in earlier chapters). No other approach is likely to differentiate as effectively between two crucially different groups. On one hand, there are those teenage killers who are so deeply troubled and have been so profoundly mis-socialized that they cannot recover in the context of a therapeutic juvenile detention program (some of whom may well never recover, as I pointed out in chapter 5). On the other hand, there are kids who would and could recover as juveniles because the murder they committed is best understood as an adolescent crisis—the sort of crisis that can and will pass "quickly" with intensive therapy and social support. The former need sentences long enough to undergo maturation and post-traumatic growth, with parole coming ten, twenty, or even thirty years down the road (or, in the rarest cases, not until a miracle occurs). The latter can be kept in the juvenile justice system and quietly "age out" at eighteen or twenty-one.

Perhaps we should adopt the Norwegian system (outlined in chapter 3) for those who need more than juvenile treatment, namely twenty-one years as the maximum sentence, but with the possibility of the state arguing for additional five-year terms after that sentence is completed, if absolutely necessary. This would allow for the continued incarceration of those who have not undergone rehabilitation and transformation (or who continue to be "unsafe" because of incapacitating mental health problems). Such an approach presumes that rehabilitation and change can happen, and thus focuses institutional resources on making it happen. Of course, a long-term program of research to validate my hypothesis about this sentencing issue would be crucial to assess its validity. Implementing it would certainly stand the current American system of parole on its head, putting the burden of proof on the state to a make a case for continued confinement, rather than on the inmate to make a case for release. It makes developmental sense, and I think it would have well served John Christianson and many thousands of others like him. It would serve the cause of justice and safety in America well, too.

This idea is particularly compelling given the terrible realities of the parole system in relation to juvenile killers. A report prepared by the American Civil Liberties Union (ACLU) in 2016 found that parole boards typically—and, in most cases, *inappropriately or illegally*—focus on the crime committed (which occurred perhaps twenty years or more earlier) rather than the progress the individual has made since committing that crime as a teenager. As the ACLU notes, the purpose of parole is

> to provide an incentive and a path to earn release from prison. Instead, in many states, the parole system is defective and reflexively denies release even to model prisoners who went to prison as teenagers, have already served decades in prison, and no longer pose a safety risk . . . finding that the promise of parole is an illusion, no matter what they do to prove their worthiness for release.

The report cites data from two states to illustrate this travesty: 0.05 percent of juvenile lifers granted parole in Florida, and none (0 percent) in Maryland in a twenty-year period! "Prisoners incarcerated since their youth are routinely denied parole, long after they've grown, matured, atoned, and been rehabilitated, and in many cases, solely because of the crime they committed in their youth—not because of who they are now."

If the parole system was broken before Miller's Children started coming forward to appeal for release, how will it manage when the initial trickle of cases becomes a flood? And what if the Supreme Court continues down the path that leads to outlawing *all* life-without-parole sentences—even those that are discretionary? This should keep all of us who love justice and are committed to compassion up at night—as it does many of Miller's Children, their families, and their advocates.

The Supreme Court's ruling in *Tatum v. Arizona* in 2016 was a direct rebuke to judges whose pro forma review of *Miller* cases constituted a perfunctory rubber-stamping of the original life-without-parole judgment. But judicial policy will be insufficient if it is not accompanied by a change of mentality on the part of parole boards—an alteration of mind and heart. Too many guys are coming before parole boards in good faith and with hope, only to be summarily dismissed and invalidated. That must stop! No man who has overcome the struggles of his fractured and damaged childhood and adolescence to become a recovered and transformed adult should hear what many of the men dismissed by a parole board have heard when they appeared before the parole board and were told, in effect, "It doesn't matter what you have accomplished. It doesn't matter who you are now. You don't matter." It's a devastating message to hear for anyone who has devoted himself to rehabilitation and transformation, as so many of Miller's Children have.

In any case, once we have figured out how to impose developmentally appropriate sentences for teenage killers, we will still have to face up to at least three impediments to doing so as a matter of comprehensive policy and practice:

Ego, incompetence, and hardness of heart among prosecutors and judges—
Can prosecutors and judges see through their own self-interest (political considerations in which they fear being seen as "soft on crime"), ego considerations (stubbornly refusing to admit that the original sentence was a mistake), and harsh, moralistic, judgmental positions regarding rehabilitation and transformation? And can the whole system admit that many of Miller's Children were themselves victimized by inadequate counsel at the time of their initial sentencing, and some were even wrongly convicted in the first place?

Refusing to see that adolescence does not end the day a kid turns eighteen—
Even as the system works through the backlog of *Miller* cases—many thousands across the United States—it must come to terms with the fact that it makes little developmental sense to draw a bright legal line between the 365th day of a seventeen-year-old's life and the first day of an eighteen-year-old's. Why stop at eighteen, when brain maturation continues, on average, until age twenty-six?

Violating the right to treatment and a spiritual path for teenage killers that includes post-release support—Simply exhorting teenage killers to rehabilitate and transform is not enough. While some very few can "reinvent the wheel" of therapeutic intervention and heal themselves, most need supportive resources. The guys who have made it through tell me this often, which raises the issue of there being a "right to treatment" for teenage killers. Affirming that right leads naturally to a discussion of what troubled and violent kids need to become good men and women, to become "safe."

Simply releasing Miller's Children back into the world as a result of judicial resentencing is not enough, of course. Post-release planning and support is crucial for their success. This is true even for younger men, now in their mid-thirties, who have been incarcerated for twenty years. They may never have learned to drive, never had a checking account or learned to balance a budget, never held a regular job. It may have been more than twenty years since they ate in a restaurant and had to make choices from a menu. For older men, who may have served four decades or more in prison for their juvenile crime, the problem is compounded by issues of aging.

My colleague Kathleen Heide puts it this way: "My big concern is if these men get out of prison at fifty to sixty years old, how will they make it in society? They will not have much credit towards social security . . . they may not have marketable skills and/or a solid education." For Miller's Children to succeed upon being released, they will need programs, such as residential halfway houses that teach them basic skills and help them deal with the enormous emotional challenges of making the shift from life in prison to life in the community. But they will also need a society that welcomes them back, with open arms if possible, but at the very least without hostility. It is to these impediments that I turn our attention next.

EGO, INCOMPETENCE, AND HARDNESS OF HEART

Scarboro State Prison, Muncie, Indiana: Maria H. was sixteen when she conspired with her boyfriend to kill her parents, and twenty-seven when I met her in preparation for her *Miller* resentencing hearing. Like so many kids who kill, Maria was best understood as an untreated traumatized child inhabiting a teenager's body. Despite the comparatively positive family environment provided by her adoptive parents, Louise and Tom H., the traumatic and neglectful nature of her early adverse experiences during infancy and early childhood had a serious negative effect on Maria's emotional life and development. With an ACE score of seven, she was among the 1 percent of American kids who have experienced the most childhood adversity.

Maria's affect was muted throughout our interview, even when discussing intense subjects (e.g., when a teenage boy attempted to rape her, when a man pointed a gun at her when she was eight years old—while visiting her father—and when she spoke of Louise using a belt and a hanger to punish her). When I asked her about her feelings, she said, "I've never been much of a crier when it comes down to my case. I didn't cry when dad died or when my grandparents died." To reinforce the point, she said, "I was used to losing people. It was normal to me." She seemed dissociated, and like many kids who adopt a strategy of dissociation, Maria said of her relationships, "I am not trusting of people close to me because they come and go, but I am okay with strangers."

The poor quality of care Maria experienced during infancy and early childhood was due to poor parenting. Her father neglected her to the point that she had animal bite marks when "rescued" by her mother from his "care." As for her mother, her problems with substance abuse were the cause of her absence from Maria's life in the first place and certainly would have compromised her ability to serve as an effective parent had she been present. Her mother's problems led her to give up custody of Maria once she had taken her from her father. That was how she ended up in the care of Louise and Tom H.

Louise and Tom made no bones about telling Maria that her biological parents were both "losers." They harped on the fact that her father was a drug dealer who died under mysterious circumstances when Maria was ten. Her mother was lost to the world of substance abuse. As if that wasn't enough, Maria was told that she was conceived via the rape of her mother by her father. Finally, Maria was biracial but living in an all-white community and in an adoptive family that made no secret of their racism. It came as no surprise to me that she dealt with her life through a chronic habit of dissociation and ambivalent attachment. Both of these "risk factors" for successful relationships came to fruition during adolescence as very serious issues with identity, socio-emotional immaturity, and depression. These problems, coupled with the cognitive and emotional issues common to adolescence, set the stage for her involvement in the plot to murder her adoptive parents.

Maria H. was convicted by a jury of first-degree murder (of Louise), attempted murder (of Tom), and conspiracy to commit murder. Under the law in effect at the time, the court imposed a mandatory sentence of life without parole. None of her powerfully mitigating factors was presented to the court at the time of her initial trial. From looking at the record and being informed of the larger social environment in which she was convicted and sentenced, it seems clear that her defense attorney was weak—both in the sense that he was cowed by the cozy relationship between the prosecutor and the judge, and in the sense that he himself had no understanding or compassion for what Maria's life had been like. Ten years later, in response to the *Miller v. Alabama* decision, the trial court was ordered to hear the case for mitigation—and possible resentencing. Maria's case was taken up by a juvenile law clinic sponsored by the state's elite law school, and they arranged for me to testify at the hearing.

On one side was the team from the university—law school faculty and staff whose appointments included the juvenile law clinic as part of their responsibilities. With them were a group of earnest young law students, most of whom idealistically looked forward to legal careers emphasizing "social justice" in one form or another. I had met the lead attorney from the juvenile law clinic several years earlier and can attest that he is as good-hearted a lawyer as any that ever walked into a courtroom seeking justice for his client. In short, these were the "good guys"—warm, compassionate, and smart to boot. On the other side stood the local prosecutor, his assistant, and the judge. They were the same team that had originally tried, convicted, and sentenced Maria.

Under the guidance of the lead defense attorney, I offered my developmental analysis of Maria's life up to the point where she engineered the terrible crime that resulted in the death of her adoptive mother and the near fatal assault on her adoptive father. When he cross-examined me, the prosecutor's questions were dripping with sarcasm as he disputed the developmental significance of Maria's early life experience, even suggesting that I was "defaming" the good name of her dead father, that her adoptive parents were saints, and that Maria was just a "spoiled bitch."

When it was his turn for redirect questioning, Maria's lawyer tried to correct the distortions of fact introduced by the prosecutor's questioning. This included information about the troubled relationship of her adoptive parents, that Maria had been traumatized as a child and had suffered through a serious identity crisis and mental health problems as a teenager, and that her biological father had a long criminal record as a drug dealer and was most likely murdered in a drug-related crime.

Then it really got ugly. In open court, the prosecutor turned to the group of law students who were sitting in the second row and addressed them directly, saying that the defense counsel should be ashamed of themselves for even bringing this matter to court. He said that these "professors" were disgraceful human beings, that the students could learn nothing of value from them, and that they should all go "back where they belong" and never come into "his" courtroom again.

Remarkably, the judge allowed this, and then, after testimony was completed, quickly reimposed Maria's sentence of life without the possibility of parole. While extreme, this demonstration of ego-driven miscarriage of justice is not unique. It is always an issue when prosecutors and judges have a personal stake in the validity of the very sentences that *Miller v. Alabama* called into question.

It takes a big person to admit that he or she was wrong, and in the criminal justice system, it seems to me, such people are all too often in short supply, despite the ethical obligation that accrues to being a prosecutor or judge. As Ronald Miller and Brent Turvey put it in their excellent contribution to an ethical handbook for attorneys,

> Post-conviction, prosecutors have an ethical, and sometimes legal duty. . . . They must be open to the examination and testing of newly discovered evidence; have the character to reconsider findings and decisions in the light of any new evidence test results; and be willing to admit mistakes when they have been made.

However, sitting in court for *Miller* resentencing hearings, either awaiting my turn to testify or listening to the testimony of other witnesses, I often wonder about the motivation of the prosecutors who reaffirm the state's position on sentencing, and the judges who are asked to weigh the evidence presented by the two sides. Setting aside the issue of giving life sentences to juveniles in the first place (dealt with in chapter 3), I find myself asking two tough questions: Why do the prosecutors so often and so fiercely argue against resentencing? And why do judges reject the defense's data regarding the rehabilitation, transformation, and redemption of their clients?

As I said in chapter 3, some of their motivation is philosophical, moral, or religious in nature. In the wake of the Supreme Court decisions that invalidated the death penalty for juvenile killers, they may have accepted the decision that "an eye for an eye" cannot be applied to juveniles, but they have yet to disengage from the proposition of "a life for a life." This is *their* truth, and any truth about the convicted killer's life—presented in mitigation of the crime and in developmental analysis of who the killer has become since the crime—often seems to be dismissed as irrelevant. I know it sounds a bit naive (particularly after participating in more than forty *Miller* resentencing cases), but sometimes I just don't get it, this unwillingness to search for the truth of rehabilitation in the lives of Miller's Children. That's why I think there is more to it than moral, philosophical, and religious objections.

For a start, there are certain cognitive issues that stimulate prosecutors to dismiss positive evidence of rehabilitation and to embrace evidence of recalcitrance. Young or old, people don't make "rational" decisions as rationally as we, and they, might like to think. Even a quick reading of research on this topic—for example, the extensive review provided in 1993 by Scott Plous—confirms this. Unconscious forces can influence powerfully the range of behavior an individual may choose. For example, research on what psychologists call "confirmation bias" reveals that most people will continue to "choose" to behave consistently with a position toward which they are predisposed, even when the empirical evidence before them is inconsistent with that hypothesis or is so mixed that no conclusion can be drawn objectively.

For example, a study conducted by Charles Lord and colleagues found that when proponents and opponents of the death penalty were given brief descriptions comparing murder rates in states with and without the death penalty, they were inclined to shift a bit in the direction of the study's conclusion. However, when the researchers followed up with a more detailed description of the studies, almost all the participants returned to their original belief, regardless of the evidence presented. How did they do this? They focused on details that supported their original belief and disregarded contrary evidence in the data. They discounted the validity of methods and results that ran counter to their original belief and embraced methods and data that supported it. Prosecutors (and, in many cases, the family members of victims) are prone to this in their efforts to oppose resentencing hearings. Of course, the same might be said of those on the other side who argue *for* Miller's Children. We must guard against that same impulse toward confirmation bias.

I think that beyond these cognitive processing problems, there are issues of ego and self-interest involved. The self-interest is partly political in nature. One of the more effective ways to invalidate someone in an American election (be it for district attorney, judge, member of Congress, or even president) is to paint them as "soft on crime." If there is one area in which most

Americans demand "toughness" in public servants, it is in their dealings with crime and criminals.

In an interview after the publication of the report "Life Goes On," Ashley Nellis, a senior research analyst with The Sentencing Project and the report's author, argued that the large and increasing number of prisoners serving life sentences has to do with political posturing over "tough on crime" measures. "Unfortunately, lifers are typically excluded from most sentencing reform conversations because there's this sense that it's not going to sell, politically or with the public," Nellis said. "Legislators are saying, 'We have to throw somebody under the bus.'"

Even in the twenty-first century, when the mistaken hysteria of the "super-predator" scare of the early 1990s has been shown to have been bogus, anyone who argues for "getting tough" and for treating teenage killers as "monsters" appears to be on solid cultural ground in the United States. But I think there is more to it than just overt political self-interest. I think there are issues of personal ego involved as well.

The scorn, sarcasm, and vitriol that have come my way in court when I have presented my analysis of rehabilitated teenage killers in *Miller* resentencing hearings are intense. They are there in the initial trial, of course, even in death penalty cases—but somewhat muted, I think, by the recognition that the best outcome possible for the defendant is life in prison (usually without the possibility of parole). Thus, death penalty hearings are, in a sense, a win-win situation for all but the most bloodthirsty of prosecutors. Much as they would like a verdict of "fry the bastard" whenever they can get it, life without parole is often palatable to them.

Of course, when death sentences are appealed it is a different matter. Then, there is always the implicit or explicit message that the first trial got it wrong—usually because of "inadequate representation" on the part of defense counsel (which can include ineffective expert testimony) or some form of explicit or implicit prosecutorial misconduct. When I testify in such cases, I usually feel the heat from prosecutors who are invested in the correctness of the death-penalty verdict, and they don't want to give it up easily. Often it seems to be very personal for them, because beyond any issue of inadequate representation by the defense is the implicit argument that the prosecution should not have sought the death penalty in the first place. Thus, when the sentence is appealed, they seem to take it as a personal affront—and they take an altered sentence as a professional rebuke. This makes sense to me as a psychologist: they are emotionally invested in the fruits of their legal labor, and to have those fruits challenged in court feels like a personal repudiation to them as people.

Miller cases seem to take this even further. Why? I think some of it has to do with the fact that for a resentencing decision to remove the automatic life-without-parole sentence opens the door to either life *with* parole or a fixed term (which often includes time off for good behavior, or "gain time" as it is often called). There is a sense in which this may force the prosecutor and judge to do more than simply violate their "life for a life" moral code with respect to young killers. It may be tantamount to telling them in open court, and in the court of public opinion (that is, in the mass media), that they were wrong in the first place. It may have been ten, twenty, thirty, or more years ago that the case was tried. The sentence may have been legally mandated by the statute in effect at the time. It may actually have been a colleague or a predecessor who was "wrong," but it nonetheless was a wrong in which each prosecutor and judge has his (or her) nose rubbed by the decision of the Supreme Court in *Miller v. Alabama* (and the follow-up decisions such as *Montgomery v. Louisiana* and *Tatum v. Arizona*). This, I think, is a significant source of the ego-driven anger I see and hear at resentencing hearings on the part of the prosecutors who examine and cross-examine witnesses (including me). The judges are generally more circumspect, of course, more "judicial," but I doubt they are always immune to these same ego-driven feelings about admitting that the original decision was a mistake, at least from the perspective of developmental psychology.

The case of Adolfo Davis (briefly noted in chapter 1) provides a stark example of the range of possibilities from the judicial perspective. In this first *Miller* resentencing case in the state of Illinois, Judge Angela Petrone heard the evidence and then promptly resentenced Davis to life without the possibility of parole. In a very interesting turn of events, a retired judge, Abner Mikva, actually testified *on behalf of Davis*. After Petrone's verdict was rendered, Mikva spoke to the press, saying, "This was a mockery of a hearing. This was not what [the Supreme court case] *Miller* was supposed to do, and she embarrasses my profession." I agree, but I am still positively stunned by his candor. As the press report concluded, "Davis' attorneys plan to appeal the judge's decision. In the meantime, Davis will be transferred back to prison." Davis is not alone in that—either in the decision or in the mockery.

There are exceptions, of course. In a highly publicized case in Florida in which I was involved, judge and prosecutor came together with the defense attorney to negotiate the release of thirty-nine-year-old Floyd Lafountain after twenty-two years in prison. (Note that I use Floyd's real name here, because of how highly publicized the case was and how successful the outcome). The judge, Chet Tharpe, resentenced Floyd to the twenty-two years he had already served (and added on fifteen years of probation). Of course, this was an "easy" case: sixteen-year-old Floyd had been involved in the robbery that led to the murder but had not pulled the trigger (making this a "felony murder" case), had more than a decade of exemplary behavior leading up to his release, and had been accepted into a highly regarded, faith-based transitional program to support his post-release adjustment to life on the outside. But there are positive examples to be found even in "hard" cases (where the individual being resentenced actually did the killing).

For example, when a new district attorney entered Dennis D.'s case, thirty years after the initial sentencing (see chapter 3), he brought with him a new openness to seeing Dennis for who he had become since he committed murder at age sixteen. To the delighted shock of both Dennis and his attorney, this new prosecutor was sympathetic to Dennis and what he had accomplished as he changed from a sixteen-year-old killer to a forty-six-year-old exemplary human being. To prepare for the upcoming resentencing hearing, the new DA drove three hours to visit with Dennis and arrived with a positive stance and an open mind. Here's what Dennis wrote to me after that meeting:

> OMG!! I should probably wait to send this because I'm still trying to wrap my brain around what just happened but in a word: AMAZING!! My horoscope read today: "A few well-chosen words could make the difference between selling your idea and going back to the drawing board. You are capable of disarming your harshest critic." An hour after seeing that I met with the new DA for 2 hours. He thanked me for the way I have served my time and asked me: "What are you going to do when you get out?" The other DAs want to talk to him as the hearing gets closer. They will undoubtedly give him an earful about the crime, but he appears to have no interest in discussing any of that. Over all, I think it could not have been better. I think he made up his mind long ago that I should not be in prison any longer and intends to say something along those lines. He had a few things he wanted to talk to me about related to the crime, but I think he just wanted to be sure he addressed those issues so they couldn't say he didn't. He did make two or three pages of notes, but it was clear that he's interested in rehabilitation, change and the future. I am stunned speechless. This feels like a dream.

But four months later, when Dennis had his hearing, even this positive district attorney reverted to form. His statement to the court contained little of the positive attitude toward Dennis that had been there in his conversations with me over the phone and with Dennis and his attorney in person. Instead, he toed the party line and while he did acknowledge the progress Dennis had made, his tone was grudging, not enthusiastic. In my testimony at the hearing, I said that no one I had ever met had transformed and rehabilitated so fully and so beautifully as Dennis. I was joined by a long list of volunteers and professionals who had known Dennis over the years. Nonetheless, it seemed that the political connections of the victim's family (who spoke at the hearing) carried more weight: three months after the hearing, the court issued its ruling, and the original life sentence was reaffirmed. Hopes were dashed, but Dennis found a way to crawl back into a place of light and wisdom, which only served to emphasize how despicable the court's ruling was.

BOYS OR MEN: WHY STOP AT EIGHTEEN?

August 24, 2016

Dear Dr. Garbarino:

I write to you in the concern that you may be able to give me some information that I am seeking on raising the legal age of juveniles over 18 years of age. I was told by someone here at the prison that you told him that you all were trying to do something for those who were over 18 years old at the time of their crime. As I was 18 when I was arrested and have spent over 21 years in prison since my arrest in 1995 this would greatly affect me and others like me. I was a very immature and physically and mentally abused juvenile with a very low education of around sixth grade who was for years in slow learning disability classes. My time in prison has been greatly used to transform me into someone who has not only received a GED, vocational and college degrees, along with a spiritual transformation with remorse, compassion and a greater love of Christ, but one who had dedicated myself into being someone who Society can benefit from. A leader, speaker and a facilitator/mentor for the youth. Please, I humbly ask you [to] assist me in finding and obtaining any and all information of raising the legal age of juveniles. May God bless you! Sincerely,

James L.

My concern with Miller's Children goes beyond the cases for which the Supreme Court mandated resentencing hearings, in two directions. First, it includes juveniles who are given *discretionary* sentences of life without parole. They should be included in the ranks of those who received mandatory sentences of life without parole. But my concern does not stop there. It includes eighteen- and nineteen-year-olds (and perhaps even offenders into their early twenties) who are tried automatically as adults because they have crossed over the legal "bright line" between minors (which they were until the last day of their seventeenth year of life) and adults (which they became on the day of their eighteenth birthday). These adolescents may have been sentenced to life without parole, but they are *not* eligible for resentencing under the *Miller v. Alabama* ruling.

They constitute an important though mostly invisible population, because no matter what they do, their prospects for release are extremely remote. They can be pardoned or have their sentences commuted—usually by their state's governor. However, this has become more and more rare, according to a 2013 analysis by Maggie Clark, who found that the political consequences (accusations of being soft on crime) usually outweigh the benefits (being seen as compassionate) and are mostly limited to criminals other than killers.

How many prisoners are serving life without the possibility of parole in the United States? According to an analysis conducted by The Sentencing Project, published in the report by Ashley Nellis mentioned above, here are the facts:

> As of 2012, there were 159,520 people serving life sentences, an 11.8% rise since 2008. One of every nine individuals in prison is serving a life sentence. The population of prisoners serving life without parole (LWOP) has risen more sharply than those with the possibility of parole: there has been a 22.2% increase in LWOP since just 2008, an increase from 40,1745 individuals to 49,081. Approximately 10,000 lifers have been convicted of nonviolent offenses. Nearly half of lifers are African American and 1 in 6 are Latino. More than 10,000 life-sentenced inmates have been convicted of crimes that occurred before they turned 18 and nearly 1 in 4 of them were sentenced to LWOP. More than 5,300 (3.4%) of the life-sentenced inmates are female.

I can only assume that in the four years since this report was compiled and issued, the numbers have held steady or gone up.

As can be seen from these data, the *Miller v. Alabama* decision deals with a fraction of a fraction of the country's lifers—those who were younger than eighteen *and* received a mandatory life-without-parole sentence. Perhaps

7,500 individuals received discretionary life-without-parole sentences—what about them? And what about the even larger number of individuals who received sentences of life without parole for murders (and other crimes) committed *after* they turned eighteen?

State laws set eighteen as the upper limit of what it means to be a minor for legal purposes in the criminal justice system. Thus, killers who have turned eighteen are everywhere defined as men (or women) rather than boys (or girls). The FBI reports that of the fifteen thousand murders that typically occur in the United States each year, only about 2 percent are committed by kids thirteen to sixteen, while about 10 percent are committed by seventeen- to nineteen-year-olds, and 17 percent by those twenty to twenty-four years of age. Of the killers whose cases I have come to know (and whose stories are told in my book *Listening to Killers*), many were in the eighteen-to–twenty-four age range that accounts for more than one in four murders. All were legal adults, as much as if they had been in their thirties (the group that commits 24 percent of all murders). But were they really adults? Were they lost boys or lost men?

I have had some wrangles in court on this point of when older adolescents and younger youths are best thought of as "boys" or as "men." In the case of Jacquon J. in the late 1990s, during the prosecutor's cross-examination he sarcastically commented on my use of the term "lost boy" when I referred to the nineteen-year-old defendant. "Isn't he really a man?" he asked rhetorically. I replied that given the trauma and social deprivation that Jacquon experienced growing up, he was psychologically immature, as were many so-called "young adults" like him—impulsive, socially inexperienced beyond the toxic world of the inner-city, drug-fueled gang culture in which he lived . . . and killed. But more than that, as a nineteen-year-old, he was still years away from the developmental time when brains mature (at age twenty-six, on average). Thus, to my mind he *was* a lost boy. They all are.

In another case, the state's psychologist (who admitted in cross-examination that the sum total of his expertise in developmental psychology was "a course I took in graduate school") argued that since the defendant in the case had been seventeen-and-a-half at the time of the crime, the *Miller* principles didn't really apply to him. When I testified, I argued that he had gotten it exactly upside down, because the trend was not to push the *Miller* principles chronologically down, as he was trying to do, but rather "up" to include eighteen- and nineteen-year-olds, if not individuals in their early twenties. Indeed, legislation passed in California to amend the penal code (sections

3051 and 4801) in 2015 requires that parole boards apply the *Miller* principles up to age twenty-three.

Certainly, eighteen- and nineteen-year-olds are kids, not adults. I say this both as a developmental psychologist and as a father whose children are in their thirties and forties. The World Health Organization defines *adolescence* as extending to age nineteen. This alone would prevent Jacquon J., James L. (who wrote the letter at the beginning of this section), and many of the young killers I have interviewed from being classified automatically as adults. It's also worth noting that the United Nations cultural organization, UNESCO, defines *youth* as the period between ages fifteen and twenty-four, which makes greater developmental sense than our current laws. Were this more scientifically defensible age range to be integrated into our laws, nearly 30 percent of all killers (those in the range from thirteen to twenty-four) would fall into this category. And yet, from the perspective of the criminal justice system, all but the thirteen- to seventeen-year-olds are fully adult. That's not even taking into account the fact that many, if not most, of the kids in the thirteen- to seventeen-year-old range are treated as adults in the criminal justice system if they commit a murder.

This situation is just plain wrong, and fixing it is an important item on any scientifically based social justice agenda. This is an important area for future work, and those of us who think so are a rising chorus that includes some judges. For example, in December 2015, in overturning the mandatory life-without-parole sentence imposed on Antonio House, the Illinois Supreme Court ruled that the same principles that provided the foundation for the *Miller v. Alabama* decision can and should be applied to nineteen-year-olds. There is hope, and that hope sustains efforts to reconsider the sentences of James L. and thousands of others like him. Amen to that.

TEENAGE KILLERS HAVE A RIGHT TO TREATMENT AND A SPIRITUAL PATH

For more than thirty years, courts have asserted that juveniles in the custody of the state are entitled to treatment. According to an analysis published in the *Virginia Law Review,* the 1974 case of *Nelson v. Heyne* was a landmark in validating this position. The case, which resulted from a class action suit brought on behalf of juvenile inmates at a detention program in Indiana, hinged on the idea of a right to treatment. This is the logical extension of what has happened so far as a result of the *Miller v. Alabama* decision—which, I argue, demands a comprehensive focus on rehabilitation at the core of prison policy and practice (while at the same time securely holding inmates like the boys and men I described in chapter 5, who are too damaged to "get better").

The tension between a juvenile's right to treatment and the right to be protected from unjust incarceration is complicated, as Martin Gardner's 2016 analysis makes clear. Gardner summarizes the legal and policy implications of *Graham v. Florida* and *Miller v. Alabama* thus:

> That juvenile offenders are now entitled to: (1) systematically less punishment than that imposed on adults committing the same offenses; (2) a robust individualized presentencing hearing, taking into account, among other things, the offender's amenability to rehabilitation; (3) a disposition in the juvenile system if, at the pre-sentencing hearing, the offender is deemed to be amenable to rehabilitation and the juvenile system affords the best opportunity for its realization; and (4) a sentence offering a realistic possibility for rehabilitation and parole if the offender is deemed not amenable to rehabilitation at the presentencing hearing.

Working this out in practice is quite a challenge, given the punitive attitudes of many legislators and policy makers in the criminal justice system.

Hanging over all these matters is the issue of whether dangerous individuals can be detained and required to undergo treatment. This issue is thoroughly explored in a 2007 analysis by Edward Ra, in the context of the Supreme Court's ruling in the case of *Seling v. Young*. This case challenged a state law permitting civil confinement and mandatory treatment for sex offenders—perhaps the most thorny problem in the field of assessment and treatment because of the very high rate of recidivism among these offenders, as reported in study after study. This is especially true of psychopaths involved in sexual violence—25 percent rearrested for a new violent offense during the first year after release and 90 percent by twenty years (compared with 40 percent of those scoring low on the measure of psychopathy), according to Kiehl and Hoffman (see chapter 5).

My point in raising this issue here is to emphasize that my entire discussion of the developmentally appropriate length of sentences for juvenile murderers can run up against legal principles, policies, and precedents that argue against "indeterminate" sentences. Many legal commentators are suspicious of (and even hostile to) the idea that a juvenile's need for time to experience brain maturation, in order to establish a foundation for treatment and transformation that can result in "safe" rehabilitation, should take precedence over the "facts of their crime." Of course, as I have argued in court many times, for most adolescents, the facts of the crime (e.g., its severity) are mostly *developmentally irrelevant,* in that they do not predict long-term developmental outcomes. These facts are generally irrelevant to the prognosis for rehabilitation and transformation (perhaps the one exception being the assaults committed by chronic sexual predators). I think that the logic of indeterminate sentencing for adolescent murderers leads inevitably to an assertion of the *right* of teenage killers to state-of-the-art treatment for their issues.

Miller's Children themselves often have a profound understanding of this. Perhaps no one captured this better than Martin I., in a letter I received from him in September 2016, on the thirtieth anniversary of the triple murder he committed as a teenager. I had met Martin when I visited his prison and sat with him and a group of his peers for more than three hours in August 2016. I quote from his letter at length here because I think it lays out the agenda for us all in our response to Miller's Children.

Reflecting on the impact of the *Montgomery v. Louisiana* decision in 2015 (which extended *Miller v. Alabama* retroactively across the country), Martin I. wrote this in a letter to me:

> The Court held *Miller* is retroactive. The Court's decision went as far as to identify parole proceedings as a viable means to comply with the Eighth Amendment's ban on mandatory Juvenile Life. This small point suggests that collateral post-conviction proceedings are not the only means by which juveniles can contest their sentences. Civil rights suits might get them there. The Court's decision also brings up another question. If youth offenders are capable of reform and if they must be given a meaningful opportunity to demonstrate such reform, then what obligation does the state have to provide conditions in which youth may develop into healthy adults? If the conditions of confinement, in other words, impede a youth offender's development and maturation (their reform, so to speak), then are there grounds under the Eighth Amendment to challenge (change) state prison systems? My wheels are spinning.

Mine too.

To be incarcerated is to face the essentials of the human condition, stripped of psychically comforting illusions and the delusions of material comfort. This is what the late Buddhist teacher Bo Lozoff advocated in his 1998 book on cultivating the spiritual path, *We're All Doing Time,* and why he subtitled it "A Guide to Getting Free." For some it is "hard time," while for others it is "easy time," but we *are* all doing time, whether behind bars or not. Wherever we are, Lozoff's guide to meditative practice as a strategy for enlightenment is useful and wise.

It is for this reason, I think, that those who are incarcerated must, to some degree, choose between two paths. One is to live as a savage barbarian, in the sense of Thomas Hobbes's definition of human life as "nasty, brutish, and short." The other is to live like a monk, taking the spiritual path of mindfulness, contemplation, reflection, education, and service—whether it be inside or outside of prison. I don't mean to trivialize the enormous difference between living a life behind bars versus "in the world," but it's vitally important to understand that in an important sense, we're all doing time—it is just a matter of what kind of time we are doing and where.

In a *Miller* hearing recently, John L., a released ex-con who had served twenty-nine years in prison, spoke movingly of how he came to travel the path of a monk in prison. He was reading a book by Thich Nhat Hanh about Buddhist mindfulness and was feeling frustrated, to the point that he called out to his cellmate Larry, who had given him the book, "How am I supposed to do this. You would have to be a monk to live this way!" His cellmate replied, "John, you are living as a monk!" The message was clear and forceful, and it "took." Eight years after that conversation, John was released on "lifetime parole," and now he was back in prison testifying on behalf of Larry's resentencing. When the prosecutor asked John how confident he was that Larry would succeed if he were released, John replied, "I am sure enough to bet my parole on it, and sir, I am not a betting man."

A spiritual path can reinforce other rehabilitative resources. Dennis D.'s life in prison is notable in four respects. First, he was able to avoid some of the most traumatic experiences associated with incarceration for a juvenile, namely sexual and physical assault. Adolescents who are subjected to the trauma of violent sexual assault are likely to develop rage and/or social withdrawal that damages them psychologically and disinclines them from taking advantage of the opportunities for educational and social improvement that may be available. Second, Dennis had access to therapeutic resources that were invaluable in helping him deal with the underlying emotional issues that were linked to his substance abuse and delinquent behavior; those resources, in turn, paved the way for taking advantage of educational and social development programs during his incarceration. Third, Dennis had the ongoing support of his mother (who was a positive influence on his life throughout childhood and continued to be supportive even during his adolescent delinquent phase). And fourth, he received the grace of being considered worthy by a priest, and thus started upon a spiritual path.

Dennis has come to a mature appreciation of spirituality and has "lived it," in particular in his service work on behalf of the prison's hospice program, where he was a long-term volunteer until he was moved to another correctional facility that did not have a hospice program. He writes to me often about how he has found meaning and a "positive place to stand in the Universe" even when confronted with setbacks. As I mentioned in chapter 4, Buddhism has been a source of comfort and guidance for him.

As someone who has become familiar with Buddhism (including some of the texts that influenced Dennis), I can attest to its power to stimulate and support transformation, and I find it quite consonant with the Jesuit approach to spirituality. Father William Watson has explored this consonance in his excellent book *Sacred Story*. Ignatian spirituality, like the practice of Buddhist mindfulness, can provide a basis for stabilizing emotions and promoting prosocial behavior. Both accomplish this, in part, through "nonattachment," the letting go that so many find liberating, whether they are inside or outside prison walls. Father Watson's rendering of the Ignatian spiritual exercises and the process of introspection and prayer that Ignatians call the "Examen" provide a blueprint for anyone in need of guidance. No one needs this blueprint more than Miller's Children, of course, and this is one reason why Father Watson's work has been extended to prisons.

Aided by therapeutic intervention and spiritual guidance, Dennis chose to be a monk and a student. His study and practice of Buddhism—including meditation—has provided him with the spiritual and psychological resources necessary to live as a monk and reap the benefits of that "lifestyle" choice in prison. His experience working in the prison hospice program has crystallized these developments. But in this, as in other aspects of his life in prison, he often had to fight with and against prison policies, practices, and personalities that violated his right to treatment. This fight has included litigation at various points over the past three decades. Imagine! An inmate seeking support for rehabilitation and transformation had to contest legally with the authorities who were supposed to provide the resources he needed. That's why we need a clearly expressed national commitment to a "right to treatment" for all teenage killers.

In any case, the result of the four major positive aspects of Dennis D.'s incarceration is that he presented himself at his hearing as a mature man with a lot of positive educational and social experiences in his portfolio, and with the fruits of effective long-term contemplation, education, and spiritual development—*not* as an angry, traumatized, oppositional, and uneducated individual. He was truly a "child of God."

In her masterful exploration of *The Case for God,* religious scholar Karen Armstrong concluded that the foundation for all religion is a process of coming to a silent encounter with the infinite absolute. It is only then, in the silent awe of contemplating the universe directly, that insight into the fundamental nature of reality arises. It is the translation of this silent insight into words that is the essence of religion. Can prison be a good place to accomplish this? Yes and no.

Sit meditating for forty days and forty nights (as did Jesus) or sit meditating under the Bodhi tree (as did the Buddha) or sit alone in the desert (as did Muhammad) or go up to the top of the mountain (as did Moses), and a human being can catch a glimmer of the divine. Inevitably, the human words—and dogma, practices, and policies—that flow from this silent encounter with the divine are imperfect, because human beings are themselves imperfect and not "divine." But they can live good lives in response to that glimmer of the divine. Pope Francis captures this from a Christian perspective when he endorses the way his namesake, Saint Francis of Assisi, approached Christian religious teaching: "Preach the Gospel at all times, and when necessary use words."

It is in the implementation of universal love and awe in the face of the universe that religions are born. But the more they focus on "the word" rather than "the silence," the more religions are prone to go astray and move from spirituality to religious orthodoxy and dogma. I think of this when I listen to guys in prison talk about their reading of the Bible or the Koran. For some, it is the kind of literalism against which both Pope Francis and Karen Armstrong warn, a focus on the word rather than the spirit. For others, it becomes the gateway to a spiritual life. Those who walk through that gateway are on the path to rehabilitation and transformation. I believe they have a fundamental right to walk that pathway, a right to treatment of the highest order, a path that gives them a spiritual place to stand in the universe.

POSTSCRIPT: THEN AND NOW

Sergio Z. is a "classic" *Miller* case. At age fourteen, he shot and killed a motel clerk while robbing the front desk in broad daylight. The security video shows that the desk clerk offered no resistance; he was handing over the money when Sergio shot him once in the chest. High on the drug Ecstasy at the time, Sergio was exhibiting classic teenage behavior. The crime for which he was sentenced is a classic illustration of the kind of impulsive and stupid behavior that flows from the limitations of adolescent thinking and action, problems that are compounded by youths who have not been adequately cared for and raised by prosocial adults.

When I asked Sergio about his crime as we sat across from each other in 2016, he told me, "Everything was fuzzy. The only thing I really remember is him looking to the side. And then I shot him. The gun shot. I wasn't in my right mind." It would appear that Sergio took the clerk's "looking to the side" as somehow threatening. As he now recognizes, it was "stupid." But that is the point: adolescent brains are particularly stupid when they are on drugs and faced with emotionally intense situations coupled with ambiguous social cues.

At the time of the shooting, Sergio was at a point in his development when the area of the brain involved in regulating the intensity of sensation (the nucleus accumbens) reaches its peak (declining after mid-adolescence and into adulthood). As I have noted previously, the research of developmental psychologist Laurence Steinberg and others demonstrates that in mid-adolescence, *everything* feels more intense than it does before or after. But there is more. Beyond their heightened emotional sensitivity, teenagers like Sergio are likely to have difficulty accurately assessing others' emotions as well as their own. This is well established in research on adolescent brain development (of the sort that figured prominently in the Supreme Court's decision in *Miller v. Alabama*). In this sense, there is nothing particularly special about Sergio's case. Similarly, a review of his social history reveals a very common pattern in *Miller* cases:

Mis-socialization (in his case, criminals abounding in his extended family)

Gang involvement (by age thirteen, he was involved in the local branch of the Crips and actively participating in drug sales)

Parental rejection and abuse (a psychologically unavailable father and a troubled mother whose beatings left scars)

Difficulty in school (although bright, he was bored and there were hints of ADHD in his records)

Compensatory substance abuse (starting at age twelve and continuing to the day he became a teenage killer)

Classic *Miller* material, but with one exception: *Sergio committed his crime in 2015, after the Supreme Court had rendered its decision in Miller v. Alabama.* As a result, he is not one of the 125-member "lost tribe" of Miller's Children in his state. Had he committed his crime ten or twenty years earlier, he would be. But now he is not.

The judge in his case heard the mitigating evidence in my report to the court, as he was now required to do. He appreciated that *who Sergio is now does not determine who he can become in the future*—ten years from now, when his brain is mature, or twenty years from now, when he may have undergone the same process of rehabilitation and transformation that many other teenage killers have. Recognizing this, the judge imposed a life sentence with the possibility of parole after twenty years. As a result, there is hope for Sergio, and because there is hope for him there is hope for America.

As nineteenth-century Unitarian clergyman Theodore Parker wrote, "I do not pretend to understand the moral universe; the arc is a long one, my eye reaches but little ways; I cannot calculate the curve and complete the figure by the experience of sight; I can divine it by conscience. And from what I see I am sure it bends towards justice." Or as Martin Luther King Jr. put it more than a century later, "The arc of the moral universe is long, but it bends toward justice." I fervently hope so. Amen.

REFERENCES

ACLU (2016) False hope: How parole systems fail youth serving extreme sentences. www.aclu.org/feature/false-hope-how-parole-systems-fail-youth-serving-extreme-sentences?redirect = falsehope.

Albert, D., Chein, J., and Steinberg, L. (2013) Peer influences on adolescent decision making. *Current Directions in Psychological Science, 22,* 114–120.

Armstrong, K. (2009) *The Case for God.* New York: Knopf.

Arnet, J. (2014) *Emerging Adulthood: The Winding Road from the Late Teens.* New York: Oxford University Press.

Babiak, P., and Hare, R. (2007) *Snakes in Suits: When Psychopaths Go to Work.* New York: HarperCollins.

Baglivio, M., Epps, N., Swartz, K., Huq, M., Sheer, A., and Hardt, N. (2014) The prevalence of adverse childhood experiences (ACE) in the lives of juvenile offenders. *Journal of Justice, 3*(2).

Barron, I., and Mitchell, D. (in press) Adolescents in secure accommodation: Exposure and impact of traumatic events. *Journal of Aggression Maltreatment and Trauma.*

Baumeister, R. (1999) *Evil: Inside Human Violence and Cruelty.* New York: Henry Holt.

Benson, P., Roehlkepartain, E., and Hong, K. (Eds.) (2008) *Spiritual Development: New Directions for Youth Development.* St. Paul, MN: Search Institute.

Bettelheim, B. (1943) Individual and mass behavior in extreme situations. *Journal of Abnormal and Social Psychology, 38,* 417–452.

Blair, R., Leibenluft, E., and Pine, D. (2014) Conduct disorder and callous-emotional traits in youth. *New England Journal of Medicine, 371,* 2207–2212.

Bronfenbrenner, U. (1979) *The Ecology of Human Development.* Cambridge, MA: Harvard University Press.

Bryant, F., Garbarino, J., Hart, S., and McDowell, K. (in press) The child's right to a spiritual life. In B. Natasi and S. Hart (Eds.), *The International Handbook of Child's Rights and School Psychology.* New York: Springer.

Bryant, F., and Veroff, J. (2006) *Savoring: A New Model of Positive Experience.* New York: Psychology Press.

Caldwell, M., and Van Rybroek, G. (2001) Efficacy of a decompression treatment model in the clinical management of violent juvenile offenders. *International Journal of Offender Therapy and Comparative Criminology, 45,* 469–477.

Caldwell, M., and Van Rybroek, G. (2005) Reducing violence in serious and violent juvenile offenders using an intensive treatment program. *International Journal of Law and Psychiatry, 28,* 622–636.

Cameron, B. (2013) Why does Norway have a 21-year maximum prison sentence? *Slate.* www.slate.com/blogs/quora/2013/05/07/why_does_norway_have_a_21_year_maximum_prison_sentence.html.

Caspi, A., McClay, J., Moffitt, T., Mill, J., Martin, J., Craig, I., et al. (2002) Role of genotype in the cycle of violence in maltreated children. *Science, 297,* 851–854.

Clark, M. (2013) Some states speed up death penalty. www.pewtrusts.org/en/research-and-analysis/blogs/stateline/2013/06/18/some-states-speed-up-death-penalty.

Cunningham, M. (in review) Institutional violence and misconduct. In R. Morgan (Ed.), *The Sage Encyclopedia of Criminal Psychology.* Thousand Oaks, CA: Sage.

DeGruy, J. (2005) *The Post Traumatic Slave Syndrome: America's Legacy of Enduring Injury and Healing.* New York: Joy DeGruy Publications.

DeLisi, M., and Vaughn, M. (2008) The Gottfredson-Hirschi critiques revisited: Reconciling self-control theory, criminal careers, and career criminals. *International Journal of Offender Therapy and Comparative Criminology, 52,* 520–537.

DiIulio, J. (1995) The coming of the super-predators. *Weekly Standard, 1*(11), 23.

Dishion, T., McCord, J., and Poulin, F. (1999) When interventions harm: Peer groups and problem behavior. *American Psychologist, 54,* 755–764.

Doidge, N. (2007) *The Brain That Changes Itself.* New York: Penguin.

Downey, G., and Feldman, S. (1996) Implications of rejection sensitivity in intimate relationships. *Journal of Personality and Social Psychology, 70,* 1327–1343.

Downey, G., Feldman, S., and Ayduk, O. (2000) Rejection sensitivity and male violence in romantic relationships. *Personal Relationships, 7,* 45–61.

Downey, G., Lebolt, A., Rincón, C., and Freitas, A. (1998) Rejection sensitivity and children's interpersonal difficulties. *Child Development, 69,* 1074–1091.

Dunn, E., Uddin, M., Subramanian, S., Smoller, J., Galea, S., and Koenen, K. (2011) Gene-environment interaction (GxE) research in youth depression: A systematic review with recommendations for future research. *Journal of Child Psychology and Psychiatry, 52,* 1223–1238.

Dustin, A., and Steinberg, L. (2011) Age differences in strategic planning as indexed by the Tower of London. *Child Development, 82,* 1501–1517.

Eberhardt, J., and Goff, P. Atiba (2005) Seeing race. In C. Crandall and M. Schaller (Eds.), *Social Psychology of Prejudice: Historical and Contemporary Issues* (pp. 163–183). Seattle, WA: Lewinian Press.

Enright, R., and Fitzgibbons, R. (2014) *Forgiveness Therapy: An Empirical Guide for Resolving Anger and Restoring Hope.* Washington, DC: American Psychological Association.

Erikson, E. (1993) *Childhood and Society.* New York: W.W. Norton.

Fagan, J. et al. amicus brief before the U.S. Supreme Court in the case of Kuntrell Jackson. http://eji.org/.

Fallon, J. (2014) *The Psychopath Inside: A Neuroscientist's Journey into the Dark Side of the Brain*. New York: Penguin.

FalseConfessions.org

Farrington, D., Loeber, R., and Van Kammen, W. (1990) Long-term criminal outcomes of hyperactivity-impulsivity-attention deficit and conduct problems in childhood. In L. Robins and M. Rutter (Eds.), *Straight and Devious Pathways to Adulthood* (pp. 62–81). New York: Cambridge University Press.

Feldman, R., Caplinger, T., and Wodarski, J. (1983) *The St. Louis Conundrum: The Effective Treatment of Antisocial Youths*. Englewood Cliffs, NJ: Prentice-Hall.

Feldman, S., and Downey, G. (1994) Rejection sensitivity as a mediator of the impact of childhood exposure to family violence on adult attachment behavior. *Development and Psychopathology, 6,* 231–247.

Ford, J., and Blaustein, M. (2013) Systemic self-regulation: A framework for trauma-informed services in residential juvenile justice programs. *Journal of Family Violence, 28,* 665–677.

Ford, J., and Hawke, J. (2012) Trauma affect regulation psycho-education group and milieu intervention outcomes in juvenile detention facilities. *Journal of Aggression, Maltreatment & Trauma, 21,* 365–384.

Garbarino, J. (1994) *Raising Children in a Socially Toxic Environment*. San Francisco, CA: Jossey Bass.

Garbarino, J. (1999) *Lost Boys: Why Our Sons Turn Violent and How We Can Save Them*. New York: Free Press.

Garbarino, J. (2008) *Children and the Dark Side of Human Experience*. New York: Springer.

Garbarino, J. (2015) *Listening to Killers: Lessons Learned from My 20 Years as a Psychological Expert Witness in Murder Cases*. Berkeley: University of California Press.

Garbarino, J., Guttman, E., and Seeley, J. (1986) *The Psychologically Battered Child*. San Francisco: Jossey-Bass.

Gardner, M. (2016) Youthful offenders and the Eighth Amendment right to rehabilitation: Limitations on the punishment of juveniles. University of Nebraska College of Law faculty publications. Paper 192. http://digitalcommons.unl.edu/lawfacpub/192.

Gelman, A., Fagan, J., and Kiss, A. (2007) An analysis of the New York City Police Department's "stop-and-frisk" policy in the context of claims of racial bias. *Journal of the American Statistical Association, 102,* 813–823.

Gilligan, J. (1997) *Violence: Reflections on a National Epidemic*. New York: Vintage.

Goffman, E. (1959) *The Presentation of Self in Everyday Life*. New York: Doubleday.

Greenwald, R. (2005) *Child Trauma Handbook: A Guide for Helping Trauma-Exposed Children and Adolescents*. New York: Haworth Press.

Grisso, T., and Kavanaugh, A. (2016) Prospects for developmental evidence in juvenile sentencing based on *Miller v. Alabama. Psychology, Public Policy, and Law, 22*, 235–249.

Grossman, D. (1996) *On Killing: The Psychological Cost of Learning to Kill in War and Society.* Boston: Back Bay Books.

Habib, M., Labruna, V., and Newman, J. (2013) Complex histories and complex presentations: Implementation of a manually-guided group treatment for traumatized adolescents. *Journal of Family Violence, 28*, 717–728.

Haney, C. (2001) The psychological impact of incarceration: Implications for post-release adjustment. http://aspe.hhs.gov/hsp/prison2home02/haney.htm.

Hare, R. (1999) *Without Conscience: The Disturbing World of the Psychopaths among Us.* New York: Guilford Press.

Harris, G., Rice, M., Quinsey, V., and Cormier, C. (2015). *Violent Offenders: Appraising and Managing Risk, 3rd ed.* Washington, DC: American Psychological Association.

Heide, K. (2013) *Understanding Parricide: When Sons and Daughters Kill Parents.* New York: Oxford University Press.

Heide, K., and Solomon, E. (2006) Biology, childhood trauma, and murder: Rethinking justice. *International Journal of Law & Psychiatry, 29*, 220–233.

Heide, K., and Solomon, E. (2009) Female juvenile murderers: Biological and psychological dynamics leading to homicide. *International Journal of Law & Psychiatry, 32*, 244–252.

Heide, K., Spencer, E., Thompson, A., and Solomon, E. (2001) Who's in, who's out, and who's back: Follow-up data on 59 juveniles incarcerated for murder or attempted murder in the early 1980s. *Behavioral Sciences and the Law, 19*, 97–108.

Hirschi, T., and Gottfredson, M. (1983) Age and the explanation of crime. *American Journal of Sociology, 89*, 552–584.

Jakupcak, M., Tull, M., and Roemer, L. (2005) Masculinity, shame, and fear of emotions as predictors of men's expressions of anger and hostility. *Psychology of Men & Masculinity, 6*, 275–284.

Jensen, F. (2014) *The Teenage Brain: A Neuroscientist's Survival Guide to Raising Adolescents and Young Adults.* New York: Harper.

Jessor, R., and Jessor, S. (1977) *Problem Behavior and Psychosocial Development: A Longitudinal Study of Youth.* New York: Academic Press.

Jim, H., Richardson, S., Golden-Kreutz, D., and Andersen, B. (2006) Strategies used in coping with a cancer diagnosis predict meaning in life for survivors. *Health Psychology, 25*, 753–761.

Kellermann, N. (2009) *Holocaust Trauma: Psychological Effects and Treatment.* New York: iUniverse.

Khachatryan, N., Heide, K., and Hummel, E. (in press) Recidivism patterns among two types of juvenile homicide offenders: A 30-year follow-up study. *International Journal of Offender Therapy and Comparative Criminology.*

Khachatryan, N., Heide, K., Hummel, E., and Chan, H. (2016) Juvenile sexual homicide offenders: Thirty-year follow-up investigation. *International Journal of Offender Therapy and Comparative Criminology, 60,* 247–264.

Khachatryan, N., Heide, K., Hummel, E., Ingraham, M., and Rad, J. (2016) Examination of long-term post-release outcomes of juvenile homicide offenders. *Journal of Offender Rehabilitation, 55,* 503–524.

Kiehl, K., and Hoffman, M. (2011) The criminal psychopath: History, neuroscience, treatment, and economics. *Jurimetrics Journal, 51,* 355–397.

Lawler, K., Younger, J., Piferi, R., Jobe, R., Edmondson, K., and Jones, W. (2005) The unique effects of forgiveness on health: An exploration of pathways. *Journal of Behavioral Medicine, 28*(2).

Leopold, N. (1953) *Life Plus 99 Years.* New York: Doubleday.

Leopold, N. (1983) The companionship, the acceptance. *The Brethren Encyclopedia, vol. 2.*

Loeber, R., and Farrington, D. (1998) *Serious and Violent Juvenile Offenders: Risk Factors and Successful Interventions.* New York: Sage.

Loeber, R., and Farringon, D. (2011) *Young Homicide Offenders and Victims: Risk Factors, Prediction, and Prevention.* New York: Springer.

Lord, C., Ross, L., and Lepper, M. (1979) Biased assimilation and attitude polarization: The effects of prior theories on subsequently considered evidence. *Journal of Personality and Social Psychology, 37,* 2098–2109.

Lozoff, B. (1998) *We're All Doing Time: A Guide to Getting Free.* New York: Human Kindness Foundation.

Luhrmann, T., Padmavati, R., Tharoor, H., and Osei, A. (2015) Differences in voice-hearing experiences of people with psychosis in the U.S.A., India and Ghana: Interview-based study. *British Journal of Psychiatry, 206,* 41–44.

Marcia, J., Waterman, A., Mateson, D., Archer, S., and Orlofsky, J. (1993) *Ego Identity: A Handbook for Psychosocial Research.* New York: Springer.

Marrow, M., Knudsen, K., Olafson, E., and Bucher, S. (2012) The value of implementing TARGET within a trauma-informed juvenile justice setting. *Journal of Child & Adolescent Trauma, 5,* 257–270.

Mayo Clinic (2016) Reactive attachment disorder. www.mayoclinic.org /diseases-conditions/reactive-attachment-disorder/basics/definition/CON-20032126.

Miller, R., and Turvey, B. (2013) Ethical issues for criminal prosecutors. In B. Turvey and S. Crowder (Eds.), *Ethical Justice: Applied Issues for Criminal Justice Students and Professionals* (pp. 257–316). New York: Academic Press.

Monahan, K., Steinberg, L., Cauffman, E., and Mulvey, E. (2013) Psychosocial (im)maturity from adolescence to early adulthood: Distinguishing between adolescence-limited and persisting antisocial behavior. *Development and Psychopathology, 25,* 1093–1105.

Moretti, M., Odgers, C., and Jackson, M. (2004) *Girls and Aggression: Contributing Factors and Intervention Principles.* New York: Springer.

Nellis, A. (2013) Life goes on. The Sentencing Project. http://sentencingproject.org/wp-content/uploads/2015/12/Life-Goes-On.pdf.

Newman, K. (2005) *Rampage: The Social Roots of School Shootings.* New York: Basic Books.

Oltmanns, T., and Balsis, S. (2011) Personality disorders in later life: Questions about the measurement course and impact of disorders. *Annual Review of Clinical Psychology, 7,* 321–349.

Parker, T. (1853) Of justice and the conscience. In *Ten Sermons of Religion* (pp. 84–85). Boston: Crosby, Nichols.

Perry, B. (1997) Incubated in terror: Neurodevelopmental factors in the "cycle of violence." In J. Osofsky (Ed.), *Children, Youth and Violence: The Search for Solutions* (pp. 124–148). New York: Guilford Press.

Piacenza, J. (2015) Support for death penalty by religious affiliation. Public Religion Research Institute, April 9. www.prri.org/spotlight/support-for-death-penalty-by-religious-affiliation/#.VaMS__lViko.

Plous, S. (1993) *The Psychology of Judgment and Decision Making.* New York: McGraw-Hill.

Quinsey, V., Harris, G., and Rice, M. (2005) *Violent Offenders: Appraising and Managing Risk (Law and Public Policy), 2nd ed.* Washington, DC: American Psychological Association.

Ra, E. (2007) The civil confinement of sexual predators: A delicate blanace. *Journal of Civil Rights and Economic Development, 22,* article 8.

Reavis, J., Looman, J., Franco, K., and Rojas, B. (2013) Adverse childhood experiences and adult criminology: How long must we live before we possess our own lives? *Permanente Journal, 17*(2), 44–48.

Rivard, J., Bloom, S., Abramovitz, R., Pasquale, L., Duncan, M., McCorkle, D., and Gelman, A. (2003) Assessing the implementation and effects of a trauma-focused intervention for youths in residential treatment. *Psychiatric Quarterly, 74,* 137–154.

Rivard, J., Bloom, S., McCorkle, D., and Abramovitz, R. (2005) Preliminary results of a study examining the implementation and effects of a trauma recovery framework for youths in residential treatment. *Therapeutic Community: The International Journal for Therapeutic and Supportive Organizations, 26,* 83–96.

Rohner, R., Khaleque, A., and Cournoyer, D. (2005) Parental acceptance-rejection: Theory, methods, cross-cultural evidence, and implications. *Ethos, 33,* 299–334.

Schneider, K. (2009) *Awakening to Awe: Personal Stories of Profound Transformation.* New York: Jason Aronson.

Search Institute (1990) Developmental Assets. www.search-institute.org/research/developmental-assets.

Shortz, J., and Worthington, E. (1994) Young adults' recall of religiosity, attributions, and coping in parental divorce. *Journal for the Scientific Study of Religion, 33,* 172–179.

Smith, P., Dyregrov, A., and Yule, W. (2008) *Children and War: Teaching Recovery Techniques.* Bergen, Norway: Children and War Foundation.

Solomon, E., and Heide, K. (1999) Type III trauma: Toward a more effective conceptualization of psychological trauma. *International Journal of Offender Therapy and Comparative Criminology, 43*, 202–210.

Solomon, E., Solomon, R., and Heide, K. (2009) EMRD: An evidence-based treatment for victims of trauma. *Victims & Offenders, 4*, 391–397.

Starr, D. (2013) The interview: Do police interrogation techniques produce false confessions? *The New Yorker*, December 9.

Steinberg, L. (2015) *Age of Opportunity: Lessons from the New Science of Adolescence.* New York: Eamon Dollan/Mariner.

Steinberg, L., and Scott, E. (2003) Less guilty by reason of adolescence: Developmental immaturity, diminished responsibility and the juvenile death penalty. *American Psychologist, 58*, 1009–1018.

Stockdale, L., Palumbo, R., Kmiecik, M., Silton, R., and Morrison, R. (2014) The effects of media violence on the neural correlates of emotional face processing: An ERP investigation. Poster presented at the 21st Annual Meeting of the Cognitive Neuroscience Society, Boston, MA.

Tedeschi, R., and Calhoun, L. (1996) The posttraumatic growth inventory: Measuring the positive legacy of trauma. *Journal of Traumatic Stress, 9*, 455–471.

Thomas, A., and Chess, S. (1977) *Temperament and Development.* New York: Brunner/Mazel.

Thomas, L., De Bellis, M., Reiko, G., and LaBar, K. (2007) Development of emotional facial recognition in late childhood and adolescence. *Developmental Science, 10*, 547–558.

Tolan, P. (1996) How resilient is the concept of resilience? *Community Psychologist, 29*, 12–15.

Tolan, P., and Guerra, N. (1994) Prevention of delinquency: Current status and issues. *Journal of Applied and Preventive Psychology, 3*, 251–273.

Tolan, P., and Guerra, N. (1996) Progress and prospects in youth violence prevention evaluation. *American Journal of Preventive Medicine, 12*, 129–131.

Tolan, P., and Henry, D. (1996) Patterns of psychopathology among urban poor children: Comorbidity and Aggression Effects. *Journal of Consulting and Clinical Psychology, 64*, 1094–1099.

Toussaint, L., Worthington, E., and Williams, D. (2015) *Forgiveness and Health: Scientific Evidence and Theories Relation Forgiveness to Better Health.* New York: Springer.

Tremblay, R., and Nagin, D. (2005) The developmental origins of physical aggression in humans. In R. Tremblay, W. Hartup, and J. Archer (Eds.), *Developmental Origins of Aggression.* New York: Guilford Press.

Turner, N., and Travis, J. (2015) What we learned from German prisons. *The New York Times*, August 7, p. A27.

van der Kolk, B., MacFarlane, A., and Weisaeth, L. (2006) *Traumatic Stress: The Effects of Overwhelming Experience on Mind, Body and Society.* New York: Guilford Press.

van der Kolk, B., Pynoos, R., Cicchetti, D., Cloitre, M., D'Andrea, W., Ford, J., et al. (2009) Proposal to include a developmental trauma disorder diagnosis for children and adolescents in DSM-V. www.traumacenter.org/announcements /DTD_NCTSN_official_submission_to_DSM_V_Final_Version.pdf.

Vygotsky, L., and Kozulin, A. (1986) *Thought and Language.* Cambridge, MA: MIT Press.

Watson, W. (2012) *Sacred Story: An Ignatian Examen for the Third Millennium.* Seattle, WA: Sacred Story Institute.

Webster, R., and Saucier, D. (2015) Demons are everywhere: The effects of belief in pure evil, demonization, and retribution on punishing criminal perpetrators. *Personality and Individual Differences, 74,* 72–77.

Werner, E., and Smith, R. (2001) *Journeys from Childhood to Midlife: Risk, Resilience, and Recovery.* Ithaca, New York: Cornell University Press.

Worthington, E., Jr. (Ed.) (1998) *Dimensions of Forgiveness: Psychological Research and Theological Perspectives.* Philadelphia, PA: Templeton Foundation.

Zagar, R., Kovach, J., Ferrari, T., Grove, W., Busch, K., Hughes, J., and Zagar, A. (2013) Applying best treatments by using a regression equation to target violence-prone youth: A review. *Comprehensive Psychology, 2*(7).

Zagar, R., Zagar, A., Bartikowski, B., and Busch, K. (2009) Cost comparisons of raising a child from birth to 17 years among samples of abused, delinquent, violent, and homicidal youth using victimization and justice system estimates. *Psychological Reports, 104,* 309–338.

Zagar, R., Zagar, A., Bartikowski, B., Busch, K., and Stark, R. (2009) Accepted legal applications of actuarial testing and delinquency interventions: Examples of savings in real life situations. *Psychological Reports, 104,* 339–362.

Zagar, R., Zagar, A., Busch, K., Grove, W., Hughes, J., Arbit, J., et al. (2009) Predicting and preventing homicide: A cost effective empirical approach from infancy to adulthood. *Psychological Reports, 104,* 1–377.

Zanni, G. (2008) Optimism and health. *Consultant Pharmacist, 23,* 112–126.

Zanni, G., and Browne, C. (2010) Coping with terminal illness. *Pharmacy Times,* August 16.

Zeier, J., Baskin-Sommers, A., and Racer, K. (2012) Cognitive control deficits associated with antisocial personality disorder and psychopathy. *Personality Disorders: Theory, Research and Treatment, 3,* 283–293.

Zinn, H. (2006) *A Power Governments Cannot Suppress.* New York: City Lights.

INDEX

ACEs (adverse childhood experiences), 11–13; Alonzo P. and, 114; Antonio R. and, 152; Baglivio, Michael and, 137; Chan L. and, 44; child abuse/neglect and, 11; David F. and, 50; emotional regulation and, 13; homicide and, 12; Johnny H. and, 129; Josiah M. and, 118; juvenile killers and, 12–13, 32; *Listening to Killers: Lessons Learned from My 20 Years as a Psychological Expert Witness in Murder Cases* (Garbarino) and, 13; Maria H. and, 156; Miguel S. and, 47–48; Muhammad T. and, 39; parents and, 113; racism and, 11, 13; rehabilitation and transformation and, 13; Robert W. and, 35; substance abuse and, 11–12, 12–13

ACLU (American Civil Liberties Union), 153

ADHD (attention-deficit/hyperactivity disorder), 90–91, 117, 172

adolescence: age eighteen and, 154; brain development and, 28–29, 46, 172; brain malleability and, 16–18, 23; childhood adversity and, 13; drugs and, 172; emerging adulthood and, 85; emotions and, 28, 46, 128, 172; group treatment and, 142; identity formation and, 147–48; imaginary audiences and, 25; impulse control and, 172; life-without-parole sentences and, 130; maturation and, 85; *Miller v. Alabama* (2012) and, 3; sexual assault and, 169; U.S. Supreme Court

on, xi, 3, 8, 19, 58; World Health Organization and, 166. *See also* juvenile killers; juvenile offenders; juvenile sentences

adolescent-onset psychosis, 123, 124, 129

adult mediation, 20–21

adverse childhood experiences. *See* ACEs (adverse childhood experiences)

African American juveniles, 26, 31, 32, 39, 40. *See also* individuals

African Americans, 39, 40, 55, 164

age eighteen, xi, 141, 146, 152, 154, 163–66

Age of Opportunity: Lessons from the New Science of Adolescence (Steinberg), 16

aging, 82–83, 84–85, 151–52, 155. *See also* age eighteen; brain maturation; emerging adulthood; maturation

aging out, 35. *See also* age eighteen

Alabama, 5, 6. *See also Miller v. Alabama* (2012)

Alabama Court of Criminal Appeals, 5–6, 74

Albert, Dustin, 86

Alito, Samuel, 7, 67–69

Alonzo P., 113–14, 115, 116, 121, 129, 138, 141

Alonzo W., 24

American Civil Liberties Union (ACLU), 153

American Psychiatric Association, 135

American Psycho (2000), 128

American Psychological Association, 6

American Psychologist, 28

Amnesty International, 8, 68

amygdala, 23

California Psychological Inventory, 83
Cameron, Bob, 57
Campaign for Forgiveness Research, 62
Canada, 127
Capital and Serious Violent Offender
    Program, 100
capital punishment, 4, 6, 72. *See also* death
    penalty
Carl O., 98–99
Case for God, The (Armstrong), 171
Caspi, Avshalom, 14
Catholicism, 55, 72, 93, 94
CDC (Centers for Disease Control and
    Prevention), 11
Chan L., 32, 41–45, 51
Chess, Stella, 91
Chicago, 1, 6, 10, 13, 78, 94, 140. *See also*
    Cook County Court (Chicago); Crime
    of the Century
Chicago Tribune, 2–3
child abuse/neglect: ACEs (adverse child-
    hood experiences) and, 11, 137; attach-
    ment relationships and, 120; Chan L.
    and, 44; conduct disorder and, 15; Ivory,
    Javell and, 2; James L. and, 163; Josiah
    M. and, 118–19; juvenile killers and, 32;
    Lamarckian hypothesis and, 139;
    MAOA gene and, 14–15; Maria H. and,
    156; Miguel S. and, 46, 47–48; Miller,
    Evan and, 23; Muhammad T. and, 38,
    39; racism and, 140; Samuel X. and,
    131–32; Sergio Z. and, 172; therapies
    and, 101; Tolan, Patrick and, 13, 140;
    violence and, 115, 140. *See also* child-
    hood adversity; childhood trauma;
    sexual abuse
child/adolescent development, 2, 9, 22–23.
    See also parenting
childhood adversity: adolescence and, 13;
    Alonzo P. and, 114; Chan L. and, 44;
    emotions and, 11; Hare Psychopathy
    Checklist and, 137; incarceration and,
    137; juvenile killers and, 9, 11, 12–13, 32;
    juvenile offenders and, 11–15; Maria H.
    and, 155–56; maturation and, 11; Miguel
    S. and, 47; Muhammad T. and, 38;
    Tolan, Patrick and, 13. *See also* ACEs
    (adverse childhood experiences)

childhood trauma: ADHD (attention-
    deficit/hyperactivity disorder) and, 90,
    91; adult mediation and, 20–21; amy-
    gdala and, 23; anger and, 23, 116; brain
    development and, 23; brain immaturity
    and, 28; Carl O. and, 98–99; child
    development and, 23; Christianson,
    John and, 145, 150; conduct disorder
    and, 15, 91; consciousness and, 104;
    cortex and, 23; depression and, 116;
    developmental exceptions and, 115;
    emotions/emotional regulation and, 23,
    116; Ivory, Javell and, 2; Jacquon J. and,
    165; Jeffrey M. and, 96; Josiah M. and,
    117–19; juvenile killers and, 25–26, 67,
    75, 98; Maria H. and, 155, 157; Martell
    A. and, 20; Miguel S. and, 46, 48;
    post-traumatic growth, 94–95; post-
    traumatic stress disorder (PTSD) and,
    115; as profound/pervasive, 115–16;
    psychopaths and, 137; Ronald B. and,
    21–22; Samuel X. and, 131–32; self-
    esteem and, 115–16; shame and, 115–16;
    spirituality and, 108, 110; substance
    abuse and, 116; suicide and, 116; thera-
    pies and, 100, 101–2; Type I, II trauma
    and, 115–16; Type III trauma and,
    115–19, 137; urban war zones and, 38–39;
    as victims, 116, 118; violence and, 115. *See
    also* child abuse/neglect; sexual abuse;
    traumatic memories
*Children and the Dark Side of Human
    Experience* (Garbarino), 143
Children and War Foundation's "Teaching
    Recovery Techniques" program (TRT),
    101
Chodron, Pema, 94
Christianity: Bible and, 53, 54; Chan L.
    and, 44; Christianson, John and,
    145–46; James L. and, 163; moral issues
    and, 134; Muhammad T. and, 36; Plun-
    kett, Craig and, 59; rehabilitation and
    transformation and, 114; religion and,
    171; Thomas W. and, 140
Christianson, John, 144–51, 153
Cicchetti, Dante, 99
Clark, Maggie, 164
classical conditioning, 105

eye movement desensitization and reprocessing (EMDR), 60

Fagan, Jeffrey, 40
Fallon, James, 15, 75, 135
false confessions, 25–26
FalseConfessions.org, 26
families: attachment relationships and, 22–23; Bobby S. and, 112; child/adolescent development and, 22; conduct disorder and, 15; confirmation bias and, 159; Dennis D. and, 163; developmental assets and, 102; 40 Developmental Assets and, 15; Josiah M. and, 119; Martell A. and, 19; psychopaths and, 137; Robert W. and, 33–34; Samuel X. and, 131–32; Sergio Z. and, 172; terminal medical diagnosis and, 107. See also fathers; mothers; parental abandonment; parental rejection; parents
family rejection, 21–22, 146. See also parental rejection
Farrington, David, 14
fathers: Alonzo P. and, 114; Chan L. and, 44, 45; Christianson, John and, 145; Craig Plunkett and, 59; Donald Z. and, 93; Eric G. and, 27; Jeffrey M. and, 97; Josiah M. and, 118; Maria H. and, 156, 157; Martell A. and, 19; Martin and, 60; Miguel S. and, 46, 47, 48; Muhammad T. and, 38; Robert W. and, 34–35, 92; Ronald B. and, 21–22; Samuel X. and, 131. See also parents
FBI, 165
fear of abandonment, 97. See also parental abandonment; parental rejection
Feldman, Ronald, 142
felony murder, xii, 1–2, 5, 32, 42, 162
females, 14, 97, 98, 120, 137, 164, 165
Fitzgibbons, Richard, 64
Florida, xi, xii, 31, 137, 153, 162. See also Graham v. Florida (2010)
forgiveness, 58–66. See also compassion
Forgiveness Therapy: An Empirical Guide for Resolving Anger and Restoring Hope (Enright, Fitzgibbons), 64
40 Developmental Assets, 15–16, 35, 102, 129, 152

Foxx, Darnell, 1–4, 52–53, 58, 61, 62
Francis, Pope, 171
Francis of Assisi, Saint, 171
Franks, Robert, 78, 79
Freeman, Morgan, 82
frontal lobe, 28, 129

gangs: ACEs (adverse childhood experiences) and, 13; Antonio R. and, 152; Chan L. and, 42; Christianson, John and, 145, 146, 148; Davis, Adolfo and, 3–4; Eric G. and, 27; Foxx, Darnell and, 3; Indiana case and, 32; Ivory, Javell and, 3; Jacquon J. and, 165; juvenile killers and, 32; Karl A. and, 87; Muhammad T. and, 36, 37, 38; Peter A. and, 89–90; prisons and, 104; Sergio Z. and, 172; sociopaths and, 133; therapies and, 101; Thomas M. and, 25; urban war zones and, 46. See also individual gangs
Gangster Disciples (gang), 1
Garbarino, James: Catholicism and, 94; Chan L. and, 41–45; Christianson, John and, 144–51; Florida and, xii; Foxx, Darnell and, 4; hope and, 143; Illinois and, xii; Ivory, Javell and, 2–3, 4–5; James L. and, 163; moral exceptions and, 74–75; rehabilitation and transformation and, 30, 159; resentencing and, 30, 160; Robert W. and, 36. See also Listening to Killers: Lessons Learned from My 20 Years as a Psychological Expert Witness in Murder Cases (Garbarino); Lost Boys: Why Our Sons Turn Violent and How We Can Save Them (Garbarino)
Gardner, Martin, 167
GEDs, 3, 27, 34, 36, 92–93, 163
Gelman, Andrew, 40
genocide, 57
Germany, 57, 105
Ghana, 124–25
Gilligan, James, 89
Goff, Phillip Atiba, 26, 40
Goffman, Erving, 25
Goodlatte, Bob, 125
good v. evil beliefs, 71, 72
Gottfredson, Michael, 82–83

Jane P., 50
Jefferson, Thomas, 134
Jeffrey M., 95–97
Jensen, Frances, 47, 128
Jessor, Richard, 108
Jesuits, 170
Jews. *See* Judaism
job opportunities. *See* employment
John 8:7 (Bible), 55
John L., 169
Johnny H., 122–26, 127–31
John P., 63
Joshua B., 24, 25
Josiah M., 116–21, 129
Judaism, 53, 54, 55, 78, 134, 141
judges: crime and, 159–60; death penalty and, 74; ego and, 154; evil and, 71, 72–73; hardness of heart and, 154; Lafountain, Floyd and, 162; Maria H. and, 157–58; *Miller v. Alabama* (2012) and, 67, 73, 158, 161; mitigation factors and, 71, 72; rehabilitation and transformation and, 158–59
juries, 71, 72, 74, 84
juvenile homicide offenders (JHOs), 9, 149. *See also* high-risk youths; juvenile killers
juvenile justice system, 151–52, 167. *See also* criminal justice system
juvenile killers: ACEs (adverse childhood experiences) and, 12–13, 32; aging and, 84–85; attachment relationships and, 23; brain immaturity and, 11; brain maturation and, 113, 149, 151, 167–68; child abuse/neglect and, 32; childhood adversity and, 9, 11, 12–13, 32; childhood trauma and, 25–26, 67, 75, 98; conduct disorder and, 84; death penalty and, 55, 56, 57, 158; domestic violence and, 32; drugs and, 32; education and, 92; emerging adulthood and, 84–85; evil and, 69, 70, 75, 78; forgiveness and, 64; 40 Developmental Assets and, 16, 102; gangs and, 32; guns and, 12–13; Heide, Kathleen and, 149; ideology and, 52; juvenile homicide offenders (JHOs), 9, 149; juvenile sentences and, 10; Khachatryan, Norair and, 149; Lamarckian

hypothesis and, 139; life sentences and, 151; life-without-parole sentences and, 31, 67, 68, 74; *Listening to Killers: Lessons Learned from My 20 Years as a Psychological Expert Witness in Murder Cases* (Garbarino) and, 66–67; as lost tribe, 30–33, 78, 165; maturation and, 113; *Miller v. Alabama* (2012) and, 11; mothers and, 120; parole and, 10, 31, 56, 57, 121, 151, 152, 153–55; psychology and, 52; race and, 32, 34; recidivism and, 10, 149, 151–52; recovery and, 152; rehabilitation and, 16, 29, 32, 57, 58, 73, 76, 77, 82, 84, 114–15, 149; religion and, 52; sentences and, 56, 152, 154–55, 167–68; services and, 73–74; social environment and, 22; super-predators and, 70, 71, 160; therapies and, 99–102, 151, 152, 155; toxic family/community environments and, 23, 32; transformation and, 77, 82, 84, 114–15, 149; treatment and, 168. *See also* individuals; violent juvenile offenders
juvenile offenders: childhood adversity and, 11–15; conduct disorder and, 83–84; criminal justice system and, 167; *Graham v. Florida* (2010) and, 31, 69; life-without-parole sentences and, 7, 8, 69; maturation and, 85; *Montgomery v. Louisiana* (2016) and the, 7; parole and, 167; police and, 25–26; presentences and, 167; rehabilitation and, 73, 167, 168; *Roper v. Simmons* (2005) and, 6, 74; sentences and, 168; *Tatum v. Arizona* (2016) and, 4; U.S. Supreme Court and, 6–7. *See also* antisocial aggression/behaviors; high-risk youths; violent juvenile offenders
juvenile sentences, 4, 7, 10, 68, 147. *See also* life sentences; life-without-parole sentences; resentencing; sentences

Karl A., 86–88
Kavanaugh, Antoinette, 3, 101, 132–33
Kellerman, Natan, 139
Kennedy v. *Louisiana* (2008), 6
Khachatryan, Norair, 149, 151–52
Kiehl, Kent, 121, 133, 134, 135, 137, 167

King, Martin Luther, Jr., 173
Koran, 37–38, 54, 171

Lafountain, Floyd, 162
Lamarckian hypothesis, 138–39
Larry F., 88–89
Latinos, 164
Lawler, Kathleen, 64
law of retaliation (Qisas), 54
Lawrence, Betty, 88
legal competency. *See* competency
legal insanity, 70
Leibenluft, Ellen, 15
Leopold, Nathan, 78–81
"Less Guilty by Reason of Adolescence"
    (Steinberg, Scott), 28
Levine, Noah, 94
"Life Goes On" (Nellis) (report), 160
Life Plus 99 Years (Leopold), 81
life sentences: crime and, 160; International
    Criminal Court and, 57; juvenile killers
    and, 151; *Miller v. Alabama* (2012) and,
    161; Norway and, 56; politics and, 160;
    Public Religion Research Institute and,
    54–55; rehabilitation and transforma-
    tion and, 51; The Sentencing Project
    and, 164; Sergio Z. and, 173. *See also*
    life-without-parole sentences
Life Skills (program), 92
life-without-parole sentences: adolescence
    and, 130; African Americans/juveniles
    and, 32, 164; age eighteen and, 164;
    Alabama and, 5; Amnesty International
    and, 8, 68; anger and, 9; Black Protestants
    and, 55; Brian N. and, 104; conduct
    disorder and, 84; Davis, Adolfo and, 3–4,
    161; death penalty and, 55–56, 67, 160;
    Dennis D. and, 78, 163; Eighth Amend-
    ment and, 6, 8, 73–74; Eric G. and, 27,
    103; females and, 164; Foxx, Darnell and,
    2; *Graham v. Florida* (2010) and, 4, 6, 7,
    31, 69; hope and, 144; House, Antonio
    and, 166; Ivory, Javell and, 2; *Jackson v.
    Hobbs* (2012) and, 5; Joshua B. and, 24;
    juvenile killers and, 31, 67, 68, 74; juvenile
    offenders and, 7, 8, 69; Latinos and, 164;
    Leopold and Loeb and, 79–80; *MAOA*
    gene and, 75; Maria H. and, 156–57, 158;

Miller v. Alabama (2012) and, xi–xii, 3, 4,
    5, 7, 74, 161, 164–65; mitigation factors
    and, 72; *Montgomery v. Louisiana* (2016)
    and the, xii, 4, 7; parole and, 153–54;
    permanent incorrigibility and, 7, 111;
    Portugal and, 57; Public Religion
    Research Institute and, 54–55; rehabilita-
    tion and transformation and, 82, 144;
    resources and, 34; Robert W., 92; Ronald
    B. and, 22; Samuel X. and, 132; The
    Sentencing Project and, 57, 164; *Tatum v.
    Arizona* (2016) and, 4, 6–7, 154; as termi-
    nal medical diagnosis, 106–7; Thomas M.
    and, 25; United States and, 8, 57, 164; U.S.
    Supreme Court and, 6–7, 18, 31, 41,
    68–69, 153–54
*Listening to Killers: Lessons Learned from
    My 20 Years as a Psychological Expert
    Witness in Murder Cases* (Garbarino):
    ACEs (adverse childhood experiences)
    and, 13; age eighteen and, 165; child/
    adolescent development and, 2; Chris-
    tianson, John and, 144; clinical diag-
    noses and, 83; juvenile killers and,
    66–67; *Montgomery v. Louisiana* (2016)
    and the, xii; Paul T. and, 30; rehabilita-
    tion and transformation and, 66; vio-
    lence and, 29
Loeb, Richard, 78–81
Loeber, Rolf, 14
Logan, John, 81
Lord, Charles, 159
*Lost Boys: Why Our Sons Turn Violent and
    How We Can Save Them* (Garbarino),
    xii, 2, 30, 41, 83, 144, 145
Louise and Tom H., 156–57
Lozoff, Bo, 168–69
Luhrmann, Tanya, 124

Mafia Insane Vice Lords (gang), 1
males: ACEs (adverse childhood experi-
    ences) and, 137; age eighteen and, 165;
    attachment disorder/relationships and,
    120; conduct disorder and, 83–84; fear
    of abandonment and, 97; life expectan-
    cies and, 31; *MAOA* gene and, 14, 15;
    violence and, 98
MAOA gene, 14–15, 75, 76

Marcia, James, 147–48
Maria H., 155–58
Martell A., 18–20, 21
Martin, 60
Martin I., 168
Marxism-Leninism, 106
Maryland, 153
Matthew 5:8 (Bible), 54, 55–56, 61
maturation: adolescence and, 85; Carl O.
    and, 98–99; childhood adversity and,
    11; consciousness and, 104; incarcera-
    tion and, 73; Jeffrey M. and, 96; juvenile
    killers and, 112; *Montgomery v. Louisi-
    ana* (2016) and, 168; Obbish, James and,
    3; school shooters and, 17; therapies and,
    100. *See also* aging; brain maturation;
    emerging adulthood
Mayo Clinic, 120
McDowell, Katherine, 109
Men Against Guns, 89
mental disabilities, 89
mental health, 13, 22–23, 94, 118, 157
mental illness, 44, 112, 125
mentorship, 10, 36, 38, 45, 92, 93–94, 103
Methuselah sentences, 8, 31
Mexicans, 146, 151
Michigan, xii
Miguel S., 32, 45–49, 51
Mikva, Abner, 161
Miller, Evan, xi, 5, 23, 74. *See also Miller v.
    Alabama* (2012)
Miller, Ronald, 158
Miller v. Alabama (2012), xi–xii, 5–9,
    18–29; adolescence and, 3; age eighteen
    and, 164–65, 166; aging out and, 35;
    Alabama Court of Criminal Appeals
    and, 5–6, 74; brain development and,
    172; California and, 165–66; Chan L.
    and, 43; competency and, 18, 29; deci-
    sion making and, 18–21, 29; dependency
    and, 18, 29; dissenting opinions and,
    67–69; Eighth Amendment and, xi;
    felony murder and, 42; Florida and, xi;
    Foxx, Darnell and, 3; Gardner, Martin
    and, 167; Grisso, Tom and, 3; hope and,
    9, 30, 144; Illinois and, xi, 161; Ivory,
    Javell and, 3; Jeffrey M. and, 96; judges
    and, 67, 73, 158, 161; juvenile killers

and, 11; juvenile sentences and, 10;
    Kavanaugh, Antoinette and, 3; life
    sentences and, 161; life-without-parole
    sentences and, xi–xii, 3, 4, 5, 7, 74, 161,
    164–65; Maria H. and, 157; maturation
    and, 85; Miller, Evan and, xi, 5, 23, 74;
    Montgomery v. Louisiana (2016) and, 8,
    168; moral issues and, 67; mutability
    and, 36; offense context and, 18, 29;
    parole and, 161; peer influence and, 18;
    Petrone, Angela and, 161; prosecutors
    and, 67, 158, 161; psychopaths and,
    132–33, 141; race and, 132–33; rehabilita-
    tion and transformation and, xii, 9, 18,
    29, 130, 166–67; resentencing and,
    xi–xii, 8, 18, 67, 73, 161, 164; scientific
    foundation of, 18–29; Sergio Z. and,
    173; as social experiment, xii; state
    legislatures and, xi; super-predators and,
    70; *Tatum v. Arizona* (2016) and, 7;
    toxic family/community environments
    and, 18
minors, 68, 69. *See also* age eighteen; juve-
    nile killers; juvenile offenders; juvenile
    sentences
mitigation factors, 70, 71, 72, 73, 113
MMPI personality assessment, 83
Moffit, Terrie, 14
Monahan, Kathryn, 85
Montgomery v. Louisiana (2016), xi–xii, 4,
    6–7, 8, 18, 144, 161, 168
moral insanity, 133, 137, 141. *See also*
    psychopaths
moral issues, 52, 66–69, 134. *See also* ethics;
    forgiveness; remorse
Moretti, Marlene, 120
mothers: Bobby S. and, 112; Buckner,
    Christine, 58; Carl O. and, 99; Chan L.
    and, 44; Christianson, John and, 145,
    146; Conchita, 47; David F. and, 60;
    Dennis D. and, 169–70; Donald Z. and,
    93; Jeffrey M. and, 97; Josiah M. and,
    118, 119–21; juvenile killers and, 120;
    Maria H. and, 156; Martell A. and, 19;
    Martin and, 60; Miguel S. and, 47;
    Miller, Evan and, 23; Muhammad T.
    and, 38, 39; rehabilitation and transfor-
    mation and, 97, 120; Robert W.

and, 35, 92; Ronald B. and, 21–22; Samuel X. and, 131; Smith, Obrellia, 52–53. *See also* families; parents

Muhammad T., 32, 36–41, 51

murder. *See* homicide; juvenile killers

Nagin, Daniel, 98

narcissism, 70, 116, 123

Nargis, Jason, 81

Native Americans, 139

Natural Born Killers (1994), 122, 125

Nazi concentration camps, 105–6

neighborhoods, 14. *See also* toxic family/community environments; urban war zones

Nellis, Ashley, 160, 164

Nelson v. Heyne (1974), 166

neurobiological maturation, 37, 38, 96. *See also* brain maturation

Never the Sinner (Logan) (play), 81

Newman, Katherine, 16–17

New York Times, 57

nonverbal cues, 46

Northwestern University, 26, 81

Norway, 56, 153

Not Easily Broken (Jakes), 93

nucleus accumbens, 28, 46, 128, 172

Obama, Barack, 125

Obbish, James, 2–3, 4–5

obsessive-compulsive behavior/disorder, 123, 125–26, 128

offense context, 18, 24–25, 29

Owens, David, 4, 5

paranoia, 123, 129

parental abandonment, 21–22, 97, 146, 150, 151. *See also* attachment relationships

parental figures, 91–92

parental rejection, 23, 118, 119, 120, 172. *See also* family rejection

parental separation/divorce, 11, 27, 44

parental supervision, 47

parenting, 15, 135, 156

parents: ACEs (adverse childhood experiences) and, 113; anger and, 97; Carl O. and, 98–99; Christianson, John and, 150; Donald Z. and, 93; Josiah M.

and, 118; Lamarckian hypothesis and, 139; Maria H. and, 155–57; psychopaths and, 135; resilience and, 87, 91–92; Robert W. and, 91–92; sociopaths and, 135. *See also* attachment relationships; families; fathers; mothers

Parker, Theodore, 173

parole: age eighteen and, 165–66; aging and, 155; American Civil Liberties Union (ACLU) and, 153; antisocial personality disorder (ASPD) and, 84; education and, 155; emotions and, 155; Eric G. and, 27–28; evil and, 72, 73; Florida and, 31, 153; good v. evil beliefs and, 71; hope and, 9, 143; incarceration and, 153; Johnny H. and, 126, 130; juvenile killers and, 10, 31, 56, 57, 121, 151, 152, 153–55; juvenile offenders and, 167; Leopold, Nathan and, 81; Maryland and, 153; *Miller v. Alabama* (2012) and, 161; mitigation factors and, 72; *Montgomery v. Louisiana* (2016) and, 18, 168; prosecutors and, 56; Public Religion Research Institute and, 54–55; rehabilitation and transformation and, 31, 82, 153, 154; resentencing and, 67; Sergio Z. and, 173; *The Shawshank Redemption* (1994) and, 82; United States and, 153; victims and, 58, 67. *See also* life-without-parole sentences

Path with Heart, A (Kornfield), 93, 94

Paul, Ronald, 18–20

Paul T., 8, 30–31, 51, 130

Pavlov, Ivan, 105

Peck, M. Scott, 43

peer influence: brain immaturity and, 28; Chan L. and, 42; decision making and, 24–25; imaginary audiences and, 25; Ivory, Javell and, 2; Jeffrey M. and, 96; Joshua B. and, 24, 25; Martell A. and, 19–20, 21; *Miller v. Alabama* (2012) and, 18; positive environments and, 16; prosocial behaviors and, 16

permanent incorrigibility, 4, 6–7, 111

Perry, Bruce, 23

Peter A., 80, 89–90

Petrone, Angela, 3–4, 161

Pine, Daniel, 15

Plous, Scott, 159
Plunkett, Craig, 58–59, 61, 63–64
police, 25–26, 40
politics, 159–60, 163, 164
pornography, 127, 128–29
Portugal, 57
positive environments, 15–16
positive relationships, 47, 87
post-release, 155. *See also* parole; probation
post-traumatic growth, 94–95, 149, 151, 152
post-traumatic slave syndrome, 39
post-traumatic stress disorder (PTSD),
    94, 115
poverty, 11, 13, 21–22, 109, 143
presentences, 167
prevention, 10
prisonization, 147, 150
prisons: aging and, 82–83; conduct disorder
    and, 83; education and, 34, 49; Eighth
    Amendment and, 168; employment and,
    10, 36; gangs and, 104; libraries and, 43;
    mentorship and, 45; prosocial contact
    and, 103; race and, 104; rehabilitation
    and, 166–67; religion and, 105–6;
    spirituality and, 108–9; therapies and,
    99–102, 112; violence and, 80; Watson,
    William and, 170
probation, 17, 162
prosecutors: childhood adversity and, 12;
    confirmation bias and, 159; death pen-
    alty and, 160–61; Dennis D. and, 162–
    63; ethics and, 158; incompetence and,
    154; Jacquon J. and, 165; Lafountain,
    Floyd and, 162; Maria H. and, 157–58;
    Miller v. Alabama (2012) and, 67, 158,
    161; parole and, 56; rehabilitation and
    transformation and, 158–59, 162; resen-
    tencing and, 67, 158, 160–61
prosocial behaviors, 16, 22, 29, 90, 170
prosocial contact, 100, 103. *See also* positive
    environments
Protestants, 54–55
Prozac, 127
Psychopath Inside, The (Fallon), 15, 75
psychopathology, 109, 111–12. *See also*
    individual diagnoses
psychopaths, 112, 121–22, 131–38, 139, 141–
    42, 167. *See also* antisocial personality

disorder (ASPD); Hare Psychopathy
    Checklist; sociopaths
psychotic disorder, 123
PTSD (post-traumatic stress disorder), 94,
    115
Public Religion Research Institute, 54–55
punitiveness, 143
Pynoos, Robert, 99

Quinsey, Vernon, 82, 141–42
Quintin P., 90–91

Ra, Edward, 167
race, 32, 34, 39, 40–41, 71, 104, 132–33
race-based traumatic stress injury, 39
racism: ACEs (adverse childhood experi-
    ences) and, 11, 13; African Americans/
    juveniles and, 39, 40; *The Autobiography
    of Malcolm X* and, 37; child abuse/
    neglect and, 140; Christianson, John
    and, 151; Garbarino, James and, 143;
    Jeffrey M. and, 96; Maria H. and, 156
rage. *See* anger
*Rampage: The Social Roots of School Shoot-
    ings* (Newman), 16–17
rape, 50, 74, 156
reactive attachment disorder, 120
Reavis, James, 137
recidivism, 10, 82, 101, 122, 149–50, 151–52,
    167
Refuge Recovery (Levine), 94
rehabilitation, 9–11; Alonzo P. and, 114;
    brain maturation and, 8; Brian N. and,
    104; Garbarino, James and, 159; good v.
    evil beliefs and, 71; guilt and, 63; juve-
    nile killers and, 16, 29, 32, 57, 58, 73, 76,
    77, 82, 84, 114–15, 149; juvenile offend-
    ers and, 73, 167, 168; Leopold, Nathan
    and, 80, 81; negative behavior and, 104;
    Obbish, James on, 3; prisons and, 166–
    67; resentencing and, 34; The Risk-
    Sophistication-Treatment Inventory
    and, 101; Robert W. and, 35–36; school
    shooters and, 16–18; shame and, 63; *The
    Shawshank Redemption* (1994) and, 82;
    temperament and, 90; United States
    and, 57. *See also* transformation
rehabilitation and transformation, 9–11;

Supernatural (television), 125
super-predators, 70, 71, 160

Tatum v. Arizona (2016), 4, 6–7, 73, 144, 154, 161
Tedeschi, Robert, 94, 95, 149
Teenage Brain, The (Jensen), 47
teenage brains, 3, 11–12, 29, 46–47. *See also* adolescence; brain immaturity
teenage killers. *See* juvenile killers
television, 125, 127, 130
temperament, 12–13, 14, 87, 90–91, 113–14
terminal medical diagnosis, 106–7
terrorism, 39
Texas, 100
Tharpe, Chet, 162
therapies: Bobby S. and, 112; brain malleability and, 150; child abuse/neglect and, 101; childhood trauma and, 100, 101–2; Christianson, John and, 150; consciousness and, 104; Dennis D. and, 169; incarceration and, 100; Johnny H. and, 130; juvenile killers and, 99–102, 151, 152, 155; prisons and, 99–102, 112; psychopaths and, 121; rehabilitation and transformation and, 82, 99–100, 155; urban war zones and, 101; violence and, 101; Xavier Y. and, 127. *See also* treatment; *individual therapies*
Thich, Nhat Hanh, 94, 169
Thomas, Alexander, 91
Thomas, Bob and Mary, 59–60
Thomas, Clarence, 7, 67–69
Thomas, Joshua, 1, 58
Thomas M., 25–26
Thomas W., 140–41
Tolan, Patrick, 13, 36–37, 140
torture, 90, 113, 121
Toussaint, Loren, 62
toxic cultural environments, 127–30. *See also* pornography; social toxicity; video games
toxic family/community environments: ACEs (adverse childhood experiences) and, 13; decision making and, 11; emotions and, 11; Ivory, Javell and, 2; Jacquon J. and, 165; Jeffrey M. and, 96; juvenile killers and, 23, 32; Karl A.

and, 87; *MAOA* gene and, 75, 76; *Miller v. Alabama* (2012) and, 18; psychopaths and, 137–38; teenage brains and, 29; Tolan, Patrick and, 13; war zone mentality, 2, 104. *See also* childhood adversity; childhood trauma; urban war zones
traits, 64, 91, 132, 138–39. *See also* temperament
transformation: Communism and, 105; education and, 92; forgiveness and, 59; hope and, 9; juvenile killers and, 77, 82, 84, 114–15, 149; parole and, 31, 154; Peter A. and, 89; religion and, 141; X., Malcolm and, 40–41. *See also* rehabilitation and transformation
trauma, 139. *See also* childhood trauma
Trauma and Affect Regulation (TARGET), 101
Trauma-informed cognitive behavioral therapy, 60
traumatic memories, 58, 60, 61–63, 98, 115, 138–39
Travis, Jeremy, 57
treatment, 101, 149, 166–71. *See also* group treatment; therapies; *individual treatments*
Trembly, Richard, 98
Trop v. Dulles (1958), 68
Trump, Donald, 125
Turner, Nicholas, 57
Turvey, Brent, 158
Tutu, Desmond, 9
"12 Steps on How to Seek and Maintain the Knowledge of Self, The" (Muhammad T.), 41
Type I, II trauma, 115–16. *See also* childhood trauma
Type III trauma, 115–19, 137

UNESCO, 166
United Nations, 57, 68, 166
United States: ACEs (adverse childhood experiences) and the, 12; crime and the, 160; death penalty and the, 53, 57; guns and the, 125; homicide and the, 165; incarceration and the, 56; life-without-parole sentences and the, 8, 57, 164; parole and the, 153; psychopaths and